David

Congratulations!
And many thanks.

Adam
&
Peter

# ADVERTISING WORKS 3

# ADVERTISING WORKS 3

*Papers from the IPA Advertising Effectiveness Awards*

Institute of Practitioners in Advertising, 1984

*Edited and introduced by*

## Charles Channon

1985

HOLT, RINEHART AND WINSTON

LONDON . NEW YORK . SYDNEY . TORONTO

Holt, Rinehart and Winston Ltd: 1 St Anne's Road
Eastbourne, East Sussex BN21 3UN

**British Library Cataloguing in Publication Data**

Advertising works 3.
1. Advertising—Great Britain—Case studies
I. Channon, Charles
659.1'11        HF5808.G7

ISBN  0-03-910619-5

Typeset, printed and bound in Great Britain by Butler & Tanner Ltd, Frome and London

Last digit is print no: 9 8 7 6 5 4 3 2 1

# Contents

## SECTION 1   NEW CONSUMER GOODS AND SERVICES

## SECTION 2   ESTABLISHED CONSUMER GOODS AND SERVICES

# CONTENTS

# IPA
# Advertising Effectiveness Awards
# 1984

The IPA Advertising Effectiveness Awards 1984 constituted the third competition in the series begun in 1980, and first repeated in 1982. Selected papers from the first two competitions were published in book form under the respective titles *Advertising Works* and *Advertising Works 2*, both edited by Simon Broadbent, and published by Holt, Rinehart and Winston in 1981 and 1983.

Like its predecessors, this book of the 1984 Awards is a selection, though, as for 1982, only two of the commended papers have been omitted. It appears under the same publisher's imprint as before, but for the first time with a different editor.

It would be difficult to overestimate Simon Broadbent's contribution to the successful establishment and achieved stature of these Awards in his multiple roles as Chairman of the working party, member of the judging panel, and editor for publication of the 1980 and 1982 competitions. He has also helped to spread the word about the principle and practice of successful competition entry through speeches and through the recent publication of a selection from the first two Awards schemes, intended for use in colleges and for trainees in marketing and advertising: Simon Broadbent (ed), *20 Advertising Case Histories*, Holt, Rinehart and Winston, 1984. The present editor has benefited from his continued membership of the working party for the 1984 Awards. The industry owes a great debt to his clarity of mind, undoubted expertise, and sheer determination.

## THE PURPOSE AND FORMAT OF THE AWARDS

The objectives of the Awards remain unaltered. The IPA guide to the entrants summarised them as follows:

1.  To demonstrate that advertising can be proven to work against measurable criteria (eg sales revenue) and show that it is both a serious commercial investment and a contributor to profit, not just a cost.
2.  Through this demonstration, to improve understanding, particularly outside the industry, of the crucial role advertising plays in marketing generally as well as in specific applications.

3. To achieve a closer analysis of advertising effectiveness and improved methods of evaluation, and thereby to inculcate ever-improving professional standards among those within the advertising industry.

As before, entries were called for in the form of written case histories which described the contribution made by an advertising campaign for a product, or service, within its marketing context.

The competition closed in July 1984 and the results were publicly announced in November. A total 59 entries were received from over 30 agencies. Eight entries were awarded prizes totalling £13 000 and a further 13 entries received a commendation. The list of successful papers and their authors is given on pages xiii–xv.

Although there is no mandatory format for entries, the format suggestion contained in the entry form for the Awards is a good (though not invariable) guide to the likely content of most of the successful papers and to the ordering of their argument, namely,

(a) business background;
(b) marketing and advertising objectives;
(c) description of the campaign, including creative and media strategies;
(d) campaign evaluation;
(e) conclusions on the success or otherwise of the campaign, on the way the advertising worked, and on the methods used.

In view of the stated objectives of the Awards, it will be clear that the evaluation of the campaign and the conclusions drawn from this (see (d) and (e)) form the decisive part in any entry. It is only here that the submitted papers can provide the convincing demonstration of advertising effectiveness that is of paramount importance both to the judges of the Awards and to that wider audience which will judge the advertising industry by its apparent contribution to the growth, competitiveness and profitability of the businesses it exists to serve.

Naturally, any evaluation will relate closely to the objectives which have been set in the first place. In this sense, objectives set the 'agenda' for evaluation and form part of it, though there will be times when the *overall* objective of increased sales and profitability is achieved in ways not wholly envisaged by the initial marketing and advertising strategy – the paper on Hellmann's Mayonnaise in this book is a case in point.

It is also true that the business background and the creative strategy and execution are necessary to make the demonstration of effectiveness comprehensible in its context, but these remain subsidiary to the central focus of these Awards on the proven worth of a campaign in its effects in the market-place.

Entries for the 1984 Awards were called for in four categories, of which one was new to the Awards scheme:

1. Consumer goods and services – established.
2. Consumer goods and services – new.
3. Small budgets (any campaign which has been supported by advertising on a budget of less than £250 000).
4. Special (any campaigns not covered in categories 1–3, for example: international, financial, recruitment, corporate; also any campaign run overseas).

## PROBLEMS OF SMALL BUDGET EVALUATION

Category 3, Small Budgets, has been introduced as a separate category to try to encourage entries for brands or markets where the market context and the typical resources available for cost-effective evaluation are much more limited and limiting than those which have classically come to represent what is required for convincing demonstration in higher-budget, fast-moving consumer goods.

In fact, it has always been clear that the criteria for the Awards do vary in their application according to the circumstances of an individual brand or service and the market conditions in which the brand or service operates. Thus, deliveries may have to stand for sales in certain markets; public-service campaign evaluations may have to offer surrogates for the measurement of their direct behavioural objective; corroborative inter-mediate data may have to be dispensed with where they have not been perceived as making a cost-effective contribution to the client/agency advertising decision, and so on.

The creation of the small budgets category is not in this sense, therefore, a change of policy but rather a *clarification of it*. It signals the commitment of the Awards to fostering case histories which convince, at a level which is appropriate to the nature and size of the specific business problem with which they are concerned and to the resources generally available to such an advertiser. Nevertheless, simply to state this principle is not to resolve the practical problems that arise from trying to implement it. It cannot mean, for example, that with a small budget and limited resources 'anything goes', though three entries from one agency clearly took it to mean just that. Demonstration and the resulting conviction of proven worth are not infinitely elastic concepts. Just what are *appropriate* rigour and thoroughness in these cases is hard to define in general terms. Almost certainly the proper place to find that definition is not in the entry rules, but specifically *within* each entry of this kind as submitted, arguing explicitly for its own particular limitations and for the thoroughness and rigour which it has attempted to exercise within them.

Very few of the entries in this category attempted to do this, and even fewer did so successfully. And of the three entries that were successful, in fact, only one *needed* to argue its case in this way, since the other two were, quite legitimately, small-budget evaluations in the big-budget style.

This kind of problem will take time to resolve and its resolution will only come through the patient accumulation of successful papers as models which provide illustrations of how it can be done. In other categories those models already exist and have begun to have some effect. This was particularly noticeable in the 1984 Awards in the high average standard of entries for the category 1 (Consumer Goods and Services – Established) but was less consistently in evidence in categories 2 and 4 (Consumer Goods and Services – New, and Special, respectively) where, with some conspicuous exceptions, the quality was uneven. Nevertheless the prizewinners in these latter categories show just what can be done – and done superlatively well – to demonstrate advertising effectiveness.

## THE ACHIEVEMENT OF THE AWARDS

With the publication of the 1984 Awards, the IPA will have published a total of 55 case histories and has a further bank of some 130 or so entries available for study at the IPA.

This represents an achievement of some consequence, both within the industry and outside it.

It is easy to forget that in the late 1970s – just prior to the institution of the Awards – brand advertising had seemed to be under increasing threat. In a recessionary environment margins were being squeezed by price-dominated competition. Advertisers needed more than ever to protect their bottom line and, faced with escalating costs (not least in media costs), seemed to be looking for a quicker pay-off from their *total* marketing spend. In this situation, there was a strong temptation to raid the advertising budget to pacify the demands of the retailer and a wish to see greater cost-effectiveness and accountability in the brand media-spend that remained.

Of course there were countervailing influences, like the belief in the power of sheer creativity (and the salience in the market-place which this could achieve) to restore the balance of the marketing mix or even to reverse it in favour of above-the-line. After all, Beecham's AMTES experiments (Area Marketing Test Evaluation System) had seemed to suggest that sales effects were more responsive to differential creativity than to differential weight. And to comfort those in advertising who saw in this tribute to agency creativity an implicit threat to agency profitability, there was the belief that those advertisers who had drastically cut their advertising in the recession of 1973–74 had suffered for it compared with those who had taken a longer view and maintained support levels.

Nevertheless, it is hard to escape the impression that thorough-going evaluation in general, and the statistical modelling techniques now quite frequent in the demonstration of advertising effectiveness in these Awards in particular, first presented themselves in wolf's clothing. It is in no small measure due to these Awards that the 'wolf' has been adopted in the industry. It has not thereby become a sheep. Anything which adds to our ability to demonstrate advertising success also adds to our ability to detect (or suspect) failure. Evaluation is necessarily a two-edged sword. But we are stronger, and perceived to be so, because of it.

Looking back, it seemed at one time as if the 1970s were likely to develop what Tony Twyman[1] called a *folklore* of the *in*effectiveness of advertising, which was to offset or destroy the folklore of its effectiveness. The latter had received fresh impetus in the heady and prosperous years for the industry following the introduction of a commercial television channel in the mid-1950s. Now in the 1980s, the industry can point to an accumulating body of evidence which is an antidote to cynicism outside the industry and at the same time a prophylactic against complacency within it.

The fact that this body of evidence is updated at regular intervals is essential both as a demonstration of the industry's continuing commitment to the seriousness and importance of the marketing case for advertising, and to the part that the Awards must play in educating the industry in what should be its own professional disciplines of planning and evaluation.

Arising out of this, however, is a special value to our industry in the Awards' format. Awards have long been an important and familiar currency of inter-agency competition and comparison in the creative area. The IPA Effectiveness Awards are not a rival to creative awards but a complement to them, providing some of the same excitement and prominence for less glamorous but equally necessary disciplines in the multi-disciplinary process that is advertising. For all those specially responsible for the 'think' input within advertising, these Awards offer an arena which is specially their own and peopled first and foremost by their peer group. And this is true whether they are researchers, account planners or account handlers.

The publicity for this year's Awards (account directed by Michael Hockney and created by Chris Inge) drew heavily on this parallel and complementarity between the two types of awards and summed it up in the headline 'You still need one more for effect'. Not least of the achievements of these Awards has been to provide a focus and dynamic not only for the issue of advertising effectiveness as such, but also for those who are its guardians within the agency account team.

## EFFECTIVENESS AND CREATIVITY

The old polarity between 'creative' and 'effective' is beginning to be seen for the false opposition that it really is. It is not only *possible* to be both but likely that it is *optimal* to be both.

Nonetheless, we must be absolutely clear that creativity *as perceived by the industry* cannot be a criterion in making these awards. 'Creativity' as perceived by the consumer may be potentially relevant to a proper understanding of the strategy and execution which is being evaluated and some examples of this will be found among the papers published here. But this is creativity as an audience requirement; their perceptions of it may or may not coincide with those of the industry. We cannot treat the latter as a proxy for or confirmation of the former. Trade awards are somewhat different (as may be their perception of creativity), and there are circumstances when they may constitute *part* of the evidence for an extremely important indirect effect of consumer advertising.

Creativity as a target audience perceives it and requires it may become more of an issue in the strategy and creative development sections of future entries, though this is a view that would not necessarily command universal approval in the industry. But it is only in this perspective that advertising *creativity* can take its proper place in the development of case histories of advertising *effectiveness*, which is what these Awards are all about.

In this volume, incidental comments on the papers submitted for the 1984 Awards are taken up in the more general context of the section on *Comments on advertising and its evaluation*, on pages 1–6.

It should be noted that prizes and commendations are given to papers in the form in which they are originally submitted. Where necessary, they have been modified for publication by the authors themselves for the sake of clarity or brevity, or to secure uniformity in certain minor matters of practice; some supporting detail has been omitted in a few cases, while in others the treatment of certain issues has been expanded where this seemed potentially helpful to the reader.

Of the two commended papers omitted for reasons of space from this selection, one is a sequel to a paper already published in *Advertising Works 2*, while the other evaluates a successful and original price-led regional campaign for 11 superstores in the North East, belonging to a national chain.

This collection of the 1984 winning essays opens with category 2, 'Consumer Goods and Services – New', as the Grand Prix winner, ICI Dulux Natural Whites, was from this category.

### References

1. Twyman, W.A., 'Are long-term effects possible or measurable?' ESOMAR Congress 1978, Session 1, page 2.

## IPA ADVERTISING EFFECTIVENESS AWARDS WORKING PARTY

Mike Grant Reynolds, Vice Chairman, Benton & Bowles Ltd (*Chairman of the IPA Marketing Group*)

Michael Hockney, Director, The Boase Massimi Pollitt Partnership Ltd (*Chairman of the Working Party*)

Simon Broadbent, Vice Chairman, Leo Burnett Ltd

Charles Channon, Vice Chairman, Ayer Barker Ltd

Chris Inge, Chetwynd Haddons Ltd

Mike Ironside, Chetwynd Haddons Ltd

## 1984 JUDGES

Sir Terence Beckett, Director General, CBI (*Chairman*)

James Best, Director, The Boase Massimi Pollitt Partnership Ltd

Charles Channon, Vice Chairman, Ayer Barker Ltd

Professor Peter Doyle, Professor of Marketing, University of Bradford Management Centre

Stephen King, Director, J. Walter Thompson Co. Ltd. and Chairman, MRB International

Nick Phillips, Sales Director, Granada Television

## ACKNOWLEDGEMENTS

The success of the 1984 IPA Advertising Effectiveness Awards Scheme is in no small measure due to the media who gave free advertising space:

| | |
|---|---|
| *Admap* | BRMB |
| *Campaign* | Capital Radio |
| *The Economist* | LBC |
| *Financial Times* | Piccadilly Radio |
| *Marketing* | |
| *Marketing Week* | |
| *Media World* | |
| *The Times* | |

Many people worked on this scheme but it owes most to the untiring efforts of Michael Hockney (Chairman of the Working Party) and, from the Institute of Practitioners in Advertising, Janet Mayhew, Research Officer, Secretary to the Marketing Group and the Working Party, Penny van Weede, Public Relations Officer and Julia Steell.

The Editor also wishes to thank Dr Neil Barnard of the London Business School for helpful advice and discussion.

# Prizes and Commendations

## NEW CONSUMER GOODS AND SERVICES

FIRST PRIZE AND GRAND PRIX

*ICI Dulux Natural Whites*
Kevin Green and Richard Dodson
   *Foote, Cone & Belding* for *ICI*

CERTIFICATES OF COMMENDATION

*How advertising helped Wall's establish a new sector in a mature market*
Tim Russell
   *SSC&B: Lintas Worldwide* for *Birds Eye Wall's*

*The effect of advertising on the launch of Shakers Cocktails*
Simon Clemmow and Damian O'Malley
   *Gold Greenlees Trott* for *Hedges & Butler*

## ESTABLISHED CONSUMER GOODS AND SERVICES

FIRST PRIZES

*Breaking the bran barrier – Kellogg's Bran Flakes 1982–84*
Jeremy Elliott
   *J. Walter Thompson* for *The Kellogg Company*

*Hofmeister: a study of advertising and brand imagery in the lager market*
Peter Field and Adam Morgan
   *The Boase Massimi Pollitt Partnership* for *Courage*

SECOND PRIZE
*The repositioning of Hellmann's Mayonnaise*
Paul Feldwick
> *The Boase Massimi Pollitt Partnership* for *CPC (UK)*

CERTIFICATES OF COMMENDATION

*Fulfilling the potential of St. Ivel Gold*
Evelyn Jenkins
> *J. Walter Thompson* for *St. Ivel*

*Building a business through advertising: Zanussi's appliance of science*
Roger Clayton, Estelle Williams and Rick Bendel
> *Geers Gross* for *Zanussi*

*Cadbury's Fudge: how advertising has built a brand*
Peter Carter
> *Foote Cone & Belding* for *Cadbury*

*Paul Masson California Carafes: 'they're really jolly good'*
Leslie Butterfield
> *Abbott Mead Vickers/SMS* for *Seagram*

*Curly Wurly: The effect of an advertising relaunch*
Mo Fisher
> *Leo Burnett* for *Cadbury*

*Defence proves the best form of attack for Cuprinol*
Dr. Laurence Hagan
> *Everetts* for *Berger Nicholson*

*Kraft Dairylea: the transformation of a brand's fortunes*
Terry Bullen
> *J. Walter Thompson* for *Kraft*

*Kellogg's Coco Pops: a 'storybook' success*
Jill Greenop
> *J. Walter Thompson* for *The Kellogg Company*

## SMALL BUDGETS

**SECOND PRIZES**

*The relaunch of Cow & Gate babymeals*
Linda Caller
    *Abbott Mead Vickers/SMS* for *Cow & Gate*

*Rebirth of the English Riviera*
Dinah Bisdee
    *Pictorial Publicity* for *The Torbay Tourist Board*

**CERTIFICATE OF COMMENDATION**

*Fine Fare North-East: an original approach to retail advertising*
David Meneer
    *Young & Rubicam* for *Fine Fare*

## SPECIAL

**FIRST PRIZE**

*Advertising's part in the regeneration of London Docklands*
Damian O'Malley, Simon Clemmow and Tim North
    *Gold Greenlees Trott* for *London Docklands Development Corporation*

**SECOND PRIZE**

*Chip pan fire prevention 1976–84*
Chris Cowpe
    *The Boase Massimi Pollitt Partnership* for *Central Office of Information*

**CERTIFICATES OF COMMENDATION**

*Home protection revisited: the national rollout of a regional test*
Sandra Yarwood and Chris Cowpe
    *The Boase Massimi Pollitt Partnership* for *Central Office of Information*

*The Lloyds Bank Personal Loan – accessible borrowing*
Jane Fiori
    *Lowe Howard-Spink Campbell-Ewald* for *Lloyds Bank*

# Comments on Advertising and its Evaluation

The two previously published volumes of these Awards have described and discussed the general principles, disciplines, and approach that are proper to the convincing evaluation of advertising effectiveness. They have also commented on the uses of evaluation in the continuing cycle of the advertising process within the agency, and the incidental lessons for parts of that cycle that may be drawn from the strategy and creative development sections of the published entries.

In view of this, the present editor has not attempted another overall review of the groundwork. The interested reader and, most particularly, the would-be entrant for future Awards are referred to those essays in their original context of *Advertising Works* and *Advertising Works 2*, so that some grasp of their content is taken for granted in the notes which follow.

The notes below are very much a miscellany covering a number of issues raised by the entries themselves or by problems that come to mind in making judgements on them. Some concern matters of principle while a few are more in the nature of practical tips.

## THE 'JIGSAW' OF THE EVIDENCE AND THE EXPERT WITNESS

Advertising is a multi-disciplinary business and so too, though sometimes less obviously, is the marketing function which it serves. It has always been clear that the proper audience of these Awards is (directly) all interested and informed parties concerned with the advertising process itself, plus (indirectly) those not formally connected with it whose opinions and actions may, nevertheless, affect the legislative, budgetary, or simply the presumptive environment within which advertising has to operate.

These Awards, therefore, are for the sort of convincing demonstration that would command *general* assent among the reasonably informed in advertising and marketing. They are not designed to be 'technical' awards, which would only be of interest to and, more important, only be found convincing by those who were themselves experts in the technicalities deployed. Specifically, they are not awards in statistical modelling and econometric analysis though, as the Introduction makes clear, these are a welcome and valuable addition to the armoury of advertising evaluation. And where they are used, they certainly require that we should give the expert witness a careful hearing.

Of course peer-group judgement, among the reasonably *but only generally* informed, accepts and acknowledges the contribution of the expert in respect of certain types of evidence and technique. But it must reserve to itself the right to weigh that contribution alongside other less technical aspects of a case and make its own judgements.

Because of the notorious difficulty of disentangling advertising effects on sales (and profitability) from those of other variables operating in the market-place (particularly those of price, distribution, seasonality, competitive activity, and of what we might call the underlying basic trend – in which advertising may or may not play a part), we are usually obliged to *build* a case, piecing together all the evidence into a mutually corroborative thrust which we hope will be accepted in its totality as reasonable and convincing proof of the effectiveness of a campaign. By the same token, a technique of analysis such as econometrics which offers to quantify (simultaneously) the relationships between variables in time series data would appear (rightly) to be a powerful additional resource to clinch our case *if* the relevant data is available in a suitable form, at the right level of aggregation, and with a sufficient number of readings.

However, we should be very careful to see statistical modelling and econometric analysis as a servant of evaluation and not its master. All the experts in this field are absolutely clear on this point. A marketing model should be designed to represent in testable form a marketing theory. In this case the theory is that a particular campaign worked. The validity of that model is dependent not only on its technical propriety in the eyes of the experts in statistics, but equally on its plausibility and adequacy to the characteristics of the market-place in the eyes of those who are working in this environment. *In the context of an entry for the Awards, this judgement on the non-technical plausibility and adequacy of a model must be derived from the way the rest of the paper builds up the case in question and with it a picture of the dynamics of the market-place.* So a model is very far from superseding other evidence or the separate examination of the variables it incorporates. If anything, because of the risk of spurious relationships – and, by definition, we can only guard against the ones we have thought of and not the ones we haven't, (though area tests with statistical modelling are slightly better off in this respect) – it is likely that the most convincing models will derive from cases that are already pretty convincing.

The central thought here was already implicit in Simon Broadbent's stress, in the second volume of these Awards, on the need to present the findings of modelling in a way that is 'intuitively obvious' and in his trenchant comment to the effect that 'if you can't see it, it isn't there'.

These principles simply reflect accepted practice where modelling is used to guide management decision-making for the future and is not simply a justification for past action (which is its inevitable role in entries for the Awards). In the world of decision-making a model must make sense in terms of its variables and in the relative size of its coefficients. The same is true here: it must make *basic* sense in the light of our *prior* knowledge before we can reasonably take notice of any *additional* sense that it may make. In providing that prior knowledge for the reader, the 'classical' arguments in the papers – particularly the arguments from inspection and elimination – have a very important part to play.

The fact that, as has been well said, 'market modelling is an artistic act within the domain of science'[1] does not lessen the importance of ensuring expert testimony on its technical merits. In particular we need to be aware of where it departs from 'normal' practice and, if that departure is significant (as in the case of St. Ivel Gold in this volume), it may be preferable to argue its pros and cons within the paper, particularly in respect of the interpretation that is to be put upon its 'findings'. The decision in the St. Ivel Gold paper to attempt to model the underlying *long-term* upward sales trend by deploying straight cumulative TVRs (undecayed) as the independent variable, which might 'represent' that effect within the model, is unconventional. It may be doubted whether other expert opinion would be as willing in this context to use as a *proxy* a variable which at the *literal* level might seem to be claiming the *whole* of the underlying upward trend as a long-term effect of advertising. Nevertheless, the interpretation of the model very carefully avoids this pitfall. The perspective of the learning process in which that paper presents its model is scrupulously correct and its overall case for effectiveness does not stand or fall on its treatment of this issue.

In general, of course, it is likely to be true that a strong case will be blurred and weakened by too much technical in-fighting. But given judicious interpretation and provided that modelling is seen in its proper perspective *as one part of a learning process which itself has to be corroborated by other parts of that process*, such in-fighting should not often be necessary. Certainly, there are other published papers where some experts in modelling would have done differently, but this is not important in the total context of a strong, thorough, balanced and well-argued case.

## ADVOCACY, HONESTY AND CRITICAL AWARENESS

In a review of *Advertising Works 2*, the present editor remarked that although the QED quality of entries may seem very unlike what happens in real life, there was one part of real life in any agency to which that very quality was highly relevant, namely that point (typically a major presentation) where we 'get the show on the road' with everything neatly packaged and tied up, leading inexorably (we hope) to one single goal: our appointment as the new agency, or the acceptance of a major recommendation by an existing client.

If is, of course, obvious that we can learn a lot from these papers about the *art* of advocacy, but that very fact reminds us that, as Simon Broadbent put it in his introduction to the selected case histories for students and trainees, '*The papers printed here are not impartial.*' This must of necessity be true and yet it is also true that *any evidence of partiality in the presentation of the case will count against it.*

Not all entrants have yet grasped this paradox. A small minority seem to have taken the parallel with the agency presentation rather too literally and substituted the looser disciplines (and style) of selling for the rather more rigorous requirements of demonstration. More common is a simple failure to address certain issues which are critical to a particular case. Obviously, selectivity is one thing but plain inadequacy is quite another.

It is in the nature of the market-place and of the complex difficulties posed within it for the evaluation of the sales effect of any single variable, that an *absolute* case for effectiveness is most unlikely. If it were otherwise there would scarcely be a need for these Awards. However, just because what is required is simply a convincing case, *the need for honesty, the ability to play devil's advocate, and a critical awareness of the nature of the relevant evidence and of the weight that it can bear* are of supreme importance in making advocacy work for the case that is being presented and not *against* it. This must be true wherever evidence must be persuasive but cannot of its nature be coercive. All the papers in this book have in varying degrees grasped this simple principle.

## CRITERIA OF EFFECTIVENESS FOR NEW CONSUMER GOODS AND SERVICES

With the one outstanding exception of the case history for ICI Dulux Natural Whites (first prizewinner in the category and winner of the Grand Prix for 1984 Awards), and the partial exception of the two commended papers in the category, it is still apparent that the problems of a brand or variety that has no past and a future where there is nowhere to go but up pose special difficulties for the full and convincing demonstration of effectiveness.

In the first volume of the Awards, Stephen King was quoted at length on the kind of criteria for success that apply in this situation. In his notes on this category to the other judges in the 1984 Awards he once more summarised the appropriate criteria and I cannot do better than, with his permission, to quote them in full:

*Criteria*

I've followed, as far as I can, the guidelines set out in Simon's 'How to win'. But new brands are a little bit different from established brands. I discount the value of the following arguments in an award for *advertising effectiveness* for new brands:

(a) 'The brand was successful against targets.' Yes, but were the targets right? And how far was it due to the advertising?

(b) 'Sales went up.' Where else could they go?

(c) 'We couldn't have launched the brand without advertising.' True, but trivial – you can say the same about distribution, packaging, sales force etc, etc.

What I've looked for, apart from more general values, is some *evidence* or at the very least *argument* on the following five criteria:

(i) Some effort to *isolate* the effect of advertising from the effect of other elements of the marketing mix. For instance, I don't think a crude association of advertising expenditure and sales/share increase for a new brand is wholly convincing, unless there is an attempt to eliminate the effects of, say, increasing distribution and relative pricing during the relevant period.

(ii) Some attempt to compare the effect of advertising and not advertising – ideally by some sort of area experiment, but at the least by before/during/after measures.

(iii) Some hard market data compared to existing brands (sales, share, price etc). The indirect/soft data (awareness, attitude) may be valuable for explaining *how* the advertising works, but the award is for showing that it *does* work.

(iv) Evidence or argument about the advertising's contribution to building a brand that has saleability (or unique positioning or a price premium or added values or potential profitability). In today's market conditions of rapid copying/private label/generics it is surely not enough for advertising to contribute noise and volume sales to the launch: it must start to build a brand that people will value beyond the naked product. Here comparative soft data can provide evidence.

(v) If possible, some indication that the client has got or will get more *profit* from the level of advertising budget used than from some smaller amount.

## SOME PROBLEMS AND SOME POINTERS

### *The problem of being premature*

One or two very promising entries failed to get commended (or better) simply because they were premature. In evaluation, as elsewhere, truth is to some extent the daughter of time.

### The advantage of breadth in evaluation

Simon Broadbent has stressed elsewhere the great advantages which are potentially conferred on evaluative programmes which are planned and instituted from the outset; one of these advantages is that it is possible to plan for completeness as far as possible and for coverage of all the angles. In real life, however, circumstances in general or the research budget in particular, may rob us of these advantages and where this happens it inevitably places a proportionately greater weight on the evidence that remains to us. Thus, for example, while it is true that the evidence from intermediate variables like awareness, attitudes, and advertising recall carries an intrinsically lower weight in the demonstration of effectiveness than the direct inspection and analysis of other elements in the marketing mix, it is also true that the absence of any corroborative intermediate data places a greater strain on the classical arguments from inspection and elimination or on the argument from experimentation if we have had the opportunity. Quite simply, the narrower the basis of the evaluation the more watertight it has to be in the evidence that remains to it and the fewer the presumptions that will be acceptable.

### The 'Rosser Reeves' fallacy[2]

Rosser Reeves was an important figure in the development of advertising and the kind of thinking applied to it. The interaction of variables and the implications of this for the direction of cause and effect were not, however, the strongest points in his armoury. In particular, his concept of 'usage pull' failed to take account of the fact that variables like advertising recall and claimed exposure were in principle just as likely to be the *result* of usage as they were to be the *cause* of it. The fallacy was widely recognised at the time and it is still a fallacy.

### Laws and limitations in intermediate data

Quantified data from intermediate variables like attitudes can often provide valuable evidence of how a campaign might be working and, in the process, help to strengthen the presumption that it is indeed doing so. However, in so far as such data has certain law-like relationships with usage within a product field, its use as corroborative evidence can in certain circumstances seem naive unless such relationships are recognised and allowed for in its interpretation. To say that certain attitudes 'went up' is only additional evidence when it is clear that the increase is more than would be expected from the increased number of users (or increased frequency of use). The mere fact of differential increases within an image battery is not necessarily sufficient to establish this. Significantly, some of the most enlightening comments on intermediate data in the 1984 Awards have been made when these variables have not behaved as expected (eg the comments on brand image in the Hofmeister paper and the comments on advertising awareness in the paper on Cadbury's Fudge).

### Some comments on papers entered in Category 4 (Special)

In his notes to the other judges, Professor Peter Doyle made three succinct comments on the criteria in Category 4, which I have asked to be able to quote direct. They do not, of course, apply to the papers from that category which are published. What he has to say should remind us that there is a body of academic knowledge which has direct relevance to our professional skills and this is of course true whatever the category or product field that we are working in.

If any advice is to be given to next year's entrants, I suggest the following, on the basis of the presentations I have reviewed:
1.  Be more rigorous and analytical in describing the background and results.
2.  Many of the presentations showed no acquaintance with the elementary principles of experimental design. Some such knowledge is crucial for any rational evaluation of advertising's effects.
3.  Contenders need to show some knowledge of key marketing principles such as market segmentation and buyer behaviour theory where appropriate.

## References

1.  Parsons, Leonard J. and Schultz, Randall L., *Marketing Models and Econometric Research*, New York: North Holland, 1976, page 123.
2.  Reeves, Rosser, *Reality in Advertising*, New York: Alfred A. Knopf, 1961, page 18 *ff.*

# Section One

*New Consumer Goods and Services*

# 1

# ICI Dulux Natural Whites

## INTRODUCTION

This is about the national launch of Dulux Natural Whites, a new paint product range from ICI. The range was sold in from February 1982, and advertised from March 1982. We look at the period 1980–84.

The range fulfilled and exceeded its objectives, and now holds brand leadership of a new market sector. Indeed within the long-established white emulsions market, it has achieved a 17 per cent volume share in the first quarter of 1984, two years after launch.

The launch advertising campaign was wholly original. Consumers identify TV advertising as their prime medium for awareness of and propensity to purchase the range, and its role in the continuing success of the range is demonstrated here.

## THE UK RETAIL DECORATIVE PAINT MARKET

Between 1970 and 1980, the decorative paints market enjoyed dramatic volume growth from 90 million litres to 115 million litres. This is attributable to three key factors:

1.  Consumer expenditure increased, along with a propensity to decorate.
2.  The overall stock of houses grew considerably.
3.  There was a significant move away from wallcoverings to the use of paints, which are seen as more convenient and cheaper to use.

The retail value of the market also increased, but less so. The growth of specialist DIY chains created strong price competition and a consequent reduction in value growth.

Since 1980, whilst consumer expenditure has continued to rise the decorative paint market has remained static in volume. The number of new houses being built has slowed, as has the move from wallcoverings to paints.

### Dulux's Position and Performance in the Market-place

Throughout the 1970s Dulux held brand leadership, averaging 28 per cent market share, and volume sales grew by 35 per cent between 1970 and 1980. In 1980 the Dulux brand as a whole reached 29 per cent volume share, its highest since 1973. However, in whites the share increase in 1980 was only from 25 to 26 per cent, and within that white emulsion had only 23 per cent, a severe decline in the most dynamic market sector.

The dilemma for Dulux was that in a now static market, with its major share product, Brilliant White Emulsion, competing in a heavily price-promoted sector, and with overall pricing being dictated by multiple DIY retailers, share growth through more aggressive pricing would simply lead to a reduction in profit margins. Dulux not only wanted to re-establish dominance in the significant whites area, but also needed to restore profit levels in this specific high volume sector.

### Problems with Dulux Brilliant White Emulsion

However, for some time there had been no product improvements in Dulux Brilliant White Emulsion, so purchasing *Dulux* had become of lower priority, or more commodity orientated. Not only that: reactions to the 1981 Brilliant White TV advertising in qualitative research compared with qualitative findings during the late, as against the early, 1970s showed that whites advertising was beginning to be criticised on the grounds of lack of impact and humanity, and of coldness – positive responses were milder and weaker than in the past.

By 1981, Brilliant White was clearly no longer new, no longer, in its starkest usage, fashionable. Although used on most decorating occasions it was no longer considered to make a marked contribution to the overall effect of the decor, and had become an automatic choice largely based on habit and tradition. Would it be possible to excite consumers about white paint again and if so, how?

Finally an examination of the consumer profile for Dulux highlighted further weaknesses. Dulux's relative strength has always been amongst older, up-market men. The own-label profile countered Dulux's orientation with a bias towards women, the young and the down-market. Long-term business for the brand would have to be ensured by strengthening Dulux's appeal in those specific weak areas.

### ACTION

How, then, in the short term, could Dulux restore brand share and re-establish dominance and profit levels in the significant, high-volume whites area? In the immediate short term (1981) it was planned to achieve this by attacking the competition on price grounds. Secondly, how could Dulux find a way of reducing the price-promoted brilliant whites sector as a market in itself?

It is this second issue to which we turned our attention, for, in the absence of a new product-based story to tell – which would take Dulux out of the commodity arena – any innovation we introduced to differentiate ourselves from the competition would have to come from the creation of an image, *and be advertising-led*. A number of actions were put into effect:

1. In 1981, a major market-research exercise into why consumers used white paint and their attitudes to it.
2. A detailed technical review of potential product improvements: this indicated that whilst there were a number of technical improvements available, none was felt to be

*sufficient* to warrant the consumer paying a *premium*, or to meet the objective of reducing the overall price promoted sector of the market.

3.  A review of Dulux's other paint markets around the world. This provided a clue in the shape of a colour card including a range of *tinted* whites.
4.  Consultations with decor experts.

### *The Solution*

This action indicated that the concept of a range of *tinted* whites with the exciting feel of *colour* might meet our longer-term objective. Such a range would offer something new, interesting and aesthetic – it would also be unique. More importantly, reassurance that using the shades would lead to successful results would have to be the job of the advertising.

### *Towards a Positioning – Whites or Colours?*

We had to clarify where such a range of tinted whites should be positioned. Would the role of white paint be upgraded by the juxtaposition of white with colours? Further qualitative research was conducted to investigate this area.

Whilst in research admirers of the new range referred to the paints both as 'near whites' and as 'delicate colours', there was little doubt as to their likely role. The common assumption was that they would be a substitute for brilliant white, ie light and airy, but less stark and harsh – and still a safe option in an integrated colour scheme. Certainly, the lack of courage of the target audience must not be forgotten. We were talking to whites-users, many of whom felt that magnolia was far too dangerous and bold a shade to use. Our target group needed reassurance; what better security than to *know* that the new paints from Dulux would be *white* paints.

However, for two reasons, it was vital that the new range was not felt to be simply an alternative to brilliant white:

1.  Other research revealed indications that consumers were demanding more:

    It's nice to have something that isn't dead white.

    It'd make you want to change your other colours to match, whereas with real white, it just goes with anything.

2.  In strategic terms, we had to move away from the passivity which is involved in the choice of a brilliant white; otherwise the new whites would quickly assume the same unimportant background role.

In 1980 qualitative research identified the most motivating and differentiating proposition for Dulux as an emotional one of 'personal renewal'. The state of consumers' knowledge was that the leading brands offered the same range of paints, based roughly on the same technology. It appeared that any attempt by any manufacturer to lay claim to differentiation on rational grounds would be viewed with active suspicion.

Reinforcing the belief that Dulux paints are superior to others, especially premium brands, would therefore entail an *emotional point of differentiation* which would centre around the assurance of a beautiful end result and the feelings of renewal which accompany redecoration.

### The Creation of the Range

A creative consultant was briefed to produce a range of tinted whites that would meet the criteria set out above. Three whites were produced – Apple White, with a hint of green; Rose White, with a hint of pink; and Fleece White, with a hint of cream.

The agency developed the concept, and also worked with packaging designers to develop appropriate can liveries. When the creative approach was finalised an animatic was produced, together with a number of concept cards and large-scale panels of the paint. These were then qualitatively researched. The tinted whites concept was eliciting encouraging results.

Dulux R&D were briefed to produce three shades of paint, clearly discernible from brilliant white, and yet not pastel colours – colours which would have to be reproducible on a large scale.

Meanwhile, the production of a launch strategy ensued.

## THE LAUNCH STRATEGY

The advertising brief was to develop an approach which would set the range apart from all other paint advertising, which would be distinctive, which would communicate the subtlety of the paint, and which would be more cosmetic and thereby less functional than previous advertising. The point-of-sale (POS) brief asked that material would reflect the advertising idea.

Fleece White had developed into Pearl White and finally into Lily White. Similarly, can designs were refined so their hue indicated the colours of the shades more precisely. Pricing policy was then developed on the basis of research and it appeared that consumers would pay about 15 per cent more for tinted whites than for brilliant whites. This was a fundamental part of the plan in order to meet profit objectives. Volume forecasts were prepared on the basis that these shades would sell along the line of Dulux's previous best selling pale *colours* like Magnolia and Buttermilk.

It was decided that the range would be fully supported, with a spend of £2 800 000 on advertising and £400 000 on POS and display material. The first cans were released on 1st February 1982. Within three months, 75 per cent sterling distribution had taken in the range. The advertising began in March 1982.

## THE ADVERTISING AND MEDIA STRATEGIES

### Marketing Aim

To increase Dulux share of the whites market in the face of heavy promotion from Crown – the main premium competitor – and the continuing threat from the cheaper paints, particularly own-label.

## Advertising Objectives

To reawaken consumer interest in white paint, lifting it from a low-priority commodity area where decisions are taken on the basis of habit and price, to assume a more important role in the decorating process, requiring a more conscious and positive choice.

Within this, to increase interest in and commitment to Dulux white paint by announcing the launch of 'a new range of whites from Dulux'.

## Target Audience

*Users of white paint, whether premium or commodity.* They are likely to feel less than happy about their continued use of white paint, but are not prepared to make a move into the more exciting but far riskier area of colours. In demographic terms this represents a very broad sample – BC1C2, under 55 – but women are likely to play the major role in decision-making.

## Creative Strategy

### PROPOSITION

Now there's an exciting but safe way to transform your home.

### REASON WHY

—because Dulux has developed a new range of whites
—so you can have a white with a touch of pink – Rose White; a touch of green – Apple White; and a touch of cream – Lily White

### TONE OF VOICE

Soft and reassuring.

### CONSUMER RESPONSE

I *know* these paints are whites, so I can feel confident in using them; I *believe* they are colours, so I can take a real interest and pride in their effect in my home.

### EXECUTIONAL CONSIDERATION

The unobtrusive inclusion of the Dulux dog, an extremely effective and emotive branding device, will enable us to concentrate on the overall proposition whilst indisputably linking Natural Whites to the Dulux brand.

## The Media Strategy

To launch Natural Whites at a competitive weight and then to maintain a strong presence. A combination of TV and posters was used to gain high product awareness rapidly (see

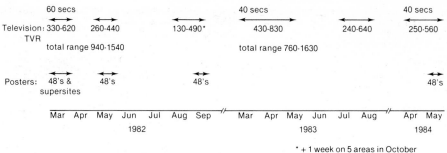

Figure 1. *Natural Whites: Launch Media Plan*

Figure 1). Three factors were essential in the scheduling of TV advertising for Natural Whites:

1. Because the range is based on an advertising property rather than a product development and is therefore creative-led, the creative requirement for a 60-second time length was paramount, but was not allowed to influence the setting of TV rating targets. Therefore, the campaign was launched at an entirely competitive weight in the market.
2. The majority of TV exposure would be concentrated just prior to and through the main Easter sales period.
3. There would be a return to advertising to support the important August Bank Holiday period.

It was also considered that impact would be further increased if Natural Whites appeared in discrete bursts without overlap with other products. The target market was essentially all adults, therefore a time-buying strategy was observed which would ensure a balance particularly across social class.

The decision to support TV with another medium was based on the wish to increase and prolong presence of the campaign. Posters were chosen as the most suitable medium and a mixture of 48-sheets and supersites was used. The campaign ran in March and May to provide maximum impact during the launch period and in September to prolong the campaign period to the end of the major paint buying season. In all cases only high quality poster sites were selected to ensure maximum exposure and the best 'environment' and presentation for the brand.

## THE ADVERTISING

The focus of the work was on the three images created for Rose, Apple and Lily White. These images were used in all creative material, from the can design through to advertising and POS.

The Natural Whites launch commercial follows on page 15. The range was presented through animation – a completely new form of expression for Dulux – which, it was felt, best fitted the need to provide a strong but reassuring emotional point of differentiation for the range.

The whiter shades of pale.

THE WHITER SHADES OF PALE

| *VIDEO* | *AUDIO* |
|---|---|
| Open on a display of three new Dulux cans: Rose White, Lily White and Apple White. | 1½ seconds silence. |
| *Title:* WHITE? | |
| Add *title:* NOT QUITE. | *Sfx* Fade in piano theme: 'A whiter shade of pale'. |
| Dissolve to continuous animation sequence, opening on the interior of an elegant drawing-room. | *Sfx* Outdoor: Birds, grasshoppers, bees etc, under. |
| Pan along the furnishings as far as a lace-covered table on which a single rose has been placed. | |
| Freeze and *title:* ROSE WHITE. A RO-MANTIC WHITE, WITH A DELI-CATE SHADE OF PINK. | |
| Continue panning through the French win- | *Sfx* Bring up level slightly. |

dow to the flower bed, comprising wall-flowers, delphiniums, then lilies.

Freeze and *title:* LILY WHITE. A RICH WHITE, WITH A SOFT AND CREAMY TINT.

Pan along the flower bed, then follow a butterfly across the lawn – we see a sheep-dog rise and walk towards camera – to the shade of an apple tree, where a table is set. On the table is a plate with two apples on it, with one of the apples cut in two.

*Sfx* Woof!

Freeze and *title:* APPLE WHITE. WITH A SUBTLE SHADE OF GREEN.

Dissolve back to the three Dulux cans.

*Title:* THE WHITER SHADES OF PALE and ICI Dulux logo.

*Mv/o* 'Rose White, Lily White, Apple White. The whiter shades of pale. Fresh from Dulux.'

## THE EVALUATION

### Data Sources

ICI's Marketing Research Services group at Paints Division operates a field force of over 300 interviewers and has run a consumer panel of some 4 500 households since 1969. In addition, this group carries out a Price Distribution and Display check (PDD) in some 700 retail outlets three or four times a year, as well as *ad hoc* studies. These services and other qualitative and quantitative research data, in conjunction with the media expenditure information, provide the base data for our analyses.

### Historical Trends Prior to Launch of Natural Whites

Figure 2 demonstrates that over the period January 1980 to January 1982 the total emulsions market remained basically static, although displaying both seasonal and random fluctuations from month to month. Figure 3 illustrates, for the same period, the Dulux share within the white emulsions market.

The declining Dulux share was largely caused, as has been stated, by strong price competition. This is clearly demonstrated by Figure 4, which compares the average price for Dulux vs. Crown brilliant white emulsions. (This chart runs into the first few months of the Dulux Natural White launch to further illustrate the extent of the problem.)

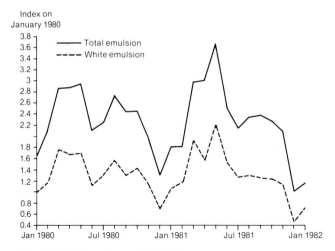

Figure 2. *Trends in the emulsion market 1980-1982*

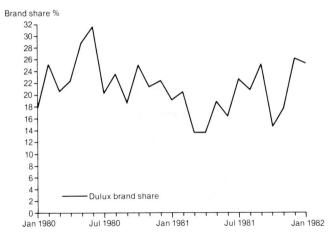

Figure 3. *Dulux share of white emulsion market 1980-1982*

## Evaluation of Results

It is important here to restate a fundamental point made earlier. Natural Whites were not in any structural way a new product. They were a new product concept. As such they would be extremely easy to copy, and indeed lookalikes appeared within nine months. Both for this major reason, and also the dependence on a small number of major national retailers, it was not possible to area-test prior to the national launch.

This fact makes it extremely difficult to isolate the individual contributions to the product's success from all the different factors involved. In particular the correlation between sales and distribution-linked variables is open to debate as to which factor is causal.

As has been explained, *the whole concept relied on the communication of the idea and the reassurance it requires by the advertising.* Therefore, we shall first look at the results in

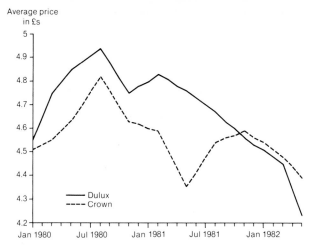

Figure 4. *Trends in average price 1980-82 (Crown and Dulux Brilliant Whites)*

broad terms and demonstrate the success of the launch. Subsequently, we look in more detail at the individual factors involved.

## Overall Launch Success

The launch was successful against all criteria.

1.  The dominance of heavily price-promoted brilliant white in the emulsions market was reduced to 51 per cent in 1983 from 58 per cent in 1980–81.
2.  Dulux increased its brand share in the white emulsions sector from a low of 18 per cent in 1981 to 36 per cent in 1983, whilst maintaining its share of the colours sector (29 per cent in both 1981 and 1983). The 37 per cent achieved during the first half of 1983 was the highest Dulux share in this sector for a decade.
3.  Natural Whites has maintained an average premium of 17 per cent above the Crown Plus Two brilliant white price, and 13 per cent above Dulux's own brilliant white price (the two 'premium brands' in the brilliant white sector).
4.  Both share and premium have been maintained despite launches of competitive lookalikes.
5.  The product has attracted new and younger users to Dulux emulsions.
6.  Above all, the launch was profitable. Over the period 1982–83, Dulux invested £2.9 million more on advertising than had historically been spent in the whites market. However, in 1982 Natural Whites obtained a 13 per cent brand share and in 1983 an 18 per cent share, whilst Dulux brilliant whites lost only 1 per cent. The net effect was a major gain in white emulsion sales over the two years. Compensating for this gain was a small loss of sales for colours caused by a general shift in the emulsions market. Even allowing for the advertising spend, larger profit margin on colours compared to Natural Whites, and non-advertising launch costs, *the resultant benefit in gross profit over the two years is significantly larger than the short-term investment.*

And this ignores the current strength which will maintain very substantial benefits well into the future.

## *The Success in Detail*

### THE REDUCTION IN DOMINANCE OF BRILLIANT WHITE

Figure 5 plots the annual share of the emulsions market accounted for by brilliant whites and Natural Whites. The former illustrates the declining importance of brilliant whites.

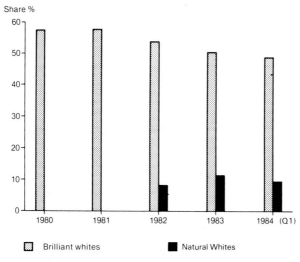

Figure 5. *Emulsion market. Brilliant white & Natural White shares*

### INCREASING DULUX BRAND SHARE

Figure 6 plots monthly and three-monthly moving-average, total brand shares for Dulux in the white emulsions market, along with the Natural Whites brand share. Obviously,

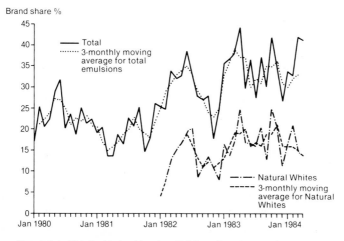

Figure 6. *Dulux White Emulsion brand shares (monthly & 3-monthly moving averages)*

the nature of the data is such that fluctuations can be expected with monthly figures, but the trends are clear. It should be noted that competitive tinted whites were launched, particularly by Crown, during the Summer of 1982. In addition there was heavy discounting on 3-litre and 5-litre brilliant white, by Crown, during the Autumn of 1982. Neither of these activities affected the long-term growth of Natural Whites, although short-term effects were discernible.

NATURAL WHITES PRICE PREMIUM

The aim of achieving a 15 per cent premium for Natural Whites over brilliant whites has been more than met when compared to Crown Plus Two, as shown by the relative price index in Figure 7. Against Dulux's own brilliant white the premium is, on average,

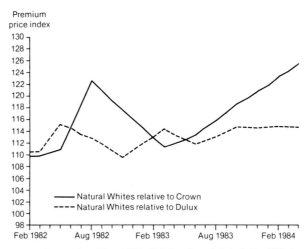

Figure 7. *Price premium of Natural Whites (Relative to Crown & Dulux Brilliant Whites)*

slightly below 15 per cent, but this is due to the ability to maintain a premium for brilliant white vs. Crown Plus Two on the strength of Natural Whites.

NEW, YOUNGER, FEMALE USERS

During April and May 1982, 295 interviews were undertaken with users of Natural Whites. The findings of this study included the following user-profile comparisons with 1981 Dulux emulsion users shown in Table 1.

TABLE 1:    USER PROFILE COMPARISONS 1982

|  | *Natural Whites* % | *1981 Dulux Emulsion* % |
|---|---|---|
| male | 35 | 49 |
| female | 65 | 51 |
| under 35 | 37 | 28 |
| 35–54 | 43 | 38 |
| 55 + | 20 | 34 |

In addition, of the users questioned only 61 per cent claimed Dulux to be the brand they most frequently purchased *prior* to buying Natural Whites. Importantly also, 84 per cent of users claimed they had decided to buy Natural Whites *before* entering the store, and 79 per cent of users claimed to have first heard of the product through TV advertising.

PROFITABILITY

Table 2 shows the emulsion market breakdown, Dulux brand shares and the Dulux advertising expenditures for the period 1980–83.

TABLE 2:    EMULSIONS MARKET 1980–83

|  | 1980 | 1981 | 1982 | 1983 |
|---|---|---|---|---|
| *all emulsions* | % | % | % | % |
| colours | 42.5 | 42.2 | 37.9 | 38.1 |
| brilliant whites | 57.5 | 57.8 | 53.9 | 50.6 |
| Dulux Natural Whites | – | – | 8.2 | 11.4 |
| *white emulsion* | | | | |
| Dulux Brilliant Whites | 23.3 | 18.4 | 16.6 | 17.4 |
| Dulux Natural Whites | – | – | 13.3 | 18.5 |
| Dulux total whites | 23.3 | 18.4 | 29.9 | 35.9 |
| *colours* | | | | |
| Dulux | 34 | 29 | 30 | 29 |
| *Advertising* | 1980 | 1981 | 1982 | 1983 |
|  | £m | £m | £m | £m |
| Dulux Brilliant White Emulsion | 1.2 | 1.4 | 0 | 1.0 |
| Natural Whites | – | – | 2.8 | 1.7 |
| *total* | 1.2 | 1.4 | 2.8 | 2.7 |

From these: the total market volumes and the gross profit margins for Natural Whites, brilliant whites and colours, the approximate gross profit contribution can be calculated. For reasons of confidentiality the precise numbers cannot be divulged. However, as stated earlier, after allowing for the lost share on brilliant whites, the decline of the colours market, and the launch costs, the profit contribution from Natural Whites is still substantial.

*Regression Analyses*

The success of Natural Whites is demonstrated conclusively by the annual results and trends. Inherent in these sales figures is the success of the advertising, since the whole concept revolved around the communication of an emotional stance. However, we have also attempted to quantify the advertising benefit more precisely using some simple modelling techniques. The variables investigated were:

—*Advertising Expenditure* indexed to 1980 levels. This was used rather than some audience measure since the media schedule consisted of multiple media.

—*Share of Shelf Footage* in store.
—*Share of Displays* in store.
—*Relative Price* for both Natural Whites and Dulux Brilliant Whites, relative to Crown Plus Two.

Several analyses were performed which investigated the Dulux share both before and after the Natural Whites launch. For brevity these are not all discussed here, but the key findings are given below and the regression results for the final analysis over the whole data period are shown in the Appendix. The main conclusions were:

1. Prior to the launch of Natural Whites both relative price and Dulux Brilliant White advertising had significant effects on brand share.
2. After the launch Natural Whites advertising and Natural Whites share of shelf footage also showed significant effects.
3. The Dulux Brilliant White price elasticity reduced after the launch from approximately 0.8 to 0.6.
4. Advertising expenditure produced short-term sales effects equivalent to one brand share point for each £100 000 (1980 prices) for both Dulux Brilliant White and Natural Whites.
5. Each 1 per cent of shelf footage allocated to Natural Whites accounts for about $1\frac{1}{2}$ brand-share points.

### SUMMARY OF ANALYSES RESULTS

The analyses essentially attribute the sales success to the advertising and shelf footage levels. However, the growth in shelf footage correlates extremely highly with the cumulative advertising levels (as will normally be the case for a successful new product launch). Bearing in mind the research result previously stated, that 84 per cent of purchasers had decided on Natural Whites before entering the store, it seems probable that it was advertising-generated sales which supported the growth of the shelf footage levels, rather than these levels growing independently and leading to sales. However, once established, high shelf-footage produces sales even in the absence of advertising. This could therefore be thought of as a long-term sales benefit from advertising.

Finally, it must be said that these analyses were designed as supporting evidence for the case and not as numerical proof which would have been extremely difficult, given the circumstances of the launch. In this context they are very informative.

## SUMMARY OF EFFECT AND FURTHER DEVELOPMENT

The success of the launch is attributable to three key factors:

1. Thorough analysis and accurate interpretation of the market situation.
2. The identification of a real opportunity.
3. The development of a creative package which was consistent in its approach and highly appealing to consumers.

The launch has succeeded in reducing the brilliant white sector of the market, and with it the move to a commodity type market.

The effect of the UK retail decorative paints market has been considerable. Apart from creating a third major market sector over and above brilliant whites and colours, Natural Whites have enabled manufacturers to improve their profit margins and to bring a new dynamic to the market-place.

Dulux has continued to exploit and develop the Natural Whites range with a number of new activities: these products have subsequently been introduced in both gloss and non-drip gloss finishes. In January 1983, Natural Whites were added to the Dulux Weathershield Exterior Masonry paint range, and to the Dulux Professional Decorator range of paints. The range has been extended by a further three shades: Bluebell, Apricot and Barley White, presented in a similar way to the original three shades. Additionally, to match all the Natural Whites, a range of wallcovering borders has been introduced. The new market will provide yet more opportunities in the future.

## APPENDIX

### Regression Analysis

Dependent Variable: Dulux Brand Share (White Emulsion)
Independent Variables: Relative Price
Share of Shelf Footage (SSF)
(Natural Whites)
Advertising Expenditure
(Dulux Brilliant White & Natural Whites)

Results:

| | Coefficient | t-Statistic |
|---|---|---|
| Constant | 79.5 | 3.5 |
| R Price | −56.5 | −2.6 |
| SSF | 1.6 | 7.9 |
| Advertising Brilliant White | 0.01 | 1.3 |
| Advertising Natural Whites | 0.01 | 2.3 |

Goodness of fit: $r^2 = 0.62$

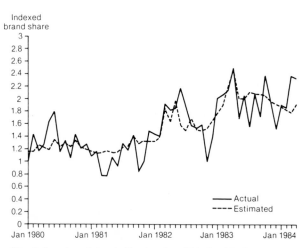

Figure 8. *Regression analysis results (Actual v. estimated Dulux brand share)*

Figure 8 shows the plot of actual brand share and the estimated brand share from this regression analysis.

# 2

# How Advertising helped Wall's Establish a New Sector in a Mature Market

## INTRODUCTION

Wall's introduced Viennetta, their new patisserie-style ice-cream dessert, into the UK market in April 1982. The product was a technical breakthrough since for the first time it brings elaborate patisserie concepts to the ice-cream market.

It was designed to pioneer and develop a new sector in the ice-cream market. As such it had to prove itself as a strongly-branded, complete ice-cream dessert which provided genuine added-value and possessed all-year-round sales potential. In establishing the brand, Wall's was prepared to accept no more than 30 per cent substitution of its existing ice-cream products.

Advertising for Viennetta therefore had to build a strong market position by communicating its unique brand benefits without substantially drawing purchasers away from other company brands.

Through a process of careful expansion over 21 months, Viennetta established itself as Wall's top selling product and developed a new market sector with sales of £15 million at RSP. TV advertising has paid for itself consistently while on air, at all stages in the evolution of the advertising campaign for this brand – at the initial Anglia test stage, the London extension and, ultimately, nationally.

We need to make one additional point. All markets differ in the amount of data available. Traditionally the ice-cream market is not as comprehensively measured as many other grocery markets due to the extremely seasonal nature of the market, and therefore this case is not as fully endowed with figures as would otherwise be possible. We have used all the data at our disposal and are convinced that this case demonstrates outstanding advertising effectiveness.

One further point to note is that all press and TV advertising expenditure quoted hereafter is at *full* rate card and does *not* take into account any discounts negotiated against rate card. Where advertising payback is mentioned, it is calculated against the *actual rate* paid (*including discount*), *not* against full rate card.

## BACKGROUND

### *The UK Take-Home Ice-Cream Market*

The UK ice-cream market divides between traditional handheld 'impulse' products (eg Cornetto, ice lollies etc) and ice-cream to be stored and eaten at home, 'take-home' products (eg Italiano, family $\frac{1}{2}$-litre bricks, 2-litre and 4-litre packs).

In volume terms the take-home sector has been gaining an increasing share of the total market, rising from 60 per cent in 1979 to 70 per cent (223 million litres) in 1983. But this growth has been accompanied by a much slower growth in share by value, with the result that in 1983 the sector was worth £202 million but accounted for only 48 per cent of sales value.

One of the principal reasons for this has been the inroads made by own-label into the volume shares of the two market leaders, Wall's and Lyons Maid. Minimal technical innovation and market investment had resulted in a classic commodity market dominated by price sensitivity and large bulk packs, of which Wall's share had fallen from 30 per cent in 1979 to 25 per cent in 1982. Importantly, the greatest decline within the take-home market had taken place in the more profitable, traditional, small pack ($\frac{1}{2}$-litre) sector. This sector was clearly long overdue for revitalisation.

Wall's decided to fight back with a major investment in technical development and strong branding. A product was needed which, through its complex formulation and powerful added-values, would leave competitors far behind.

## MARKET OPPORTUNITY

Back in 1979, Wall's had identified patisserie as an area of potential interest. The frozen desserts market, which included frozen gateaux, had doubled both in volume and value between 1978 and 1979 and was almost to treble in value again by 1982. It was clear that people were prepared to pay significant amounts of money for fresh and frozen gateaux, well over £1.00 for a typical cake giving four to six portions – but no company had ever sought to mass-market an ice-cream product with similar patisserie values.

Wall's considered that a re-creation and enhancement of the basic *mille-feuilles* concept was potentially the most interesting. Over a period of about 18 months, Wall's developed a product consisting of white vanilla ice-cream layers interleaved with thin, crisp chocolate-flavour layers. The presentation was extremely attractive – the fluted and piped effects on the side combined with the contrasting dark brown and white layers to produce a hand-finished patisserie effect. The product offered a unique taste and texture sensation – the soft ice-cream contrasting with the thin, chocolate-flavour layers.

It was perceived that housewives would regard the product as a novel and complete ice-cream gateau providing high-quality eating properties and excellent value for money at a price of 80–90p. At this price it was hoped that customers would regard the product as a regular rather than occasional purchase.

The company believed that a distinctive name which both described the product and implied continental heritage was essential. It had already enjoyed substantial success with its Cornetto and Italiano brands and it decided to continue along these lines with the new name. The particular advantage of 'Viennetta' was that it had associations with continental origins, and connotations of both Italian ice cream and Viennese patisserie.

The manufacturing process was both unique and sufficiently complex for a patent application to be made. A British patent was duly granted on 19th December 1984. The physical appearance of the product was regarded as so new and original that a Registered Design was granted. Furthermore, the brand name, too, was registerable, thus enhancing the branded opportunity.

In April 1982 Viennetta was ready to be launched as a sophisticated product, designed to appeal to adults and to bring in all-year sales.

A test market was impractical, partly because of the investment required in plant for the new product but also because it would allow time for competitive response. Wall's, therefore, decided on a national launch.

## THE ROLE OF ADVERTISING

Advertising had a crucial role to perform within the marketing strategy. It had to have the impact to position Viennetta as a unique ice-cream dessert with taste and texture sensations that matched its presentation. It also had to create a new sector which provided genuine added-value in terms of aspiration and sophistication for the key target market of BC1C2 housewives. The key objective was to achieve a balanced image that turned an everyday meal into a special occasion that was at the same time accessible and affordable.

### *Marketing and Advertising Objectives April 1982*

The key objectives were defined as follows:

#### MARKETING OBJECTIVES

To create a new added-value sector with all-year sales potential and to build incremental volume, allowing for 30 per cent substitution with existing products.

#### POSITIONING OBJECTIVES

A strong adult positioning with implied sophistication.

#### ADVERTISING OBJECTIVES

To build high awareness rapidly and induce trial of Viennetta.

## PHASE 1   NATIONAL PRESS CAMPAIGN

### *Market and Media Implications*

The uncertainty of the market potential for Viennetta meant it could not justify a heavy-weight advertising campaign in its own right.

It was decided that Viennetta should be launched with a medium-weight women's colour press campaign. The budget was fixed at £95 000, which could be upweighted or superseded by TV at a later date, depending on consumer response.

*Creative Strategy and Execution*

TARGET MARKET

The prime target group was defined as BC1C2 housewives aged 25–45 who buy ice-cream regularly, and who occasionally buy fresh or frozen patisserie and gateaux as a special treat for the family.

MAIN CONSUMER BENEFIT

The main consumer benefit was expressed as:

> Wall's Viennetta is a unique ice-cream dessert that gives you a delicious, luxurious taste and texture every bit as sophisticated as its presentation. One slice is never enough.

Based on this strategy, Lintas developed a press campaign featuring a close-up of Viennetta on a silver salver. The body copy concentrated on the product, with major emphasis on its quality. The copy used emotive terms: 'looks luscious', 'spectacular dessert', 'tastes sumptuous', 'luxurious layers of rich vanilla ice-cream interleaved with tempting crisp, choc tiers'. A key line was that it was 'an extravaganza with only one modest feature – its price'.

*National Sales Results April–September 1982*

From the national launch in April 1982, sales consistently exceeded expectations and Wall's gained incremental volume with very little substitution. This confirmed Wall's hypothesis that Viennetta would create a new market sector. It was now judged that Viennetta had considerably greater market potential and Wall's decided to proceed with an investment in heavier advertising support, with a regional TV test.

## PHASE 2   ANGLIA TV TEST

*Media Selection*

TV's key advantages were:

1. In creative terms, it allowed for clear and succinct expression of the key product benefits while adding enormously to the product's stunning visual presentation and unique taste and texture appeal, through the use of movement and colour.
2. High and fast coverage of the target audience.
3. TV is intrusive, which was important in building high awareness of this unique product breakthrough.
4. TV is appreciated by both the retail trade and the sales force as a sign that the company is making a serious attempt to build a brand.

*Creative Strategy and Execution*

Lintas retained and developed the focus on the product and the positioning of implied sophistication.

# Introducing Wall's Viennetta.
# Ice cream that's really something else.

You must agree Viennetta looks luscious.
A spectacular dessert piped and fluted with great artistry.

It also tastes sumptuous. Luxurious layers of rich vanilla ice cream interleaved with tempting crisp, choc tiers. An extravaganza with only one modest feature - its price.

Viennetta from Wall's. And only from Wall's. Really something else.

STAY'IN FOR
AN EVENING OUT WITH
WALL'S VIENNETTA.

Wall's Viennetta is such a spectacular ice cream dessert that it gives a night at home a rather special flavour.

Its rich vanilla ice cream interleaved with deliciously crisp choc layers makes Viennetta a luxuriously unique way to end a meal.

And a luxurious way to enjoy an evening in.

# BIRDS EYE/WALL'S—VIENNETTA

1½ SECONDS SILENCE
(SFX UNDER: Dinner party
clatter and chatter. Appreciative
noises, polite conversation. Soft
background music – dramatic
and exciting.)

MVO:
(Fairly soft and close so back-
ground is still audible)
WALL'S HAVE CREATED A
SPECTACULAR ICE CREAM
DESSERT . . .

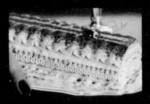

. . . CALLED VIENNETTA.

BUT, DESPITE ITS
DELICIOUSLY . . .

. . . RICH ICE CREAM . . .

AND ITS IRRESISTABLE
CRISP CHOC LAYERS,

VIENNETTA COULD LEAVE
YOU . . .

(SFX: Clatter and chatter
dies down.)
. . . WITH ONE SMALL
PROBLEM.

(SFX: Complete hush except
for the music which is therefore
now more audible and creates a
certain tension.)

MVO:
WALL'S VIENNETTA.
ONE SLICE IS NEVER
ENOUGH.

A 30-second commercial was produced using an elegant dinner party setting showing only the participants' hands. The commercial focused in close-up on the product's unique appearance and the textural contrast of the soft ice-cream and the crisp, chocolate-flavour layers. The voice-over and music track underscored the sophistication of the product and helped build up tension for the finale: 'One slice is never enough'.

*Area Choice - Anglia*

It was decided to use Anglia because:

1. Anglia's share of Viennetta sales from launch corresponded very closely with its share of UK household. The August–October average of Viennetta sales was 6.3 per cent, and 6 per cent of UK households are in the Anglia region.
2. It offered a relatively compact area for evaluating TV effectiveness without significant financial risk.
3. Wall's distribution area (Peterborough, Norwich and Colchester depots) corresponds almost exactly with the Anglia catchment area. Only 15 per cent of the Peterborough depot's distribution falls outside Anglia.
4. Anglia contains a good mix of major national accounts and a representative profile of independent grocers and CTNs.
5. Anglia's share of the UK ice-cream market is in line with its share of population.
6. All major competitors are sold in Anglia – Lyons Maid, distributors' own brands and other brands.
7. Media costs were very reasonable and good test market discounts were offered.

*The Media Plan*

The TV campaign started on 1st November 1982 and ran for seven weeks achieving 666 TVRs, 7.4 OTS (housewives). The rate card cost of the campaign was £138 000 (see Figure 1).

CAMPAIGN EVALUATION

Only ex-depot sales for the Anglia and London TV test areas have been included in the evaluation to ensure strict accuracy.

ANGLIA EX-DEPOT SALES RESULTS

The success of the TV test is shown clearly in Figures 1 and 2, and Tables 1 and 2. Viennetta's sales in Anglia during the TV support period increased by a factor of more than 10 (national sales increased by a factor of three during the same period). Before TV, Viennetta sales in Anglia were between £6 000 and £11 500 @ RSP per month. Sales then rose to £120 000 @ RSP per month. The result was that within four weeks Anglia's share of national Viennetta sales went from August–October 1982 average of 6.3 per cent (Table 1) to a peak of almost 25 per cent during the week commencing 22nd November 1982, and during the TV support period, Anglia's share of national Viennetta sales were on average three times greater than their previous share of national sales.

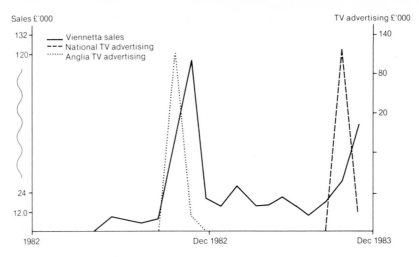

Figure 1. *Viennetta ice cream — Anglia depots*
*Source:* Birds Eye Wall's

TABLE 1: THE EFFECT OF TV ADVERTISING ON COMPANY
VOLUME SHARE FOR VIENNETTA IN ANGLIA REGION

| *1982* | Anglia's share of Company Viennetta Volume % |
|---|---|
| August to October | 6.3 |
| week ending: | |
| November  5 | 4.2* |
| November 12 | 8.4* |
| November 19 | 22.5* |
| November 26 | 24.3* |
| December  3 | 24.2* |
| December 10 | 20.5* |
| December 17 | 19.4* |
| December 24 | 24.4 |
| December 31 | 28.7 |
| January  7 | 15.2 |
| January 14 | 13.7 |
| January 21 | 13.3 |
| January 28 | 10.1 |
| February  4 | 13.0 |

\* TV support (average share 17.6 per cent)
Source: Bird's Eye Wall's

Depot comparisons display an equally dramatic picture and link the sale improvement even more closely with the advertising. Two depots, Exeter and Taunton, in the TSW catchment area, which received no TV support during this time and which had a similar share of households and former Viennetta sales to Anglia, were used as a financial control during November–December 1982. In November, the percentage of total national Viennetta sales from Anglia sales was over three times greater than that of the Exeter/Taunton

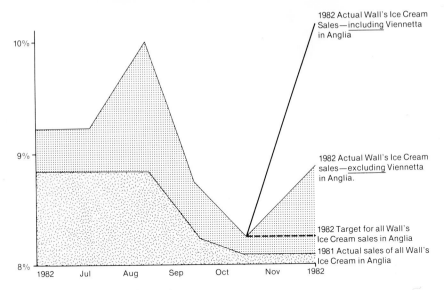

Figure 2. *Anglia as percentage of company ice cream turnover*
*Source:* Birds Eye Wall's

TABLE 2:   1982 ANGLIA VALUE CONTRIBUTION TO NATIONAL
                    VIENNETTA SALES

|                          | Nov    | Dec    |
|--------------------------|--------|--------|
| Anglia                   | 18.4%  | 31.5%  |
| Control (Exeter/Taunton) | 5.3%   | 8.6%   |

Source: Birds Eye Wall's

depots – 18.4 per cent vs. 5.3 per cent – and in December it was virtually four times greater than that of Exeter/Taunton – 31.5 per cent vs. 8.6 per cent (Table 2).

Even after TV support was withdrawn in Anglia, Viennetta sales remained at a high level and in fact reached their peak during the week commencing 31st December 1982, over two weeks after the TV burst ended (Table 1). Even two months after the commercial was last shown, in the week commencing 3rd February 1983, Viennetta sales, although lower, were still more than *twice* their previous rate .in August–October 1982 (Table 1).

In addition, substitution was minimal. In fact, Viennetta TV advertising had a '*halo effect*' (Figure 2) which helped pull all Wall's ice-cream sales in Anglia considerably *above* the 8.25 per cent targetted share for Anglia in November 1982 to 8.75 per cent actual share, excluding Viennetta, or just over 10 per cent *including* Viennetta – 6 per cent and 17.5 per cent increases respectively (Figure 2).

ANGLIA ADVERTISING PAYBACK

Substitution was minimal and significant incremental volume was achieved: virtually 10 times greater than the August–October level. Furthermore advertising was paid back in terms of direct trading profit in just over four weeks after the start of TV support.

Wall's and Lintas are convinced that TV advertising was a key contributor to the brand's success.


## PHASE 3   LONDON TV TEST


*Marketing and Advertising Strategy – January–May 1983*

In view of the success of the Anglia TV Test it was decided to test TV advertising in a larger area, while maintaining a modified women's press campaign (£70 000 expenditure) for the whole of the country.


### AREA CHOICE

London was selected as the largest and most competitive test area. The same commercial was run at a similar weight as Anglia's, during Easter 1983.


*Media Plan*

555 TVRs 6.4 OTS (housewives) at £385 000; 30-second commercial.


### LONDON EX-DEPOT SALES RESULTS

Before Easter 1983, sales had been running at around £26 000 @ RSP per month. With TV support, sales increased almost eightfold to just under £225 000 @ RSP per month (Figure 3).

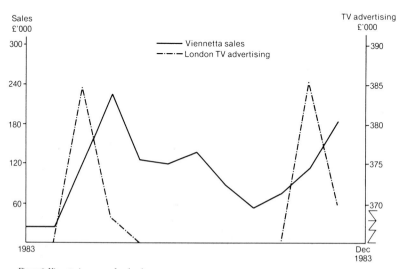

Figure 3. *Viennetta ice cream — London depots*
*Source:* Birds Eye Wall's

## PHASE 4   NATIONAL TV

*Marketing and Advertising Strategy – November–December 1983*

The considerable success with the Anglia and London TV test areas encouraged the use of national TV support in the pre-Christmas 1983 period.

### MEDIA PLAN

The strategy adopted in London areas replicated nationally: national, 550 TVRs, 6.4 OTS (housewives); £1 845 000 spend. The same 30-second commercial was used nationally. In addition a 10-second reminder was used in areas which had had prior TV exposure, ie Anglia and London. Experience had shown that more spots, irrespective of length, created greater awareness and interest.

### NATIONAL SALES RESULTS

Sales for the period prior to November–December 1983 averaged £435 000 @ RSP per month. During the TV support period they increased by more than a factor of five to around £2 375 000 @ RSP per month (Figure 4). It is of particular significance that Viennetta sales during November and December 1983 were *four* times greater than June–July 1983 – traditionally the peak selling season for ice-cream. Furthermore, November–December sales alone represented 50 per cent of 1983 Viennetta sales. It is also interesting to note that this was the first time ever that ice-cream was advertised on this scale nationally on TV during the winter.

During 1983, Viennetta substantially increased Wall's share of the ½-litre family pack sector. Furthermore, it rejuvenated the whole sector and reversed the declining volume trend. Sales in Quarter 4, 1983, for the total ½-litre, family pack sector (all brands) were

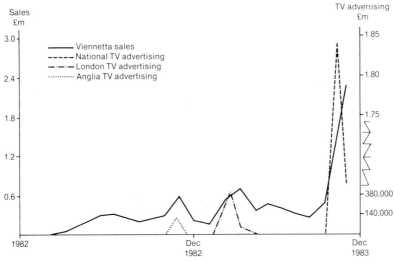

Figure 4. *Viennetta ice cream – UK*

*Source:* Birds Eye Wall's

21 per cent higher than Quarter 4, 1982, entirely due to the effect of Viennetta (Table 3). Within this sector, Wall's brand share by volume had moved from 28 per cent in Quarter 1, 1982 (ie pre-Viennetta launch) to 60 per cent in Quarter 4, 1983 (Table 3).

TABLE3:  $\frac{1}{2}$ –LITRE FAMILY PACK SECTOR – PERCENTAGE BY VOLUME

| 1982 | Q1 | Viennetta launch Q2 | Q3 | Anglia TV Q4 |
|---|---|---|---|---|
| Wall's | 28 | 35 | 33 | 35 |
| Lyons Maid | 27 | 19 | 18 | 13 |
| all others | 45 | 46 | 49 | 52 |
| sector volume % change vs previous year's quarter | − 25 | + 15 | − 13 | + 6 |

| 1983 | London TV Q1 | Q2 | national TV Q3 | Q4 |
|---|---|---|---|---|
| Wall's | 34 | 48 | 40 | 60 |
| Lyons Maid | 15 | 11 | 16 | 9 |
| all others | 51 | 41 | 44 | 31 |
| sector volume % change vs. previous year's quarter | + 6 | − 16 | + 14 | + 21 |

Source: Attwood

In view of the consumer demand generated for Viennetta, trade response has been consistently enthusiastic. As a result, Viennetta currently has the widest distribution of any ice-cream product in the UK. Viennetta's impact and effectiveness have been acknowledged in the 'Supermarketing Top 20 Awards 1982' and the 'Supermarketing Quality Food Award 1983'. In both instances it was the highest placed dessert product.

Following its success in the UK, the Wall's Viennetta technology has been exported to 12 Unilever ice-cream companies around the world. Viennetta has become an international brand in two years.

## CONCLUSIONS

1.  We started with an outstanding product, and an attractive price.
2.  Advertising (especially TV) consistently accelerated the rate of sale by a factor of between five and ten (as the figures presented demonstrate).
3.  The advertising worked by presenting a unique product in a way that allowed the qualities of the product to speak for themselves. The setting enabled the consumers to bring their own aspirations and imagery to bear, enhanced by the music which won a Clio bronze award in 1983.
4.  No additional factors existed that could explain an increase in rate-of-sale of this order (there was no couponing, nor unusual weather conditions). Indeed, the growth of Viennetta defied the norms that hitherto defined the ice-cream market.

5. Substitution with existing products was always far lower even than had been predicted.
6. Viennetta has become, in less than two years, the major brand in the take-home ice-cream market. Advertising played a critical role in this success, and the brand continues to grow.

# 3

# The Effect of Advertising on the Launch of Shakers Cocktails

## INTRODUCTION

This paper attempts to assess the part played by advertising in the launch of Shakers Cocktails. It is difficult to isolate the effect of advertising on any new-product launch, since the results of the marketing effort cannot be compared with historical brand performance – the only possible direction is up! What we have done in this case is to compare the performance of the brand in advertised and non-advertised areas with its overall performance nationally, and in doing so we believe that the positive effect of the advertising has been conclusively demonstrated.

Although Shakers is now an established brand, having been in national distribution for two years and having received the support of two TV commercials and a radio campaign, we have restricted ourselves to the first year of national distribution (July 1982–June 1983) for the purpose of this paper. The discussion therefore concerns the first television commercial only.

## THE CLIENT: HEDGES & BUTLER LTD

Founded in 1667, Hedges & Butler Ltd is probably London's oldest wine merchant. (It is very difficult to prove otherwise, since all records were destroyed in the Great Fire the previous year!) Today, the company is a wholly-owned subsidiary of Bass plc (the largest brewery company in the UK), and has two main responsibilities:

1.  The purchase of wines and spirits for the Bass UK operating companies (including 1 100 off licences and 7 500 pubs).
2.  The free-trade sales of wine and spirits to all other brewers, multiple and independent grocers and off licences throughout the UK. In this capacity, Hedges & Butler act as agents for the owners of several major brands, including Bacardi Rum, Dewar's Scotch Whisky, Zamoyski Pure Vodka, Emva Cyprus Sherry, Mateus Rosé, Mouton Cadet and Hirondelle Table Wines.

# BACKGROUND: TWO IMPORTANT TRENDS IN THE UK ALCOHOLIC DRINKS MARKET

Towards the end of the 1970s, two important trends in the UK alcoholic drinks market became particularly marked, and they have continued into the early 1980s.

## The Cocktail Boom

An increasingly experimental consumer began looking for drinks which were 'new' and 'different'. Younger drinkers cheerfully cast aside the habits of their parents, and the fashion-conscious in particular required drinks which were in keeping with their outgoing, gregarious lifestyle. The growth of restricted licences and theme pubs, sales of mixers, and the success of brands such as Pernod, Southern Comfort and Bailey's Irish Cream reflect this trend.

As part of this, there was a revival of interest in cocktails. Specialist cocktail bars began to appear not just in London but in provincial cities and towns. There was an increase in the number of discos, hotels and even pubs selling hand-made cocktails. There was a great deal of editorial activity and press coverage, particularly in women's magazines. And omnibus surveys confirm that increasing numbers of consumers are claiming to drink cocktails (see Table 1).

TABLE 1: 'DO YOU EVER DRINK COCKTAILS?'

|            | 1982    | 1984    |
|------------|---------|---------|
| 'All adults' | 18%     | 20%     |
|            | (7.8 m) | (8.7 m) |

Source: NOP

| | £583m 1972 | £2179m 1979 | % change | % change in annual turnover |
|---|---|---|---|---|
| Brewery-owned | 32% (£184m) | 27% (£585m) | +218 | +293 |
| Free specialists | 38% (£219m) | 34% (£738m) | +237 | +243 |
| Multiple/Co-op grocers | 20% (£117m) | 27% (£597m) | +410 | +377 |
| Others | 10% (£63m) | 12% (£259m) | +311 | +122 |

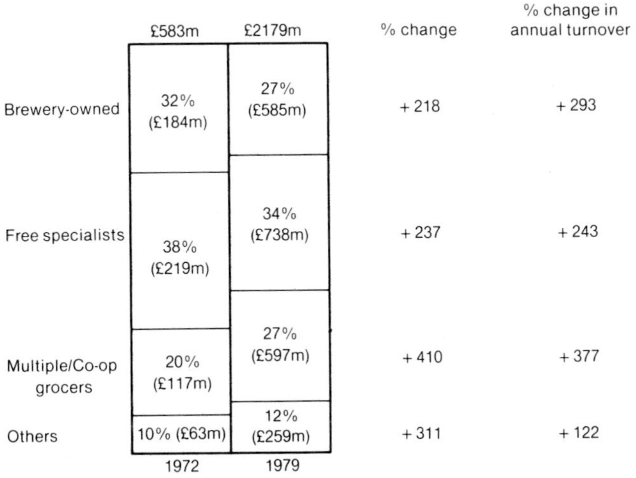

Figure 1. *Turnover in alcoholic drink by outlet type (off trade)*
*Source:* Stats MR

*Increased In-home Consumption*

Parallel with this trend towards greater experimentation, another significant change was occurring in the alcoholic drinks market. This was an increased emphasis on in-home drinking, and a corresponding decline in the use of the traditional British pub. The big grocery multiples – who began acquiring licences to sell liquor from about 1970 – became major outlets for alcoholic drink as it became increasingly an off-trade purchase (see Figure 1).

## PRE-MIXED COCKTAILS IN THE USA

It was against this background that a particular phenomenon was observed by Hedges & Butler in the USA: the very buoyant performance of pre-packaged cocktail mixes.

In 1978, the market for these 'pre-mixed' cocktails in the USA was both mature (the product category had been in existence for about 20 years) and large (sales were steady at about 3 000 000 cases a year). There were two major brands in the market: Heublein's 'Club' and Schenley's 'Cocktails For Two', each of which offered an extensive range. In addition, there was a multiplicity of other products in sachets, cans and bottles. There were both alcoholic and non-alcoholic mixes. Advertising expenditure was some $10 million a year.

## MARKET OPPORTUNITY

Hedges & Butler felt that the nature of the trends in the UK market at that time provided an excellent opportunity for such a product. They envisaged a range of pre-mixed cocktails which would sell in the on-trade, but which would be aimed primarily at the take-home sector.

## DEVELOPMENT

In 1979, an exhaustive research programme was initiated. A rolling programme of qualitative research involving dozens of group discussions was undertaken. In the early stages the nature of this research was kept as broad as possible: many demographic sub-groups of the population were sampled, and the product stimuli covered a wide range. Later, recruitment became more specific as the prime target audience for the product became more defined, and product types and packaging ideas began to be short-listed. For the purpose of this discussion the development programme can be broken down into two main stages.

*Stage One*

Initially, around 40 different cocktail products were put into research. These were selected according to the rank order of popularity of cocktails in the USA, and consisted of a wide range of Coladas, Daiquiris, Punches, Sours and so on. Many different packaging ideas were also researched. A whole variety of shapes (including existing US and British containers as well as new ideas) were investigated in different materials (plastic, glass, tin). Scores of potential brand names were examined. The key findings from this exploratory research were:

1. A great deal of interest was expressed in the concept of pre-mixed cocktails, and the take-home opportunity was largely confirmed. Women in particular expressed enthusiasm for the idea.
2. Interest was particularly high amongst the younger age groups. Social class did not appear to be a key discriminator – rather, it was lifestyle and attitude to cocktail drinking that was important. The type of lifestyle and attitude that appeared to offer the greatest potential for the product was found to be most prevalent amongst the 'middle classes' of C1C2.
3. It was clear that the product would have to be firmly positioned as a 'real' cocktail if it were to realise its full potential, rather than just being another 'new drink'. It was therefore essential to imbue it with the 'cocktail values' of excitement, fun, glamour and a little sophistication.
4. The packaging therefore became extremely important. Conventional bottle shapes were rejected as being too 'boring', and the importance of the 'right' name was paramount.
5. Some of the products were 'approved', and some rejected on taste grounds.

*Stage Two*

In the light of these findings, the second stage of research took place amongst a much narrower audience (demographically 18–24 and 25–34, C1C2 women) who had been identified as the prime target market. This time, the take-home opportunity was confirmed beyond doubt, and potential drinking occasions were defined (such as parties, anniversaries, moments of self-indulgence, any kind of 'treat'). It appeared that although the product was viewed as being for 'special occasions', the number of different types of special occasion for which it would be suitable was large.

The package design which emerged as most strongly delivering the promise of a 'real' cocktail was the now famous mini-cocktail shaker in silvered glass. The contest between two potential brand names which had both been strong contenders (Slingers and Shakers) was therefore now resolved almost by default, and an embryonic brand was born. The products were short-listed to a final four: Pina Colada, Margarita, Rum Punch and Whisky Sour.

## TEST PANEL

In autumn 1981, the brand was progressed to a national test panel consisting of 75 off licences and 90 pubs within the Bass Group. Although viewed primarily as an off-trade proposition, it was felt that an extended test in on-trade outlets would be a good way of identifying any potential negatives in the name, pack or product, testing price levels and assessing volume potential. The brand's performance in these test outlets was carefully monitored between October and December 1981. The key findings were:

1. The packaging was extremely successful in creating visibility and stimulating interest at point-of-sale.
2. The pack size and price were satisfactory. The bottle size of 160 ml was sufficient for two glasses, and this was seen as good value at a price of around £1.30 in the pub. (This price level would allow the brand to retail at about £1.00 in the off-trade.)
3. All the product varieties were popular, but different ones appealed to different people. It was clearly important to offer a range.
4. Pina Colada and Margarita were the best-known and best-liked names. Rum Punch and Whisky Sour were found to be less exciting. Further qualitative work was therefore undertaken in this area, and these names were subsequently changed to Sundowner and New Yorker respectively. The final Shakers range is shown below.

Overall, the results of the test panel were very encouraging. Volume forecasts were extrapolated from rate-of-sale data (see 'Marketing Objectives' below), and a national

launch was set for summer 1982, with advertising support, beginning on a regional roll-out basis, planned for the autumn.

## NATIONAL LAUNCH

Regional roll-out commenced in April 1982, and by July all areas had at least some distribution. The brand's progress in the off-trade was monitored by means of a bi-monthly retail audit through Stats MR.

Price was set at 99p and maintained at this level until April 1983, when the Budget measures necessitated an increase to over £1.00.

## MARKETING OBJECTIVES

The results of the test panel enabled volume forecasts to be made for the brand, and sales objectives were set in both the on- and off-trade to be achieved in the first full year of national distribution (July 1982–June 1983). Unfortunately, absolute volume figures cannot be revealed for reasons of confidentiality, but we will show later how the brand performed relative to these forecasts.

It was recognised that steady distribution gains would have to be made if volume targets were to be achieved, and target national sterling distribution levels were set at 40 per cent by Christmas 1982 and 50 per cent by June 1983 (although it was recognised that these levels might not be met by every region individually).

## ADVERTISING STRATEGY

The development research had shown that there was a great deal of interest in the concept of a pre-mixed cocktail, once it was understood. Clearly, the role for advertising was to educate the target market by communicating the concept in a way that was empathetic to both the audience and the product. That achieved, the evidence was that the product would almost sell itself. Branding was obviously of crucial importance, since Shakers had to claim all the generic benefits of the category. It was also important to communicate the range.

The primary target market was defined as young (18–30), female, C1C2. Those for whom Shakers would have the strongest appeal would tend to be outgoing and style-conscious, and probably already drinkers of hand-made cocktails. For these people, Shakers would perform the role of a 'take-home cocktail', and as such the advertising would have to reflect the cocktail values of fun, excitement, glamour and a little sophistication.

The main advertising objective was to build awareness of the brand. Once this was done, and the concept clearly communicated, research indicated that trial would be naturally stimulated. Objectives were set for post-advertising brand awareness levels of 30 per cent spontaneous, 45 per cent prompted, and for trial levels by the end of the first year of 10 per cent amongst all adults, 15 per cent amongst the 18–34 age group.

TV was almost self-selecting as the advertising medium. Shakers was not only a new brand but a new product category in itself, and impact, intrusiveness and high coverage

Making cocktails used to be such a chore,

but with Shakers Cocktails all you need to do . . .

. . . is shake . . .

. . .

. . .

Shakers: real cocktails in a couple of shakes.

were the order of the day. In addition, the medium had to support an exciting, dynamic creative execution. TV was the medium which could best fulfil these requirements.

## CREATIVE EXECUTION

The creative execution revolved around the idea of a waiter at a cocktail party, standing in an exercise belt, carrying a tray displaying the range of Shakers' cocktails. The belt shook the waiter (and hence the tray) so much that not only did it render the Shakers cocktails perfectly ready for drinking, but it reduced the waiter in size from a somewhat plump figure to nothing at all after 30 seconds (only his uniform and spectacles remained on the carpet)! Meanwhile, the hostess delivered the sales pitch in which the four varieties were introduced. A storyboard representative of the commercial is shown on page 44.

Qualitative research was used to check the communication and executional treatment. The findings were that the product concept was being clearly communicated, branding was excellent, and the scenario appeared to have captured the required balance between humour and sophistication.

## MEDIA LAYDOWN & TVR ACHIEVEMENT

It was felt that the conurbation areas of London, Birmingham, Manchester and South Wales offered the greatest immediate volume potential for Shakers, and it was decided

TABLE 2:   MEDIA SUPPORT AND WOMEN TVRS BY REGION

|  | 1982 | | 1983 | |
| --- | --- | --- | --- | --- |
|  | Nov | Dec | Jan | Feb |
| London |  | D6–J2 576 |  |  |
| Southern |  |  |  | J31–F27 515 |
| Central | N1–N28 587 |  |  |  |
| Anglia |  |  |  |  |
| Harlech | N1–N28 636 |  |  |  |
| Westward |  |  |  |  |
| Granada | N1–N28 531 |  |  |  |
| Yorkshire |  |  |  | J31–F27 455 |
| Tyne-Tees |  |  |  | J31–F27 463 |
| Scotland |  |  |  | J31–F27 579 |

that priority for advertising support should be given to these regions. Consequently, support was planned into London, Central, Granada and Harlech in time for what was felt would be the high-demand, pre-Christmas period. The rest of the country (with the exceptions of Anglia and Westward) was covered utilising the much less expensive air-time early in the new calendar year. The actual dates of media support by region (including the number of women ratings achieved) are shown in Table 2. In this way, over 90 per cent of the country was covered with an average women TVR achievement of 579 pre- Christmas and 499 post-Christmas.

## BRAND PERFORMANCE

### Distribution

As we stated earlier, all areas of the country had at least some distribution by July 1982. Table 3 shows how distribution gains were made region by region, over the year under consideration.

TABLE 3:    SHAKERS COCKTAILS: £% DISTRIBUTION

|  | 1982 | | | 1983 | | |
|  | Jul–Aug | Sep–Oct | Nov–Dec | Jan–Feb | Mar–Apr | May–Jun |
|---|---|---|---|---|---|---|
| GB | 15 | 25 | 43 | 43 | 48 | 51 |
| London/Southern | 17 | 31 | 51 | 48 | 51 | 55 |
| Central/Anglia | 8 | 17 | 35 | 36 | 41 | 41 |
| Harlech/Westward | 8 | 10 | 28 | 32 | 34 | 32 |
| Granada | 8 | 21 | 49 | 45 | 52 | 46 |
| Yorkshire/Tyne-Tees | 24 | 35 | 47 | 54 | 55 | 64 |
| Scotland | 22 | 27 | 34 | 39 | 50 | 60 |

Source: Stats MR

It will be remembered that in order to achieve the desired sales volume, national distribution levels of 40 per cent and 50 per cent had been set for November–December 1982 and May–June 1983 respectively (although it was recognised that these might not be achieved by every region individually). Table 3 shows that despite the occasional regional weakness (notably Harlech/Westward) the national targets were met, and a solid base built from which to achieve sales volume.

### Awareness

An awareness check was carried out by means of a pre-and-post study, commissioned from market research company Survey Research Associates, in the London region. In-street interviewing was carried out amongst 200 women aged 18–44 in the London ITV non-overlap area in November 1982, and again in January 1983. A dramatic increase in spontaneous awareness of Shakers, from 12 per cent to 40 per cent was recorded over that period. The target post-advertising level of 30 per cent was certainly being met.

In January 1983, questions concerning the prompted awareness and trial of Shakers Cocktails were commissioned from the Marplan Q15 omnibus on a bi-monthly basis. This survey samples at least 1 500 respondents, demographically representative of the adult population of Great Britain. Fieldwork was conducted in mid-January, again in mid-March, and again in mid-May. The results are shown in Table 4. The target post-advertising level of 45 per cent had been achieved.

TABLE 4:    SHAKERS COCKTAILS: NATIONAL AWARENESS LEVELS

|  | Jan | 1983 Mar | May |
|---|---|---|---|
| Prompted brand awareness | 46% | 46% | 49% |

Source: Marplan

### Trial

It will be remembered that trial levels had been set for the end of the first year of 10 per cent amongst all adults, and 15 per cent amongst the 18–34 age group. In May 1983, the results of the Marplan omnibus nationally were:

|  | 'Ever drunk Shakers' |
|---|---|
| All adults | 13% |
| 18–34 | 19% |

Target trial levels, too, had been achieved.

### Volume Sales

Although for reasons of confidentiality it is not possible to show absolute figures, we can compare sales volume achieved by June 1983 with the targets set at the beginning of the year:

|  | achieved vs. objectives |
|---|---|
| Off-trade | +35% |
| On-trade | +15% |
| Total | +30% |

So, nationally, all marketing and advertising objectives had been met. Distribution was up to expectation, and target awareness and trial levels had been exceeded. And the forecast sales volume had been exceeded by 30 per cent! But what was the specific contribution that advertising had made to this spectacular success?

## ADVERTISED AND NON-ADVERTISED AREAS

Although it was not planned for this purpose, the nature of the media laydown allows us to assess the effect of the advertising by examining the performance of the brand in advertised and non-advertised areas.

For the purpose of this analysis, we have divided the country into two regional groups, as can be seen in Figure 2. It would be convenient to exclude from these groups the two regions which received no advertising support at all (Anglia and Westward), in order to construct a truly balanced comparison. This is not possible, however, since neither the Marplan nor Stats MR data allow us to separate Harlech from Westward, and in the Stats MR data Central and Anglia are inextricably linked. However, both Anglia and Westward are relatively small regions, and their inclusion will not have a significant effect on the overall results.

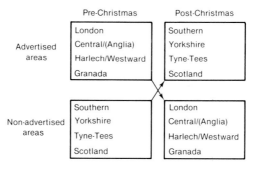

Figure 2 *Areas and period used for advertising*

### *Awareness*

Table 5 shows the regional awareness scores for January and March 1983. The boxed figures are those which are higher than the national average. It will be noticed that the pattern corresponds very closely to that of the media laydown.

TABLE 5:   SHAKERS COCKTAILS: REGIONAL AWARENESS LEVELS

|  | Prompted brand awareness* | | Seen advertised recently** | |
|---|---|---|---|---|
|  | January 1983 | March 1983 | January 1983 | March 1983 |
| GB | 46% | 46% | 34% | 38% |
| London | 54% | 46% | 53% | 34% |
| Central | 56% | 46% | 40% | 32% |
| HTV/Westward | 45% | 36% | 41% | 25% |
| Granada | 57% | 38% | 36% | 17% |
| Southern | 25% | 50% | 28% | 47% |
| Yorkshire/Tyne-Tees | 39% | 51% | 16% | 50% |
| Scotland | 33% | 51% | 8% | 53% |

*Base: all adults
**Base: all adults aware of Shakers

*Source:* Marplan

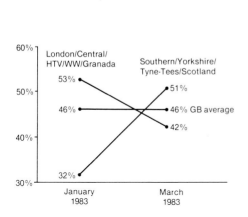

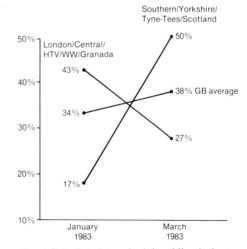

Figure 3. *Shakers Cocktails: prompted brand awareness by regional group*
Source: Marplan

Figure 4. *Shakers Cocktails: 'seen advertised recently' by regional group*
Source: Marplan

The effect is dramatically illustrated when average awareness levels for each regional group are plotted graphically. Figures 3 and 4 show awareness shifts relative to the national average. Using these as a model it can be hypothesised that if there had been no advertising, prompted awareness of Shakers would only have been 32 per cent nationally by Christmas 1982 (29 per cent below target, and 35 per cent below its level at the end of the launch year).

### Rate-of-sale

Rate-of-sale by each of the regional groups relative to the national average is shown in Table 6 (again, absolute figures cannot be shown for reasons of confidentiality).

TABLE 6:    SHAKERS COCKTAILS: RATE-OF-SALE (INDICES)

|  | Nov–Dec 1982 | Jan–Feb 1983 | Mar–Apr 1983 |
|---|---|---|---|
| GB | 100 | 100 | 100 |
| London/Central/Anglia/HTV/WW/ Granada | 108 | 103 | 91 |
| Southern/Yorkshire/Tyne-Tees/ Scotland | 82 | 99 | 122 |
| Difference between advertised and non-advertised regions | 32% | 4% | 34% |

Source: Stats MR

These indices are plotted graphically in Figure 5. It is clear that, pre-Christmas, the rate-of-sale in the advertised regions is above the national average and well above the rate-of-sale in those regions which did not receive advertising support. Post-Christmas, as advertising support is switched to the other regional group, the difference in rate-of-sale between the two groups is diminished, and then their relationship is reversed. There

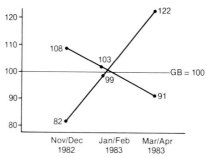

Figure 5. *Shakers Cocktails: index of rate-of-sale by regional group*
*Source:* Stats MR

is clearly a market force at work here which sustains a rate-of-sale differential of some 30 per cent.


*Volume Sales*

Our final demonstration of the effect of the advertising concerns the changes in volume sales in each of the two regional groups relative to the national average over the advertised periods. Tables 7 and 8 give the indices for the pre-Christmas and post-Christmas periods. These indices are illustrated graphically in Figures 6 and 7. They show that over the pre-Christmas period, sales in the advertised areas were 10 per cent higher than the

TABLE 7:    SHAKERS COCKTAILS: OFF–TRADE SALES NOV–DEC VS. SEP–OCT 1982 (INDICES)

|  | Sep–Oct | Nov–Dec 1982 |
|---|---|---|
| GB | 100 | 100 |
| London/Central/Anglia/HTV/WW/ Granada | 100 | 110 |
| Southern/Yorkshire/Tyne-Tees/ Scotland | 100 | 75 |

*Source:* Stats MR

TABLE 8:    SHAKERS COCKTAILS: OFF–TRADE SALES JAN–FEB 1983 VS. NOV–DEC 1982 (INDICES)

|  | Nov–Dec 1982 | Jan–Feb 1983 |
|---|---|---|
| GB | 100 | 100 |
| London/Central/Anglia/HTV/WW/ Granada | 100 | 91 |
| Southern/Yorkshire/Tyne-Tees/ Scotland | 100 | 124 |

*Source:* Stats MR

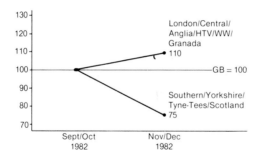

Figure 6. *Shakers Cocktails: index of volume sales by regional group, pre-Christmas*
*Source:* Stats MR

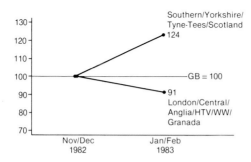

Figure 7. *Shakers Cocktails: index of volume sales by regional group, post-Christmas*
*Source:* Stats MR

national average, and in the non-advertised areas they were 25 per cent lower. Similarly, over the post-Christmas period sales in the advertised areas were 24 per cent above the national average, while in the non-advertised areas they were 9 per cent behind.

## SUMMARY AND CONCLUSIONS

We have demonstrated the positive effect of advertising on the launch of Shakers Cocktails by examining the performance of the brand in two stages.

Firstly, we have shown how, nationally, the brand launch achieved its marketing objectives in terms of distribution and volume sales. We have argued that advertising played a necessary and major part in this success by creating awareness and stimulating trial of the brand, and we have produced evidence to show how the defined advertising objectives were met.

But this is not enough in itself to 'prove' advertising effectiveness. What we have done secondly, therefore, is to compare the performance of the brand in advertised and non-advertised areas with its overall performance nationally. In doing so, we believe that the positive effect of the advertising has been conclusively demonstrated.

The regional analysis shows that brand awareness, rate-of-sale and volume sales were all higher in advertised areas relative to the national average, whereas in non-advertised areas brand performance fell behind on these dimensions. When the advertising pattern was reversed, and support switched to the other regions, this pattern of awareness and sales was reversed also. The immediacy of the response to advertising in this way reveals the contribution advertising has made to the success of the brand.

# Section Two

*Established Consumer Goods and Services*

# 4

# Breaking the Bran Barrier— Kellogg's Bran Flakes 1982-84

## MARKET BACKGROUND

Bran cereals have a long history. All-Bran has been on the market since 1922. Kellogg's added 30% Bran Flakes to their range in 1939, Sultana Bran and Bran Buds in the early 1960s. But for many years demand for bran cereals remained limited, partly because bran is not very palatable (which is one reason why it has generally been removed from processed foods) and partly because of the medicinal and laxative associations created by over 40 years of advertising All-Bran as 'Nature's laxative', associations which people have understandably attached to other brans as well.

Slowly, as public nutritional knowledge improved and a small but increasing number of people began to appreciate the contribution of fibre (or 'roughage') to health, sales of bran cereals increased to the point where it was supply, not demand, that was constraining growth. Recognising the future potential in the developing trend towards healthier eating, Kellogg's made a major capital investment in the bran sector of the cereal market by opening a new plant at Wrexham in 1978, substantially boosting production capacity.

The brakes removed, sector growth accelerated. Bran cereals' volume share of the growing ready-to-eat (RTE) cereal market, which had for long been fairly stable, rose from $8\frac{1}{2}$ per cent in 1977 to 11 per cent in 1981, a volume increase of 35 per cent in four years. Other manufacturers had by now seen the opportunity, and begun to join the bran wagon with manufactured brands or by making stores' own-label brands.

Even so, bran cereals remained minority-appeal products. Consumer attitudes were still largely negative. Many people were not prepared even to try them. Even amongst those housewives who acknowledged the benefits of fibre and recognised bran cereal as a rich source, there was reluctance to serve them to the family.

### The 'Bran Barrier'

The laxative connotations of All-Bran were automatically transferred to other cereals in the sector through the associations inherent in the word 'bran'. However, the use of laxatives was on the wane, and the sales potential of food products bought for occasional medicinal use was not going to keep the Wrexham plant busy. To raise demand we had first to break through the 'bran barrier' of prejudice, by changing the word's associations away from the medicinal aura it had towards that of a healthy, normal food ingredient.

Among the many elements of the range of marketing strategies that ensued were: continuing experimentation with TV (print, traditionally, had been the medium for bran cereal advertising) to learn how best to overcome anti bran prejudice and normalise the products; a strong push behind Sultana Bran, concentrating the emphasis of communication on its fruit content; and a major repositioning of Kellogg's Bran Flakes.

## MARKETING STRATEGY FOR BRAN FLAKES

Originally called 30% Bran Flakes, this brand had been positioned as a health product, with advertising centred on its high iron content. But we were convinced that it had much greater potential as a general appeal cereal, both because of the consumer interest we had detected in a wheat flake cereal and because we had a particularly good-tasting product. A research study in which people took home samples of the standard product, but in blank packs, confirmed that consumers, too, thought it delicious. And that a number of them, when subsequently told that what they had been enjoying so much was 30% Bran Flakes, simply refused to believe that it could have been the identical product. Such was the strength of the 'bran barrier'.

Further attitude research confirmed the brand's image as a traditional bran cereal, bought primarily for its medicinal and health qualities, and weak on taste expectation. People just assumed that because it was a bran cereal, it would not taste very good.

Kellogg's and J. Walter Thompson saw an opportunity to use the unrecognised but excellent taste of the product to break through the 'bran barrier'. In 1981, the decision was taken radically to alter the marketing strategy by:

— Dropping '30%' from the name, and redesigning the pack.
— Shifting out of magazines into TV, which had produced encouraging results in previous experiment.
— Adopting an all-family brand positioning as a pleasant-tasting, natural and healthy cereal.
— Concentrating on the *tastiness* of the product, leaving it to the word 'bran' in the product name to supply the health reassurance behind the tasty claim.

The new TV advertising was given two roles:

1. To create an image for the brand which was sufficiently strong to overcome the negative associations of 'bran' in the product name.
2. To make people see the brand in a new way which would make them want to try it.

Its target was all housewives predisposed towards natural, healthy foods, with primary emphasis on the 30–50 age group. Its aim was, firstly, to recruit new consumers and, secondly, to encourage more regular purchase.

The outcome of this brief was 'Tasty', a commercial with a bright and memorable tune and stream-of-consciousness lyrics with the refrain 'They're tasty, tasty, very very tasty', all in a distinctive, colourful and modern style. A scene from this commercial is shown on page 55.

It first went on air, nationally, in April 1982. It had run for one burst when something happened that profoundly altered public opinion about bran.

### The F-Plan phenomenon

Audrey Eyton's *F-Plan*[1] was serialised in the *Daily Express* on 18th–21st May 1982, creating an instant craze. When, shortly afterwards, it was published in paperback, it went straight up the best-seller lists. To date *F-Plan* has sold over 2 000 000 copies. One home in ten has a copy.

For the first time, a mass audience learned about dietary fibre and the importance of its function in the digestive processes. They learned that by maintaining the body's normal intestinal behaviour, high-fibre foods help to protect against some of the more prevalent Western diseases, as well as contributing to general health. They learned that a fibre-rich diet can reduce your weight. And they learned that one of the most accessible sources of fibre is bran cereals.

This produced a dramatic change in public knowledge and opinion. A check in February 1982, before the F-Plan had been heard of, showed that fibre's benefits were then primarily seen as laxative-related. After the F-Plan the emphasis had shifted: awareness and understanding of fibre's contribution to general health and well-being had advanced substantially (Table 1). The proportion of housewives claiming consciously to include fibre foods in the household meals had gone up and so had their recourse to bran cereals as a prime source of fibre (Table 2).

TABLE 1:    FIBRE KNOWLEDGE

| % housewives saying the benefits of fibre are: | Feb 1982 | Jan 1983 |
|---|---|---|
| keeps you regular | 26 | 23 |
| as a laxative | 18 | 19 |
| helps prevent constipation | 13 | 13 |
| | 57 | 56 |
| | | |
| helps keep digestive system healthy/working properly | 22 | 30 |
| provides roughage | 18 | 25 |
| generally good for health/fitness | 12 | 16 |
| helps prevent illness/disease | 1 | 2 |
| | 53 | 74 |
| | | |
| sample base | (546) | (569) |

Source: BMRB Access Omnibus Surveys

TABLE 2:    FIBRE USAGE

| | Feb 1982 | Jan 1983 |
|---|---|---|
| % housewives consciously including bran/fibre foods in diet | 42 | 47 |
| of whom, % buying with fibre in mind: | | |
|   All-Bran | 25 | 34 |
|   Bran Flakes | 13 | 19 |
|   Farmhouse Bran | 3 | 4 |

Source: BMRB Access Omnibus Surveys

Kellogg's marketing response to the opportunity created by this new interest in fibre was swift. The TV campaign for All-Bran, in area test at the time, went national from July 1982. Sultana Bran's advertising funds were increased. And Bran Flakes' national advertising campaign, which had just begun, was extended. Table 3 shows the increase in TV advertising after May 1982. In this table, as in the ones that follow, we show data for years ending May, rather than the usual calendar year. We have divided it this way

TABLE 3:    TV ADVERTISING

| network housewife ratings (TVRs) year ending: | May 1981 | May 1982 | May 1983 | May 1984 |
|---|---|---|---|---|
| Kellogg's Bran Flakes | 400 | 600 | 1800 | 1400 |
| All-Bran | 100 | 300 | 1500 | 1500 |
| Farmhouse Bran | 300 | 1600 | – | 200 |
| Sultana Bran | 1100 | 900 | 1500 | 1400 |

the better to see what happened in the two years after first publication of *F-Plan* (May 1982) compared to the two years before.

## SALES RESULTS

The effect on consumer purchasing was dramatic. In the year immediately before *F-Plan* was published, sales of bran cereals in total rose by 4 per cent. In the year after, they soared by 37 per cent. Kellogg's Bran Flakes' sales rose by 41 per cent, even though they started from a base of marginal decline the year before. More significantly, they have continued to rise by a further 23 per cent in the following year to May 1984, even though growth has slowed in the rest of the sector (Table 4).

TABLE 4:    CONSUMER SALES GROWTH

| annual % volume change year ending: | May 1982 | May 1983 | May 1984 |
|---|---|---|---|
| Kellogg's Bran Flakes | −2 | +41 | +23 |
| other bran cereals | +6 | +35 | + 9 |
| total sector | +4 | +37 | +12 |

Source: AGB Television Consumer Audit

The bran boom lasted for about a year. From the middle of 1983 the craze for fibre in the diet began to wane, and sales began to slow towards a rate of growth similar to the pre-boom rate. But not so Kellogg's Bran Flakes, which has continued to make above-average gains, and shows no signs of reverting to previous rates.

TABLE 5:    FIBRE KNOWLEDGE

| % housewives saying the benefits of fibre are: | Feb 1982 | Jan 1983 | Jan 1984 |
|---|---|---|---|
| keeps you regular | 26 | 23 | 31 |
| as a laxative | 18 | 19 | 17 |
| helps prevent constipation | 13 | 13 | 11 |
| | 57 | 56 | 59 |
| helps keep digestive system healthy/ working properly | 22 | 30 | 23 |
| provides roughage | 18 | 25 | 16 |
| generally good for health/fitness | 12 | 16 | 12 |
| helps prevent illness/disease | 1 | 2 | 2 |
| | 53 | 74 | 53 |

Source: BMRB Access Omnibus Surveys

Thus far it could be argued that the bran boom stemmed largely or entirely from the stimulus of the F-Plan phenomenon, and that advertising played little or no part. Nobody denies the crucial importance of the F-Plan in altering the climate of public opinion towards bran. But as memory of it has faded, so has the salience of the general health-related benefits of fibre; and the laxative benefits are once again to the fore. Table 5 updates Table 1 with more recent figures. This helps explain why sector growth has slowed down. But in that case why has Kellogg's Bran Flakes gone on making headway? The F-Plan boom undoubtedly contributed to its 1982–83 growth; but its 1983–84 growth has some other mainspring.

*Increasing Number of Purchasers*

In the two years before May 1982, the average number of homes buying the leading bran cereals was virtually static. (The exception was Farmhouse Bran from Weetabix Ltd, which went national during 1981.) In the following year, the year of the bran boom, they all increased penetration. But only Kellogg's Bran Flakes has continued significantly to gain more users since then, as Table 6 shows.

TABLE 6:    HOUSEHOLD PENETRATION

| % homes buying in average 4 weeks year ending: | May 1981 | May 1982 | May 1983 | May 1984 |
|---|---|---|---|---|
| Kellogg's Bran Flakes | 2.7 | 2.6 | 3.8 | 4.5 |
| All-Bran | 5.5 | 5.3 | 6.3 | 6.3 |
| Farmhouse Bran | .5 | 1.4 | 1.8 | 1.9 |
| Sultana Bran | .9 | .8 | 1.1 | 1.2 |

Source: AGB/TCA

The strong implication of this evidence is that Kellogg's Bran Flakes has, since its new advertising began two years ago, been more successful than other advertised bran cereals in persuading non-users to become users, and occasional buyers to become regular buyers: the essence of our 'breaking the bran barrier' strategy. In the year to May 1983, Kellogg's Bran Flakes' average monthly penetration increased by half, more than any of the others; while the cumulative proportion of homes buying at all in a 12-week period rose from 4.2 per cent to 7.9 per cent between the spring and autumn of 1982. During 1983–84, the number of buying homes increased still further.

But (it may be argued) this still does not prove the effectiveness of the advertising. The bran boom could have induced initial trial and the product's deliciousness could have converted the trialist into a regular consumer, all with little or no contribution from the commercial.

True, the bran boom did encourage trial, and the product itself did help build repeat purchase. So, is there any evidence to demonstrate that the television advertising did affect sales and, if so, how?

## DID THE ADVERTISING AFFECT SALES?

Firstly, sales of Kellogg's Bran Flakes have continued growing, mainly because of an increasing number of buyers each month, when the rest of the sector's growth has slowed down. Something is at work recruiting additional usage that goes beyond the bran boom.

Secondly, it can be seen from Figure 1 that penetration began to rise with the first burst of the new campaign, *even before F-Plan was first published*. Subsequent bursts, moreover, can be seen to have been lifting the numbers of purchasers.

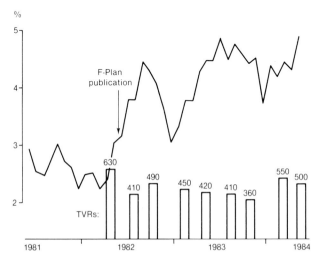

Figure 1. *Percentage of homes buying Kellogg's Bran Flakes. Four weekly*
*Source:* TCA

Thirdly, we have the findings of extensive econometric analysis. JWT built a model of brand sales, using multiple regression. This technique seeks to explain movements in the dependent variable (in this case Kellogg's Bran Flakes market share) by relating them to coincident movements in a number of other, explanatory factors. It estimates *which* of these other factors have been related to movements in sales, and the size and strength of each of those relationships.

The explanatory variables in the Kellogg's Bran Flakes model are:

— *Relative price:* since the dependent variable we are trying to explain is a relative one (volume *share* of market), we chose similarly to express the brand's price as relative to the RTE cereal market average (pence per kilo, indexed to market average).
— *Advertising:* of which there had been considerable variation, in campaign as well as in quantity: a TV campaign in 1980, a magazine campaign in 1981, the new 'Tasty' TV advertisement in 1982 followed by a further development of that campaign in 1983–84.
— *Close competitors:* the share movements of certain directly competitive brands: other bran flakes, and Special K.

— *The bran boom:* this had to be allowed for in any model. But there were no figures to quantify the intensity of consumer interest in a high-fibre diet. To approximate to it, we used the combined share growth of other bran cereals as the closest we could get to a description of consumer demand for fibre in general.

Two other explanatory variables were also examined, but in the end discarded, because they did not add significantly to the model. One was brand distribution which, vital though it is, nevertheless varied too little to have any effect detectable through multiple regression techniques. The model is therefore valid only whilst distribution remains steady. The second discarded variable was seasonality: the brand follows the market average, so its market share is seasonally stable. The data used were from the AGB Television Consumer Audit, for the period January 1980 to April 1984.

The result of this analysis was a model that fits the observed data well, with an $R^2$ of 0.91. That is, 91 per cent of observed variation in market share is accounted for by the model. The estimated share line follows the movements in the actual graph closely, as shown in Figure 2. The unexplained residuals, plotted in Figure 3, lie within the 95 per

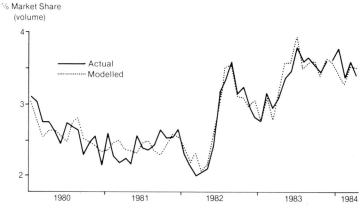

Figure 2. *Market model*

cent confidence limits, are well scattered and show no signs of systematic deviation that would suggest the presence of some other factor beyond those included in the model. The variables that are in the model have good levels of statistical reliability attached to them. The market model is summarised in Table 7.

We can draw the following conclusions:

1. *The Bran Boom:* as expected, there is a positive correlation between sales of Kellogg's Bran Flakes and other bran cereal products. Had this been fully proportional to market shares the coefficient would have been 0.4 (an increase of 0.4 in Kellogg's Bran Flakes share for every 1 point gained by other brans). The fact that the derived value is 0.2 supports the view that the bran boom explains part of the brand's growth, but is not the only factor.

2. *Close Competitors:* the negative correlation with other bran flakes denotes a competitive relationship between these very similar products. (It would have been astonish-

% Market Share

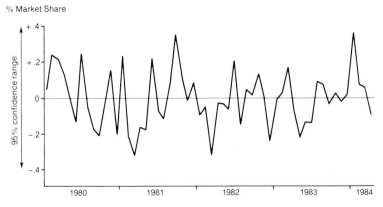

Figure 3. *Residuals*

ing had it been otherwise.) Less predictable was the observation of a competitive relationship with Special K (confirmed by brand switching analyses). On reflection though, Special K's role as a crisp, pleasant-tasting flake for adults who watch their weight can be seen as overlapping that of Bran Flakes.

3. *Price Elasticity:* this is low. Demand for Kellogg's Bran Flakes is fairly insensitive to variations in its relative price. (It is a larger factor in the competition with other bran flakes though.)

4. *Advertising Elasticities:* the effectiveness of the 1980 TV campaign, and of the magazine advertising that ran from the summer of 1981 into the first quarter of 1982, were below average for this market. By contrast, the effectiveness of the new strategy TV campaign, in 1982 and since, is well above average. These are the highest

TABLE 7: MARKET MODEL

Multiple regression analysis of AGB/TCA data Jan 1980–Apr 1984.
Dependent variable: Kellogg's Bran Flakes volume market share.

| | |
|---|---|
| *explanatory variables:* | |
| the bran boom | |
| (market share of bran cereals | |
| other than bran flakes) | +.2 per point |
| | |
| competitor brands | |
| other bran flakes market share | −.5 per point |
| Special K market share | −.6 per point |
| | |
| price elasticity | −.6 |
| | |
| advertising elasticities: | |
| TV 1980 | +.1 |
| magazines 1981 | +.1 |
| TV 1982 ('Tasty') | +.3 |
| TV 1983–84 ('Waiters') | +.4 |
| | |
| $R^2 = 0.91$ | |

elasticities we have recorded for any brand in numerous econometric studies of the cereals market.

By weakening the prejudices against bran, the F-Plan naturally made it possible for bran cereal advertising to be more effective. To that extent, the advertising was given a helping hand. But this was equally true for other brans' advertising, with less dramatic effects. It is to the credit of the Kellogg's Bran Flakes campaign that it capitalised more effectively on this change in consumer opinion, and that it has continued to match the public mood.

When we produced 'Tasty' the F-Plan had not been heard of. The commercial worked, and worked well. But consumer knowledge and attitudes were changing, and we had to keep up with the consumer. The evidence from the model is that we succeeded: 'Waiters' – the film that ran in 1983–84 – has been even more effective than 'Tasty'. 'Waiters' won a diploma at the 1983 British Television Advertising Awards.

The model argues strongly that the TV advertising worked. But we do not rely solely on the model. There is other evidence to back it up.

### How did the Advertising Work?

In 1982 the roles of the advertising were to overcome the negative associations of bran and to encourage trial. Helped by the changing climate of opinion, both these aims were quickly and largely achieved. Average monthly penetration rose by half as much again to nearly 4 per cent. Cumulative 12-week penetration doubled to almost 8 per cent. Brand attitudes shifted dramatically (Table 8). Not only did roughage and bran become much more important purchase motivators, but *liking* the product for its tastiness figured significantly more often in respondents' reasons for buying it – exactly on strategy.

In 1983 that strategy was modified for the new 'Waiters' film (see page 65). Qualitative research among consumers had confirmed a move towards greater personal respect and care. People were increasingly trying to improve the quality of their lives by taking more care of themselves. The fashion of jogging epitomised what, at a deeper level, was a more active approach to life, linked to a more relaxed appreciation of it.

The new 'Waiters' film accordingly kept the messages about general enjoyment and product tastiness, but sought to add an even greater air of freshness and activity, allied to a very contemporary expression of discerning choice. The brand's appeal was broadened as a 'healthy' cereal, in a natural and non-cranky way, and particularly enjoyable in its own right. The aim now was to combine a strengthening of the consumption habit among its existing consumers with some further recruitment of new eaters.

Research to monitor attitudes (see Table 8) showed a fall during 1983 in digestion-related reasons for purchase, a maintenance of health and taste-related reasons, and a further rise in secondary reasons: the presence of vitamins (a good measure of consumer perceptions of nutritional value), and the product flavour (which many find needs little or no sugar).

A recent image study found that Kellogg's Bran Flakes is seen – just as much by housewives who have never tried it as by existing users – as a product for modern active people of all ages who like to eat healthy foods, and who are not much in favour of traditional cereals. Only on the all-family appeal of the brand does the 'never-trieds' view

TABLE 8:    REASONS FOR BUYING KELLOGG'S BRAN FLAKES

| % recent buyers who buy because: | Dec 1981 | | Jan + Apr 1983 | | Jul + Oct 1983 |
|---|---|---|---|---|---|
| general health benefits | | | | | |
| plenty of roughage | 38 | ↔ | 50 | | 52 |
| helps keep you healthy | 37 | | 41 | | 37 |
| made from natural ingredients | 16 | | 14 | | 14 |
| rich in vitamins | 8 | | 11 | ↔ | 18 |
| digestive benefits | | | | | |
| contains bran | 38 | ↔ | 44 | ↔ | 31 |
| ensures healthy digestion | n/a | | 29 | ↔ | 20 |
| easy to digest | 10 | | 12 | | 10 |
| other benefits | | | | | |
| I like it | 23 | ↔ | 34 | | 32 |
| tastes nice | 15 | ↔ | 20 | | 20 |
| needs little or no sugar | 9 | ↔ | 14 | ↔ | 21 |
| Purchasing behaviour | | | | | |
| I buy it regularly | 14 | ↔ | 20 | ↔ | 24 |
| Sample base | (120) | | (118) | | (130) |

↔ major changes
Source: Marcos Studies

lag behind. They still see it as mainly a woman's product. This apart, the user image (Table 9) has moved a long way away from that of the elderly, costive bran-eater it used to be.

TABLE 9:    USER IMAGERY

| % housewives saying Kellogg's Bran Flakes would be eaten by: | brand buyers | never tried |
|---|---|---|
| people who like to eat healthy foods | 81 | 87 |
| modern, active people | 66 | 67 |
| people who like traditional cereals | 32 | 31 |
| young adults | 64 | 50 |
| middle-aged | 62 | 50 |
| older people | 54 | 49 |
| women | 68 | 51 |
| men | 44 | 26 |
| children | 43 | 17 |
| all the family | 45 | 26 |

Source: RBL, May 1984

Brand attitudes also show general agreement by 'never-trieds', as much as by users, that Kellogg's Bran Flakes is a particularly healthy, fibre-rich and up-to-date cereal. On the other hand, the 'never-trieds' who are ready to concede that it tastes nice, without ever having tasted it, are a minority still. Yet this itself represents a remarkable advance. Only four years ago, research found a massive expectation among those who had never tried the product that it could not possibly taste nice. Today, some 40 per cent at least are of the opposite opinion (Table 10). It was the advertising that changed their view.

TABLE 10:    BRAND ATTITUDES

| % housewives saying Kellogg's Bran Flakes is: | brand buyers | never tried |
|---|---|---|
| rich in fibre | 96 | 88 |
| a particular healthy cereal | 93 | 86 |
| a modern and up-to-date cereal | 81 | 76 |
| popular | 71 | 55 |
| tastes nice | 84 | 40 |
| appetising | 75 | 38 |

Source: RBL, May 1984

We have seen how the two commercials, 'Tasty' and 'Waiters', have helped to enhance and modify knowledge and opinion about the brand, its taste and its image. There remains one last piece of the jigsaw to fit into place: consumers' perception of the part that the advertising played.

*Advertising's Influence*

As part of the research programme to monitor progress of the brand, we asked buyers of bran cereals to tell us what had encouraged them and their families to start eating bran cereals, or to eat more of them. In January 1983, and again a year later, one respondent in five said she had been influenced by advertisements (Table 11). This, in our experience, is an unwontedly large acknowledgement of the influence of advertising, which ranks remarkably high on this list of stimuli. No less importantly, it is the younger age groups whom the advertising has impressed. Bran cereals had an older consumption profile. The aim of normalising the product required that we introduce it to younger consumers.

TABLE 11:    INFLUENCES ON BRAN CONSUMPTION

| % buyers of bran cereals who were influenced by: | Jan 1983 | Jan 1984 | 15–34 | 35–54 | 55+ | ABC1 | C2DE |
|---|---|---|---|---|---|---|---|
| advertising for bran cereals | 19 | 19 | 29 | 20 | 9 | 16 | 21 |
| newspaper articles | 16 | 22 | 21 | 29 | 16 | 25 | 20 |
| F-Plan book | 12 | 13 | 13 | 20 | 6 | 17 | 9 |
| doctor's advice | 11 | 9 | 9 | 7 | 9 | 8 | 9 |
| articles about F-Plan | 6 | 9 | 11 | 10 | 3 | 11 | 6 |
| radio commentaries | 5 | 10 | 6 | 17 | 8 | 11 | 10 |
| other influences | 26 | 17 | 14 | 16 | 20 | 17 | 17 |
| sample base | (463) | (443) | | | | | |

Source: BMRB Access Omnibus Surveys

Kellogg's Bran Flakes is the second largest brand in the bran sector. Yet it has been the top brand amongst those who acknowledge having been influenced by advertising. Table 12 shows that this supremacy of advertising effect increased during 1983, corroborating the evidence from sales and household penetration data that Kellogg's Bran Flakes pulled away from the rest of the field. Furthermore, there is an indication (though admittedly on small sample sizes) that the evident sales success of this campaign arose not only because it encouraged people to suspend their disbelief about the taste and *try* it, but also because perseverance with the campaign has encouraged trialists and occasional users to become *regular* consumers and purchasers, more effectively than any of its competitors. This is illustrated by Table 13.

TABLE 12:    ADVERTISING INFLUENCE BY BRAND

| % influenced by advertising, who bought: | Jan 1983 | Jan 1984 |
|---|---|---|
| Bran Flakes | 48 | 62 |
| All-Bran | 44 | 41 |
| Farmhouse Bran | 13 | 21 |
| Sultana Bran | 21 | 25 |
| sample base | (93) | (83) |

Source: BMRB Access Omnibus Surveys

TABLE 13:    ADVERTISING INFLUENCE ON CONSUMPTION

| % influenced by advertising who now buy: | Kellogg's Bran Flakes | other advertised brans |
|---|---|---|
| regularly | 63 | 41 |
| occasionally | 37 | 49 |
| don't know | — | 10 |
| | 100 | 100 |
| sample base | (51) | (83) |

Source: BMRB Access Omnibus Survey, Jan 1984

## CONCLUSIONS

To sum up the evidence:

1.  Since the change in strategy in 1982 and the brand's repositioning as a tasty, natural and healthy cereal for the family, sales have grown faster than the bran-cereal sector average. Sales have continued rising rapidly even though the bran boom and the growth of other brands have slackened.

2.  This has been achieved by an above-average and continued increase in the number of households buying Kellogg's Bran Flakes per month. More homes bought it to try and more homes have become regular and frequent purchasers.

3.  Econometric analysis has uncovered a strong relationship between the 1982-84 TV campaign, and consumer purchases. This was helped by the change in the climate of opinion brought about by the F-Plan diet, but the campaign's effect was not solely due to that: the advertising had begun to work before the F-Plan had been heard of.

4.  The advertising elasticities (0.3 and 0.4) derived from the econometric model are the highest we have recorded in the cereal market. Even after allowing for the bonus effect of the F-Plan, the advertising effectiveness has been remarkable.

5.  Adapting the campaign to keep up with changing consumer needs and attitudes has added even more to its effectiveness. Kellogg's Bran Flakes pulled further ahead of the field in 1983.

6.  The advertising worked by telling people, very credibly and persuasively, that the product really is very tasty - contrary to what most of them previously thought. It has worked, too, by transforming the brand image, which once was that of a traditional, semi-medicinal, older person's product, into that of a healthy food for modern, active people of all ages.

7.  Consumers acknowledge that Kellogg's Bran Flakes advertising, more than that of any other bran cereal, has influenced them and their families to start eating it, or to eat more of it.

The new brand positioning strategy we adopted in 1982, and its execution in advertising, have amply justified our faith in the brand's potential. We may not yet have totally demolished the bran barrier (there still remain some people who have never tried Kellogg's Bran Flakes because they expect it not to taste good), but we have certainly breached it, with the help of some particularly effective advertising. That extra creative effectiveness has a cash value: not one that is calculable with absolute precision, but we can make a reasoned estimate.

Supposing the Kellogg's Bran Flakes campaign had been just as effective – no more and no less – than the advertising for other bran cereals (which are themselves judged to have been successful campaigns)? Then we might reasonably have expected a sales increase in line with other types of bran cereal which, in the latest 12 months, are 35 per cent up on two years ago. In fact, though, Kellogg's Bran Flakes have gone up 73 per cent over the same period. This difference between expected and actual is worth an *additional* £3 million in sales revenue in the latest year alone.

The advertising spend at just average rates of effectiveness would have delivered a satisfactory rate of return. The above-average effectiveness that has brought in an *extra £3 million* in sales on top of that is a substantial extra contributor to profit in anybody's book. 'Very very tasty' was the message; very very potent was its effect; and very very profitable the result.

## REFERENCES

1.  Eyton, A., *F-Plan*, London: Penguin, 1982.

# 5

# Hofmeister: a Study of Advertising and Brand Imagery in the Lager Market

## INTRODUCTION

In 1983 brewers spent £44 million advertising lager brands. The market has experienced steady growth for some years, and brands are both big – up to £300 million at retail value – and profitable in relation to ales. Yet the bulk of lager volume goes through the brewers' tied pub trade. People tend to choose pubs as places to drink, rather than for the brands they serve, and even when in the pub will usually ask for 'a pint of lager' rather than a brand by name.

On face value, then, this enormous investment might well appear to be superfluous – why advertise to a captive market? What is the real role and value of all this advertising?

This case history attempts to answer both questions. It looks at Hofmeister, Courage's mainstream lager brand, which came late to the market, suffered a shaky start and subsequently struggled to catch up with the bigger lager brands it was launched to rival.

In simple terms, we will try to demonstrate that a major new advertising campaign for Hofmeister generated profit over and above its costs. In a wider context, we hope to say something more fundamental about the importance of brand imagery, even to a captive market, and the role advertising plays in creating it. We therefore confine ourselves to the tied-pub trade and exclude clubs and off-licences, where Hofmeister is also sold. The pub trade accounts for more than 70 per cent of the brand's sales.

We should make it clear at this point that we are not at liberty in this paper to disclose share or volume figures for Courage brands. These data have therefore been indexed.

## SALIENT FEATURES OF THE LAGER MARKET

For the past two decades lager has been the most dynamic sector of the British beer market, growing to capture one-third of it. Sales of draught lager alone are now worth nearly £2 billion, and even during the recent market recession lager volume has kept increasing. This trend has been to the benefit of the brewers, who derive a 20 per cent higher margin from lagers than from ales.

Lager has achieved this growth through its appeal to young drinkers: 18–34s consume two-thirds of total volume. This further enhances its importance to the brewers: not only is it their market's most dynamic and profitable product sector, it also represents the future. Drinkers tend to carry preferences established when young through the rest of their lives. It is therefore vital to a brewer to have a strong lager brand.

Not surprisingly, the brewers have responded to this opportunity by distributing and promoting a plethora of brands. To ensure the appeal of their pubs, most brewers now offer a portfolio of alternatives on the bar. New contenders frequently appear and some 30 lagers enjoy TV support. Yet, as in most markets, the first brands in have remained the leaders: 60 per cent of draught lager sales are held by the big six brewers' original mainstream brands – Carlsberg, Carling Black Label, Harp, Heineken and Skol.

In part, this persistence is explained by the major brewers' distribution muscle, but the nature of lager and its drinkers' needs also play their part. Mainstream lagers are much of a muchness in product terms, and the low temperatures at which they are served usually mask any differences that may exist between them. In blind product tests, most drinkers cannot consistently discriminate between brands. They differentiate between them on image.

Brand images are crucial in determining choice, a feature of the market highlighted in our qualitative research. And the nature of those images is bound up with the lifestyle of lager drinkers. They tend to be young, sociable and fashion-conscious. They drink in public, amongst their peer group. They prefer lager to bitter not only because its blander taste is more readily accessible, but because it is seen to be a more modern, youthful drink, with a higher price that demonstrates its higher status value.

Successful brands tend to reflect these generic market-place demands. They may have a specific product or heritage story, but they also establish an image around this story. Almost invariably, they demonstrate through the portrayal of their 'ideal' drinkers that they are contemporary, confident and sympathetic to a young man's outlook on life. Drinkers want to be sure that the brands they choose are popular and thus that they themselves are 'doing the done thing'. Big is beautiful.

Media advertising is crucial in creating and sustaining these images of success. Indeed, respondents in lager group discussions often talk of their brands primarily by reference to their advertising. In a market where products are so simple and so similar, advertising-created images provide consumers with the only means to differentiate.

## COURAGE AND HOFMEISTER

Hofmeister was a late entrant to the market. Courage already had a standard lager in Harp, whose ownership was shared amongst a consortium of brewers. Growth in the market and a desire for greater control led to the launch of Hofmeister in 1977, with a 'continental' positioning considered complementary to Harp. By 1981, the new brand had become Courage's main draught lager, replacing Harp in the majority of tied outlets.

During these years, Courage's lager sales performance did not keep up with that of its ales. Thus, on an indexed basis, Courage's 1983 ales market share was 106 compared with 100 in 1977, but its lagers share was 93 compared with 100 in 1977 (see Figure 1).

Courage lagers consistently lost ground in every year except 1981. In that year, ale

Figure 1. *Courage's retail trade share of major brewers market*
*Source:* BMS, Courage

marketing activity increased pub traffic; total pub sales increased, including lager. However, lager sales resumed their downward path thereafter. The movements shown may
seem small, but it is worth reiterating their significance for two reasons: the market is
huge and the figures, derived from a census of sales returns contributed by each major
brewer, are very accurate.

Courage had a problem. In the important lager sector it was losing share. Lagers were
'letting the side down'. Hofmeister was a £100 million brand, available in over 85 per
cent of Courage's pubs, but it was underperforming.

The key marketing objective was therefore to reverse Courage's declining lager share.
It was the inadequate performance of Hofmeister, the mainstream lager brand with
near-universal tied-trade distribution, which had apparently led to the decline; it was up
to Hofmeister to bring about its reversal. It was important to discover why Hofmeister
was underperforming and, when Boase Massimi Pollitt was appointed to the brand early
in 1983, we set out to answer this important question. We needed to explore the nature
and position of the brand and to discover whether advertising could play a role in its
revitalisation.

## UNDERSTANDING THE BRAND'S PROBLEMS

Qualitative research was illuminating in suggesting reasons for the brand's sales problem.
Hofmeister drinkers showed little enthusiasm for the brand. The only reason they gave
for drinking it was that it was served in their local. To them the brand was unremarkable,
low key and, because they could say little about it, faceless. They even felt that Hofmeister
was unpopular amongst men who didn't drink it.

Non-drinkers were indeed critical. The brand was criticised for being 'weak' and
'having no head'. Its symbol – the bear – was mischievously abused, with the brand all

too frequently being referred to as 'bear's piss'! All this, when in blind tests it was shown that the brand matched its key competitors. The justification for this criticism was perhaps that the brand had experienced early product shortcomings, but these had been rectified as early as 1981; the real problem lay elsewhere.

Quantitative research added to the understanding of the brand's problems. Hofmeister's weaknesses were apparent in a number of ways.

### Drinker Commitment

Compared with other major lager brands, Hofmeister had the lowest level of drinker commitment (see Table 1).

TABLE 1:    DRINKERS' COMMITMENT TO BRANDS

commitment = drink regularly ÷ drink nowadays

|  | % |
| --- | --- |
| Carling Black Label | 55 |
| Carlsberg | 45 |
| Heineken | 42 |
| Skol | 42 |
| Harp | 38 |
| Hofmeister | 36 |

Source: Millward-Brown Jan–Feb 1983

### Brand Awareness

Hofmeister's prompted brand awareness was comparable with other brands. However, its spontaneous awareness was very low. The brand lacked 'front-of-mindness' (see Figure 2).

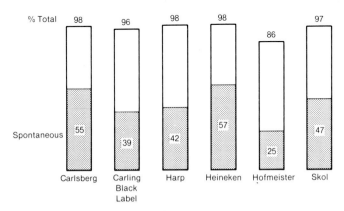

Figure 2. Hofmeister brand awareness vs. the Big 5

Source: Millward Brown Jan/Feb 1983

*Quantitative Attitude Measures*

The brand had a weak image profile compared to the other leading brands (see Figure 3).

Conventional market research interpretation would suggest that the cause of the brand's problem arose through these image weaknesses, and presumably could be put right by rectifying them. As we shall see, in the real world advertising did not work in this neat way.

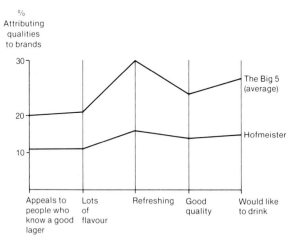

Figure 3. *Brand images: Hofmeister vs. the Big 5 competitors*
*Source:* Millward Brown Jan/Feb 1983

## THE ADVERTISING BRIEF

If Courage's lager performance was to be revitalised, then the new advertising had two essential tasks. In the short term, it had to boost the saliency and appeal of Hofmeister amongst lager drinkers exposed to the brand, primarily Courage pub-goers. In the long term, it had to raise the reputation of Hofmeister alongside that of the market leaders, amongst the wider universe of all lager drinkers.

The initial advertising objective was therefore to raise Hofmeister's profile in the market-place and to increase its franchise of frequent drinkers. Brand loyalty is weak in the standard lager market, but if the advertising could create an aura of popularity and success around Hofmeister, it could bolster the confidence of its drinkers in their choice and thus build their commitment to the brand.

The mechanism by which we believed this could be achieved was the creation of a new brand image for Hofmeister which was not only distinctive, but of genuine appeal and relevance to young drinkers.

The creative brief emerging from this initial research and thinking requested a campaign that would position Hofmeister as 'cool' and fashionable. It suggested a number of guidelines, the most important of which was to bring back 'The Bear'. Our qualitative work had consistently found this to be Hofmeister's only brand asset. Although drinkers were confused as to what the bear did, looked like, or represented, they knew Hofmeister as the 'beer with the bear' and some even claimed to ask for 'a pint of bear'. Despite its two-year absence from Hofmeister advertising, this animal symbol remained potent. What it needed was direction, a purpose and a relevance. If a new bear was to embody the brand or personalise its drinkers, it clearly had to do so in a way that those drinkers found admirable and sympathetic.

A strong character, we felt, could personify the 'cool' aspect of the brand and carry the secondary elements of intended communication, notably Hofmeister's satisfying product qualities and German heritage. It should also provide a long-term brand theme capable of translation into point-of-sale and promotional material – significant elements in drinks marketing.

## MEDIA PLANNING

### The Reason for Choosing TV

It was clear from our consumer research that a strong TV presence was an integral part of drinkers' confidence in a lager brand; to compete with the market leaders, we had to match them on that battle ground. More importantly, TV was also the natural choice for the job. Given the need to create a new, confident image for the brand, TV provided the most intrusive and influential way to reach our young drinkers. The budget of £1.7 million set for the draught product was a realistic reflection of the brand's share and less than any of our major competitors' anticipated spend. Rather than dilute this presence further, we therefore decided to put all the money into TV.

### The Media Strategy

Although Courage's pubs are distributed throughout England and Wales, 70 per cent of them are concentrated in six TV areas: London, TVS, Yorkshire, Harlech, TSW and Central. We therefore concentrated our advertising in these areas alone. Advertising for canned Hofmeister ran in these areas alongside the draught commercials.

## DEVELOPING THE CAMPAIGN

The development of the new advertising revolved around the development of a character, George the Bear. This took four stages of qualitative animatic testing, during which his personality evolved to meet young drinkers' need for a figure whom they could admire, identify with and be amused by.

The agency's original embodiment of 'cool' was a classically sophisticated, somewhat haughty bear in a dinner jacket; by the final stage, George had emerged as a stylish, 'Fonz'-type, street-smart bear, the leader of his young peer group. Trendy, extrovert, witty, fun to be with and slightly anarchic, George reflected the aspirations of young drinkers. He became at once both brand and drinker and, through this dual role, tied Hofmeister to a set of positive values that the drinkers themselves demanded of the advertising.

*Bear*: Life in a Bavarian forest was boring.
A big event was me and Ronnie Rabbit watching a leaf fall down.
*Rabbit*: (excitedly) a leaf! A leaf!
*Bear*: Hey . . .

*Bear*: Then one day I discovered Hofmeister lager with a picture of my Grandpa on it.
It had a cool cut on the back of the throat that was so good I decided to leave the forest.

And so I found . . .
companionship.

I found the left hand screw to kiss onto the pink. (SFX kiss)
But most of all I found Hofmeister on draught.

The moral is: If you want poetry stand and stare

But if you want great lager – follow the bear, hey!

*Bear*: So the cold Hofmeister is sliding down like a dream

When this girl comes up and asks me what I do.

So I tell her I'm a dispensing chemist, which really impresses her for a bear,

And I'll read her prescription any time.

Sometimes I think the medical profession is misunderstood. I prescribe Hofmeister twice nightly, hey.

Hofmeister. For great lager, follow the bear.

## RESULTS: SALES EFFECT

The year following the launch of the new campaign was a record one for lager: the hot summer of 1983 helped standard lager sales in pubs rise by 9 per cent. Over the same period, Hofmeister's pub sales increased by 25 per cent (see Figure 4). This dramatic

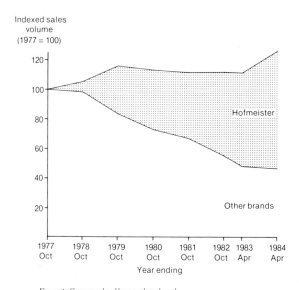

Figure 4. *Courage sales of lager to the pub trade*
*Source:* Courage

growth was not caused by a wider availability of the brand: its pub distribution only grew by 1.5 per cent. Hofmeister's rate of sale thus rose by 13 per cent more than the market. Furthermore, the brand's growth was incremental to Courage's total lager sales, rather than substitutional as it had been before. The company's share of the pub lager market therefore rose after two years of consistent decline, at a time when its ales share was static (see Figure 5). Hofmeister's brand share performance within the standard lager market in pubs was impressive, increasing by 1.24 per cent, worth no less than £10 million in this huge market.

We examined some possible causes of Hofmeister's improved performance:

1. *Product* There was no change in product specification over the period.
2. *Price* Hofmeister's price actually increased in relation to its competitors at this time.
3. *Distribution* As mentioned above, Hofmeister's pub distribution grew by less than 1.5 per cent.
4. *Promotions* There was no change in the level of below-the-line support for Hofmeister, although new promotions and promotional material were designed to complement the advertising. Indeed, enthusiasm for the advertising led to demand for branded 'George the Bear' T-shirts that surpassed all such previous offers.
5. *Presentation* The draught fount remained unchanged.
6. *Pubs* There was no change in pub investment policy over the period.

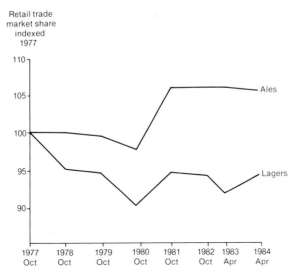

Figure 5. *Courage's retail trade share of major brewers market*
*Source:* BMS, Courage

The reasons for the uplift in sales had to lie elsewhere. The strongest indication as to the cause came from an area analysis of the sales increase, which demonstrated its association with the advertising activity. In those Courage pubs which saw no change in the lagers on offer between the summers of 1982 and 1983, *Hofmeister sales grew at almost twice the rate in the advertised areas as in the non-advertised ones* (see Table 2).

TABLE 2: HOFMEISTER PUB SALES IN UNCHANGED CONFIGURATIONS*

|  |  | 1982 | 1983 |
|---|---|---|---|
| advertised areas | Hofmeister | 100 | 139 |
|  | the market | 100 | 121 |
| non-advertised areas | Hofmeister | 100 | 120 |
|  | the market | 100 | 121 |

period: July–Aug 1983 vs. 1982
* in pubs where the range of lagers on offer did not change
Source: Courage, BMS

## RESULTS: CONSUMER BEHAVIOUR

This uplift in Hofmeister's sales was explained by marked shifts in claimed consumer behaviour relating to the brand. Over the year following the new campaign's launch, claimed trial of Hofmeister rose by 13 per cent in the advertised areas: non-advertised areas showed no rise at all (see Table 3). 'Nowadays' drinkers on the survey also increased, whilst the proportion within those who claimed to be regular Hofmeister drinkers rose as well, indicating a new commitment to the brand. The behavioural data is thus consistent with the observed increase in Hofmeister's sales *in advertised areas*. We will now attempt to explain the link between behaviour and advertising.

TABLE 3:    HOFMEISTER TRIAL AND DRINKING IN ADVERTISED AREAS

|  | Pre % | Post % |
|---|---|---|
| trial | 45 | 51 |
| drink nowadays | 17 | 21 |
| drink regularly | 6 | 9 |
| 'commitment' | 36% | 43% |

commitment = drink regularly ÷ drink nowadays
period: Jan–Feb 1984 vs. 1983
Source: Millward Brown

## RESULTS: CONSUMER ATTITUDES

That advertising had played some part in Hofmeister's improved performance appeared evident from both quantitative and qualitative research. The new campaign was unmistakably noticeable and well branded. Advertising recall shot up in response to the first burst, to levels never previously achieved by the brand (see Figure 6).

This level of awareness, moreover, was greater than for any of the 'Big Five' lager brands' campaigns, despite media expenditure lower than any of theirs. Similarly, brand awareness in advertised areas rose to higher levels than had been seen at the height of the

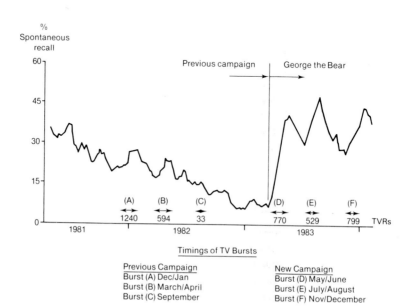

Figure 6. *Hofmeister claimed advertising recall*
*Source:* Millward Brown

1982 campaign, so that Hofmeister's consumer 'stature' came more closely in line with the other major brands (see Table 4).

TABLE 4:   HOFMEISTER BRAND AWARENESS IN ADVERTISED AREAS

|  | Pre<br>% | Post<br>% |
|---|---|---|
|  | spontaneous/total awareness | |
| Hofmeister | 31/90 | 38/92 |
| the 'Big Five' brands | 48/97 | 48/98 |

period: Jan–Feb 1984 vs. 1983
Source: Millward Brown

We sought to establish the link between Hofmeister's new consumer saliency and its observed sales increase, by examining the brand's consumer image. We found this link in qualitative research, but *not* in the quantitative brand imagery data.

### Qualitative Findings

Our findings were based on qualitative research conducted in February 1984. We found that the advertising had altered drinkers' perceptions of the brand. A faceless brand had been given a positive, desirable identity – that of George the Bear: confident, popular and enviable.

'He doesn't have to try'.
'He's cool'.
'He can do anything'.

Drinkers, moreover, had readily identified with George, bear or not:

'I don't really see him as a bear'.
'He's the sort of bloke I'd like to be'.

Drinkers were happy to drink Hofmeister because they perceived it to be popular and trendy, rather than because it was a superior product. Indeed, product perceptions – always low key amongst lager drinkers – had changed little; the advertising, after all, had deliberately provided little more than basic product reassurance. Non-drinkers of Hofmeister, on the other hand, were now reluctant to criticise the brand. Many of them referred to it as second best to their brand.

### Quantitative Findings

When we turned to the quantitative data, however, we were surprised to find that there had been no significant shift in Hofmeister's consumer standing.

To attempt to understand this anomaly, Boase Massimi Pollitt conducted a series of in-depth interviews among lager drinkers who had beforehand completed the lager tracking study questionnaire. We found that brand image and brand usage could not be separated in the way the questionnaire attempted to. This is because when answering a structured questionnaire the majority of lager drinkers will not express an opinion of a brand they have not tried or do not drink regularly. This observation has been made for other product fields.[1]

Regular drinkers of Hofmeister were content with the brand and rated it accordingly. However, because of Hofmeister's relatively small presence in the market, they were swamped by non-drinkers of the brand who were reluctant to rate it. Average ratings were thus low and pegged down by the brand's low absolute availability. Its non-drinkers were now happy with the brand, but still unwilling to praise it extravagantly on *product* grounds against better-known competitors, as they were perfectly well aware that the product was nothing special.

The in-depth interviews supported the earlier qualitative research in suggesting that Hofmeister's new appeal lay in drinkers' perceptions of it as a popular, fashionable lager; thus, the link between the brand's advertising-born saliency and its sales increase was confirmed.

## SUMMARY AND FINANCIAL EVALUATION

In the year following the new advertising, Hofmeister's sales increased at over twice the market rate on a very small distribution increase. This increase was confined to advertised areas; elsewhere the brand's sales simply rose in line with the market. This strong performance almost single-handedly reversed Courage's declining lager share; given no other variables, it seems hard to avoid the conclusion that the new advertising was primarily responsible for Hofmeister's change of fortune, and the achievement of the marketing objectives.

In an IPA competition there may be an expectation for the case history to demonstrate a massive profit payback from advertising investment. Unfortunately the vast majority of advertised brands are not afforded this opportunity. In Hofmeister's case, once the 'natural' market growth has been subtracted from the sales increase (setting aside the fact that the brand had previously performed consistently below the market rate), the incremental wholesale profit on the sales increase achieved was £1.9 million, against an advertising spend of £1.7 million over the same period.

It is worth remembering that the lager market, like many, is one in which heavy expenditure is always expected, simply to *maintain* share, and in which advertisers look gradually to recoup their initial advertising investment in following years. Yet this campaign generated incremental profit greater than the cost of the advertising in the first year alone. Nor have we considered here either the additional effect of the advertising on draught sales in the club trade, which also outstripped the market, or the considerably enhanced retail profit secured by Courage pubs at the same time.

We hope we have shown a 'real world' case where advertising has succeeded in making a significant contribution to sales and a solid contribution to profits.

## CONCLUSIONS

The tied-pub trade is a captive market, yet advertising can be shown to have a significant effect on sales within it. Even where consumer purchase can be guaranteed, advertising has a role to play. Rate of sale depends on consumer commitment to outlet and product, and a key to this is brand imagery; in the absence of any grounds for rational discrimination, advertising must play a crucial part in creating a strong brand image.

This case history suggests that the increased consumer confidence in a brand through a strong brand image *can* bring about a sales increase, even in a captive market, which more than justifies the financial investment involved.

## REFERENCES

1.   Bird, M., Channon, C. and Ehrenberg, A. S. C., *Journal of Marketing Research*, August 1970.

# 6

# The Repositioning of Hellmann's Mayonnaise

## INTRODUCTION

Most of the classic studies of advertising effectiveness start with a sluggish or declining sales graph, which is then dramatically reversed by the new campaign. Hellmann's is different: it was already a healthily growing brand and the need for a new initiative was not immediately obvious, though we believe and hope to show it was crucially necessary. And, of course, it presents a particular challenge to demonstrate advertising effectiveness under these circumstances.

## BACKGROUND

### Hellmann's importance to CPC

CPC Best Foods Division is one of three divisions of CPC (UK) Ltd, the others dealing with catering supply and industrial starch technology. Best Foods (the retail division) currently turns over some £45 million at manufacturer's selling price and the business is comprised of Mazola Corn Oil, Brown & Polson cornflour, Dextrosol, Knorr cubes, soups and sauces, Frank Cooper, and Hellmann's Mayonnaise.

In 1981 divisional strategy was thoroughly reappraised, among other issues addressing the problem of how a finite total marketing budget should be apportioned among a large number of small- to medium-sized brands. One influential tool in the analysis was the matrix originally developed by the Boston Consulting Group, by which each brand is evaluated in two dimensions: market growth and brand dominance.

Dominant brands in growing markets become 'stars' – the opportunities on which the future of the business depends and therefore priorities for investment. Dominant brands in static or declining markets are regarded as 'cash cows', which can be 'milked' to provide investment for the 'stars'. Weak brands in declining markets are described as 'dogs' (for apparent reasons); and weak brands in growth markets must be treated on their individual merits. (This is inevitably an oversimplistic description and the results are rarely as unequivocal as this sounds; it can be, nevertheless, and was here, a useful aid to decision making, as can be seen in Figure 1.)

As a result, Hellmann's (hitherto regarded as a relatively minor part of the portfolio)

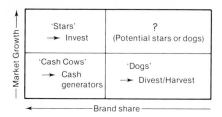

Figure 1. *The BCG matrix*

emerged as a prime candidate for investment: it dominated the mayonnaise market with a 60 per cent volume share, and the market itself had been growing for some years by 10–20 per cent per annum, being worth in 1981 some £7 million (see Figure 2).

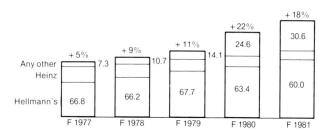

Figure 2. *Mayonnaise market trends (000/jars) & Hellmann's share*
*(NB: F 1977, etc., refers to CPC fiscal years which end*
*30 September. Thus, F 1977 refers to 12 months ending*
*30 September 1977)*

*Source:* Nielsen

## Hellmann's: Early History

Hellmann's Real Mayonnaise, originally an American brand, was launched in this country in the 1960s. At first it was very much a delicatessen product in limited distribution and continued for a number of years to develop a small but discriminating following.

It is important to understand that at the time of Hellmann's original launch, 'real' mayonnaise – ie a thick, spoonable, subtle-tasting emulsion of egg yolks and oil – was virtually unknown to the majority of the British public. The word 'mayonnaise' was widely used, erroneously, as a synonym for salad cream (a peculiarly British product with a pourable texture and highly flavoured with vinegar and sugar). This may be due to the fact that Heinz marketed until 1981 a product called 'Heinz Mayonnaise' which was very similar in taste and texture to salad cream.

Two significant circumstances followed from this. Firstly, mayonnaise became known exclusively as a salad dressing. This may still seem unsurprising to the British reader, until we remember that we are probably the only country in the world where this statement would be true: in the USA or on the Continent, there is no particular link between mayonnaise and salad.

Secondly, the early advertising history of Hellmann's was devoted by one means or another to explaining how the 'real' mayonnaise differed from salad cream expectations. By drawing these comparisons, of course, the salad usage positioning was reinforced.

*Hellmann's Position in 1981*

By 1981, Hellmann's had achieved reasonable distribution throughout the grocery trade (85 per cent £). The brand had been advertised, but not nationally or consistently: the best remembered campaign was that featuring 'Mrs Hellmann' which ran from 1976–79, mostly in London and the South. Penetration was still low and even awareness of the brand continued to be patchy. Year-on-year growth rates were encouraging (see Figure 2); but against this, it could be seen that much of this growth was simply a factor of improved distribution (see Figure 3). Calculating the actual rate of sale, this was much flatter – indeed in certain areas rate of sale could be shown to be in decline.

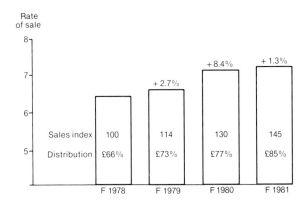

Figure 3. *Hellmann's Rate of Sale (000 jars/% £ distribution)*
*Source:* Nielsen

The original portfolio analysis had taken account of historical growth rates, but had not attempted to predict the future. Yet the logic of investing in the brand depended on the assumption that the market would, or could be made to, continue to grow. At £3.7 million (MSP), Hellmann's was not a large enough brand to justify heavy advertising expenditure simply for maintenance purposes. Its share of market was unlikely to increase, being so high already; indeed, it was almost inevitably foreseen to decline as own-label products became available, retailing considerably cheaper than Hellmann's, yet of highly acceptable quality. Before committing large sums of money, therefore, we had to address the question: what were the prospects of continued market growth?

Our analysis suggested strongly that Hellmann's, as it was at that time perceived and used, could not expect to grow indefinitely and indeed as distribution plateaued, might not grow much further. At its simplest this was predictable from the fact that the amount of salad served, while showing some growth, is finite; therefore Hellmann's would continue to compete with salad cream, and increasingly with other dressings such as French dressing which were – and are – growing from a small base even faster than mayonnaise.

The naive assumption that people would forsake salad cream as soon as mayonnaise became available to them was not borne out by the facts. Loyalty to salad cream was, and is, enormously strong. Most mayonnaise buyers were buying it in addition to, not instead of, salad cream. In fact mayonnaise was seen by the majority of its users as a 'special occasion' salad product, an occasional but not a routine substitute for salad cream.

This 'special occasion' imagery had in the past been recognised by client and agency as an important part of the Hellmann's brand: it grew out of the delicatessen origins of the brand and, in one campaign at least, had been explicitly reflected in an upper-class setting and a suggestion that Hellmann's was 'superior' or 'posh'.

However, we now began to consider whether this imagery was not a limitation as well as a strength. For users it inhibited everyday use of the product, which in any case was unlikely to take the place of salad cream totally. For non-users it was even a disincentive to purchase, especially to the C2D groups: the profile of Hellmann's at this time still being strongly AB (Table 1).

TABLE 1:  HELLMANN'S PENETRATION BY SOCIAL CLASS

| (Base: all housewives) | AB | C1 | C2 | D | E |
|---|---|---|---|---|---|
| Claim to buy Hellmann's nowadays: | 33% | 20% | 10% | 5% | 7% |

Source: TGI

It seemed likely then that once Hellmann's Mayonnaise had achieved a certain share of salad cream occasions, and a certain penetration among ABC1s, and allowing for the fact that about a quarter of all potential buyers reject the product on taste grounds, it would not have much further room to grow. And this point seemed to be not far off. If this were to be the case, it was difficult to justify the level of expenditure which were being contemplated.

## THE NEW STRATEGY FOR HELLMANN'S

All these limitations derived from the fact that mayonnaise was seen exclusively as a salad dressing. This had other limitations as well, in terms of regionality and seasonality. Salad consumption is heavily biased, of course, to the summer. For Hellmann's, with a relatively short shelf-life, this meant plant standing idle in the off-season. Also, salad consumption is greater in the South than the North. Hellmann's historical Southern bias was not a case of the South being ahead of the North; it was largely the same regional pattern as salads, or indeed salad cream.

On the other hand, if it were possible to re-present mayonnaise as a product with a wider range of uses and to divorce it from salad cream, the potential for growth would be very much greater. This would entail consumers seeing mayonnaise more in the way it is seen in the USA or Europe: as a versatile condiment. At the same time, it could be made more accessible and everyday: a condiment for snacks as well as formal meal occasions, associated with good food but not pretension.

Whether or not this aspiration was realistic or not was a difficult question for research to predict before the event. In the end, we decided on a major piece of qualitative research to probe, using individual interviews, people's attitudes to and experience of mayonnaise. This was very encouraging in that it showed little resistance to extending the versatility of mayonnaise usage, though there were clear 'no go' areas such as red meat or meals with gravy. One of the most interesting findings was that the heaviest users of mayonnaise were *already* using it in many different ways, but with considerable guilt because this was not 'proper', and almost disrespectful to a product which had positioned itself on a pedestal.

In addition to this, the new strategy seemed to fit well with some broad trends in eating habits; in particular the long-term growth in all pickles and sauces, the increase of snacking and the decline of the formal meal occasion, and an increasing willingness of the consumer to experiment and try new things.

### Advertising Development

On this basis, we proceeded to a creative brief. The objectives of the new campaign were defined as:

#### ADVERTISING OBJECTIVES

1. To encourage trial of Hellmann's (especially in areas of low salad consumption).
2. To stimulate a wider range of applications among existing trialists.

At the time, we considered two ways of approaching the objective. Either we could maintain our existing salad base and add new suggestions gradually, or we could abandon all the precedents and talk about mayonnaise as if it were a new product, with no salad antecedents. We decided fairly soon that the second approach was the only viable one: we needed to force a complete revaluation of the brand, and to do this we had to be radical, even shocking. The creative strategy was formulated as follows.

#### CREATIVE BRIEF

1. Redefine Hellmann's as a versatile, everyday 'condiment/ingredient'.
2. Divorce Hellmann's from any association with salad cream.
3. Brand Hellmann's strongly.

Guidelines:

— Feature a range of usage occasions (rather than a 'recipe' approach).
— Hellmann's is not just for good cooks – it's idiot proof.
— Hellmann's is a natural, simple product (parallel: whipped cream).

#### TARGET MARKET

1. Current Hellmann's users.
2. Non-users of mayonnaise.

The campaign that was produced was certainly different (see page 91). Not only did burgers and jacket potatoes replace delicate salads: but the black ties and silver candlesticks gave way to a Northern working-class kitchen where Mum was an awful cook and ran off with the coalman, leaving our hero (an overgrown schoolboy) to transform her inedible, boring food with the addition of a little Hellmann's.

Neither the client nor the agency could ignore the dangers of this radical approach if it misfired. Would we jeopardise all Hellmann's traditional brand strengths by debunking it like this? The campaign was extensively researched, both qualitatively as an animatic, and quantitatively as a finished film. The research showed a campaign with great impact which clearly communicated its objective of extended usage, and forced a revaluation of mayonnaise, but which also had no detectable effects on the quality perception of the brand. Indeed, intentions-to-buy scores were improved and the campaign was much liked by users and by non-users (Table 2).

TABLE 2:    INTENTION TO BUY
'How likely would you be to buy Hellmann's Mayonnaise?'

| Base: housewives exposed to: | Previous Commercial % | New Commercial 'Kitchen' % | Control (pack) % |
|---|---|---|---|
| very likely ( + 5) | 30 | 38 | 34 |
| quite likely | 37 | 31 | 19 |
| neither likely nor unlikely | 6 | 7 | 8 |
| not very likely | 17 | 14 | 9 |
| not at all likely ( + 1) | 10 | 9 | 31 |
| mean score | 3.62 | 3.74 | 3.17 |
| n = | (161) | (159) | (160) |

Source: Millward Brown

The following verbatims give examples of how consumers responded in group discussions to the new campaign at the animatic stage; the first group are C2D non-users from Cheshire.

'Terrific.'
'Really amusing.'
'It gets you to look at it.'
'Not like some dreary ones.'
'Trying to tell you you can use it on all types of food – more than you think.'
'Some of these things I would never have thought of but I'll try them.'

### The second group, from Hampton, Middlesex, are BC1 users:

'I like the Hellmann's brightening the food.'
'Goes with things you would never have dreamt of, like chips.'
'Encouraging other members of the family to help themselves.'
'I like the message that you can use it on things all the year round.'

### And the final group, from Oldham, Lancashire, are also BC1 users:

'That's very good.'
'I'd forgotten I'd had it on baked potatoes!'
'There's nothing extraordinary: it's food you eat anyway.'
'Salad cream's just for salad – with that one, it points out that you can use it with all these different things so you get your money's worth.'

*Media*

TV was chosen for its impact, and also because it addresses a family audience; we emphatically did not want a recipe campaign addressed to housewives, but a campaign to stimulate demand from all members of the family. Research suggested, for example, that teenagers making themselves snacks would be part of the opportunity.

Mayonnaise, as we have mentioned, was and still is a market with distinct regional strengths and weaknesses. A number of factors could be identified:

— the historical weight of advertising and distribution in London and the South;
— high salad consumption in the South;
— for an up-market product, the slightly different demographic profile of the South vs. the North.

Given the new strategy, however, we did not feel any of these factors constrained the opportunity. Indeed it was part of our objective to build a broader national brand than we inherited, which would not be limited by regional bias of salad consumption, nor so rigorously confined to AB purchasers.

Accordingly, the campaign was planned nationally and, in fact, the relatively cheaper airtime costs in the North of the country resulted in those areas being upweighted to the consumer. This was in line with our view that a higher weight of advertising was needed to build penetration and awareness in these areas.

The campaign was planned to break around the end of May 1982, the peak season for mayonnaise, followed by another burst in August–September. It was, however, part of our objective to develop counter-seasonal usage for Hellmann's. There had historically been a slight Christmas sales peak associated with cold turkey and seasonal indulgence: we decided to build on this by creating a special Christmas commercial (see page 93) to run for two weeks before and after Christmas, followed by two weeks of the original 'Kitchen' commercial retitled with a new end-line 'Don't save it for the summer'.

This regional pattern was essentially repeated the second year of advertising. To add new life to the campaign we made three new 20-second commercials, each tackling one new type of usage occasion: chips, coleslaw, and sandwiches (one example is shown on page 95).

## THE PROGRESS OF THE BRAND: 1982–84

At the time of writing, (May 1984), exactly two years have passed since the new Hellmann's campaign began. Let us describe first of all what has happened in the marketplace and evaluate Hellmann's progress against our objectives, which may be summarised as:

— *Primary*: major volume growth (while maintaining price).
— *Secondary*: development of weaker areas and development of counter-seasonality to be achieved by increased penetration and increased weight of purchase.

### HELLMANN'S MAYONNAISE "KITCHEN"

When I was a lad my mother was a dreary cook.

Her string beans tasted of real string.

Then one day she ran off with the coalman's humper.

Left with a wedge of rubber and one of mother's doorsteps.

I was lucky enough to spot a forgotten jar of Hellmann's.

Quickly I mixed 'em up and bingo!

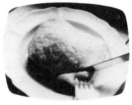

It were stupendous.

I spread Hellmann's on her carpetburgers.

They were magic.

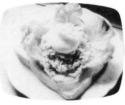

And mixed with tuna thick creamy Hellmann's transformed the limpest cloth lettuce.

Never again would her humble spud taste like it had a woolly on under its jacket.

Hellmann's. Don't save it for the salad.

*Volume Growth*

It is clear that Hellmann's has seen accelerated volume growth (Figure 4). It is true that the brand has also lost some share, but only at the same rate as we have observed for some years previously (about 3 per cent per annum): starting from such a high base this is perhaps not surprising. The share has been lost partly to own-label – in early 1983

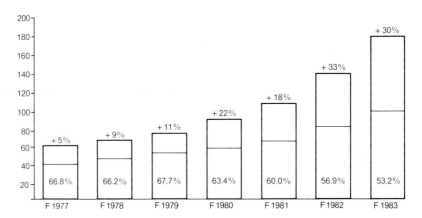

Figure 4. *Mayonnaise market trends (000 jars) and Hellmann's share*
Sources: Nielsen, 1977-81, MGS 1982-83

Tesco launched own-label mayonnaise for the first time – and to a lesser extent to Heinz, who relaunched a mayonnaise in spring 1983. This product has taken about 10 per cent of the market, although much of this replaces the share taken by Heinz Slimway Mayonnaise, on sale during 1981 and 1982. Both the own-label and Heinz products are considerably cheaper than Hellmann's, which commands a premium of some 60 per cent by weight at RSP.

Under the circumstances, it is a tribute to the strength of the Hellmann's brand that the rate of share loss has been so low: and for the last 12 months has shown signs of plateauing at around 50 per cent volume share.

What we did not predict was the rate at which the market could grow, with the result that Hellmann's ex-factory sales for the 1983 financial year were considerably in excess of the most ambitious internal forecasts made in 1981. (A 56 per cent increase compared with a 27 per cent forecast increase.)

*Development of Weak Areas*

Here the pattern is less clear cut, and complicated by problems in accurate regional measurement. Progress in Lancashire and especially Yorkshire seems to have been disappointing and all our attempts to explain this have been unsatisfactory; but other areas where mayonnaise was formerly very weak such as Harlech and the West, the Midlands and, in particular, Scotland, have shown very high levels of growth so that the profile of the brand is now more nationally based than it was (see Table 3).

## HELLMANN'S MAYONNAISE
### "TURKEY"

I'll never forget the Christmas we won turkey in raffle...

it were July before we had to feed the cat again...

Luckily Santa left me a jar of thick creamy Hellmans OOH OOH.

It were best Christmas ever.

Gran said if Dad...
ate anymore turkey, he'd end up looking like one.

Hellmanns. Don't save it for the summer.

TABLE 3:    REGIONAL BREAKDOWN OF HELLMANN'S SALES BY VOLUME

|  | 1981 Apr–Oct % | 1983 Apr–Oct % | Population, ISBA regions % |
|---|---|---|---|
| London | 42 | 33 | 20 |
| Southern | 7 | 8 | 9 |
| Wales and West | 6 | 9 | 11 |
| Midlands | 11 | 11 | 16 |
| Anglia | 5 | 7 | 6 |
| Lancashire | 11 | 10 | 13 |
| Yorkshire | 7 | 6 | 10 |
| North-East | 3 | 4 | 5 |
| Scotland | 8 | 12 | 10 |

Source: Mars Group Services

## Development of Counter-Seasonality

This is the most difficult area to evaluate. We have had two winter seasons and two very different experiences. The first winter showed an unprecedented rate of market growth, and one moreover in which Hellmann's participated fully (Table 4). This result is also remarkable for the fact that there is a high correlation between the rate of growth achieved by TV area, and the level of TVRs which our 'net homes' allocation enabled us to buy, making a strong case that this sales peak was in response to advertising (Figure 5).

The second winter, however, shows minimal year-on-year growth. Admittedly, this is starting from a high base, but in view of the continuing high rates of summer growth it means that progress towards making the brand less seasonal has apparently been wiped

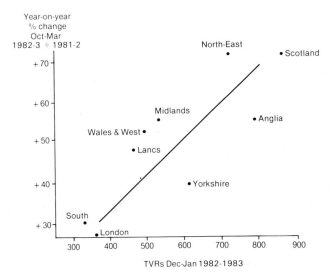

Figure 5. *Hellmann's volume growth: Winter campaign*
*Sources:* MGS, BARB

### HELLMANN'S MAYONNAISE
### "SANDWICH"

In mother's absence

hunger drove me to the four distant corners of the fridge where I discovered a 'ham frisbee'.

With my trustee jar of delicious creamy thick Hellmanns

and a trick I learned with an egg...

I fast became expert in the art of the sarnie.
OOH magic.

Hellmanns. Don't save it for the summer.

TABLE 4: SUMMARY OF HELLMANN'S PERFORMANCE – CHANGE ON PREVIOUS YEAR BY VOLUME

|  | Summer 1982 (Apr–Oct) | Winter 82–83 (Nov–Mar) | Summer 1983 (Apr–Oct) | Winter 1983–84 (Nov–Mar) |
|---|---|---|---|---|
| market | +35.8% | +43.0% | +24.5% | +7.7% |
| Hellmann's | +30.7% | +41.5% | +13.6% | −4.2% |

Source: Mars Group Services

out. Weights of advertising each year were similar, but in the second year the campaign did not break until after Christmas, while in the first year it started on 18th December. Whether this made any difference is a matter for debate, but it seems unlikely it could have accounted for such a wide discrepancy.


## THE CONTRIBUTION OF ADVERTISING

As we have seen, our primary objective – major volume growth for the brand – has been achieved. We have yet to make the case that advertising was a major factor in this growth, and that without the advertising it would have been less (we guess the market would have grown, but at a lower rate). Unfortunately the obvious demonstration of this is not available to us as the campaign has been national from the outset and hence no control exists. Given, however, that we have seen an acceleration in the rate of growth, we can build our case on the following evidence:

1.  A discussion of the other factors that might have caused an increased rate of growth.
2.  Measures of the campaign's impact on the consumer.
3.  Changes in usage pattern and user profiles which would reflect the advertising strategy.

### Other Possible Factors in Generating Growth

Let us review and, where possible, discount other factors which might have affected Hellmann's growth.

—  Distribution
—  Pricing
—  Trade stocking and display
—  Promotional activity
—  Product development


#### DISTRIBUTION

Gains in distribution were a considerable factor in Hellmann's volume growth up to the end of the 1981 financial year. The growth since has, however, come from a much more static distribution base. A calculation of rate-of-sale shows the increase in offtake post-advertising (Figure 6).

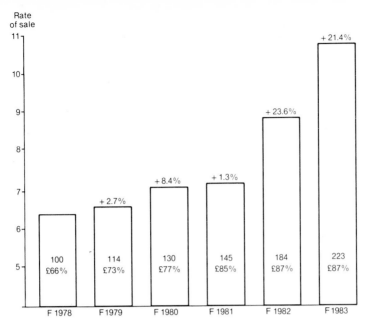

Figure 6. *Hellmann's rate of sale (000 jars/% £ distribution)*
*Sources:* Nielsen, MGS

PRICING

There was indeed a slight reduction in the retail price between 1981 and 1983, a consequence of increasing volumes being sold through the major multiples (Table 5). However,
while this may well have helped, it did little to reduce the very considerable premium of
Hellmann's over salad cream (Table 6).

Having conducted price elasticity research since, it seems unlikely that these modest

TABLE 5:   HELLMANN'S PRICE APRIL–SEPTEMBER

|  | 1981 £ | 1982 £ | 1983 £ |
|---|---|---|---|
| 200 g | 0.576 | 0.567 | 0.572 |
| 400 g | 1.04 | 1.00 | 0.982 |

Source: Mars Group Services

TABLE 6:   PRICE PER 100 g: HELLMANN'S AND
HEINZ SALAD CREAM

|  | 1981 p | 1983 p |
|---|---|---|
| Hellman's | 28.8 | 28.6 |
| Heinz salad cream | 19.4 | 20.6 |
| premium | 9.2 | 8.0 |

Source: Mars Group Services

reductions would effect 30 per cent sales increases. The market is clearly not dominated by price: if it were, Hellmann's would hardly be able to command the premium it does over own-label.

STOCK LEVELS AND TRADE SUPPORT

With increasing availability of own-label and pressure on the 'salad sector' from other brands, the amount of Hellmann's on-shelf has not increased nearly as much as the actual sales to the consumer. Mars Group Services (MGS) audit the amount of stock in the forward area: taking the period April–September 1981–83 gives us the following figures expressed as indices (Table 7).

TABLE 7:    HELLMANN'S PERFORMANCE (INDEXED)

|      | Front Stocks | Sales |
|------|------|------|
| 1981 | 100  | 100  |
| 1982 | 112  | 131  |
| 1983 | 113  | 148  |

Source: Mars Group Services

PROMOTIONAL ACTIVITY

Compared with the considerable advertising spend over this period, there was very little promotional activity and the pack design and copy remained unchanged for most of the period. An on-pack recipe book offer, while it achieved good levels of redemption, does not explain the observed rates of growth.

PRODUCT DEVELOPMENT

During the second year of advertising, in May 1983, two flavour variants of Hellmann's (lemon and garlic) were launched and had achieved a 6 per cent share of the market by September. The rationale behind the flavours is to differentiate the brand from own-label and to stimulate re-trial among lapsed users who find ordinary mayonnaise too 'bland'. As such, they may be expected to have contributed something to the brand's growth, though the extent of straight substitution for the base product is very hard to estimate. It is worth noting also that the launch of flavours has not been reflected in increased total Hellmann's facings in the retail trade. Our best conclusion must be that the addition of flavours to date has been a contribution – but not *the* major factor – in the growth picture, and this in any case applies to the last 12 months only.

    We conclude that no other factor or combination of factors can conceivably explain Hellmann's rate of volume growth.

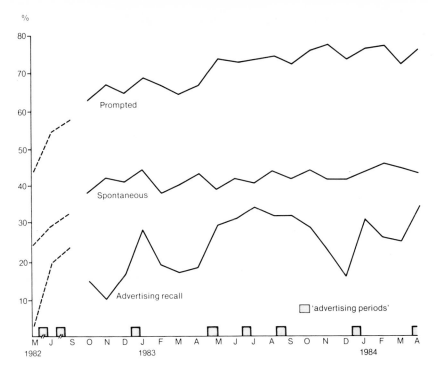

Figure 7. *Awareness & advertising recall of Hellmann's Mayonnaise*
*Sources:* ---- NOP
        —— Millward Brown

## Consumer Reactions to the Advertising

While the following data does not necessarily equate to purchasing behaviour, there is considerable evidence that the campaign has been widely seen, recalled, understood, and liked by the consumer (see Figure 7).

— Brand awareness has improved significantly since the campaign began.
— The campaign has achieved consistently high recall levels. (To put these figures into context, the high points are the highest figures (with one exception) recorded on the CPC tracking study, which includes not only all CPC's own brands but heavily and successfully advertised competitors such as Heinz and Oxo.)
— Related recall is accurate and recall of the main message is on strategy (Table 8).

TABLE 8:   RELATED RECALL OF HELLMANN'S CAMPAIGN

| (average 11 months to April 1984) | % |
|---|---|
| use of different things/not just salad | 38 |
| livens up boring meals/revives them | 24 |
| makes things taste better | 24 |
| adds flavour to ordinary food/makes more interesting | 27 |

Base: all recalling Hellmann's advertising
Source: Millward Brown

TABLE 9:    PROMPTED COMMENTS ON HELLMANN'S
            CAMPAIGN

| (average 11 months to April 1984) | % |
| --- | --- |
| it gave the impression the product would be very good | 40 |
| I liked it | 38 |
| it made me more interested in buying the product | 15 |
| it was no different from most other commercials | 7 |
| it was hard to believe | 9 |
| I'm getting fed up seeing it | 3 |
| it put me off buying the product | 1 |
| I don't like it | 2 |

Base: all recalling Hellmann's campaign
Source: Millward Brown

On a standard set of statements, the campaign is clearly liked and appreciated. Again, these figures are high compared with company norms (Table 9). These types of responses are also found in qualitative research where the campaign is characteristically received with recognition and enjoyment.

> He was lovely ... human ... you really felt sorry for him ... it's just how men are on their own.
> He's a bit scruffy ... the lazy type ... had his mum to run around for him and in a bit of a mess until he found the Hellmann's.
> He is quite nice ... down to earth type ... it somehow makes you think that anyone can have Hellmann's ... it's not just for posh people.
> It's the versatility of the product – it's not like a salad cream, you can use Hellmann's on anything ...
> It's quite stunning with him in it.

— Image ratings over time have shown increases in 'versatility' and 'everyday usage' without any loss in traditionally high-quality ratings (Table 10).

These quantified image ratings also reflect a profound change in the way people talk about mayonnaise in qualitative research. Two years ago mayonnaise was widely seen as having strong class connotations which, for many, were a real inhibition to trial. The following statements from C2 non-users in Cheshire illustrate this point:

> My husband's boss – he wouldn't have salad cream, only mayonnaise.
> We buy salad cream, they buy mayonnaise.

These barriers are now very much a thing of the past, and there is now a much more relaxed acceptance of mayonnaise as an accessible product among all social classes. This is reflected in consistent figures that show the new market entrants in the last two years to come increasingly from C2s and Ds (Table 11).

So much for the accessible image of the product, but how have usage patterns actually changed? We measured this in July 1983 and were able to make some comparisons with a survey conducted in 1980 (Table 12). While it is clear that salad remains a common denominator (though to a lesser extent than for salad cream), there have been increases in most non-salad uses. Also, the specific uses shown in the advertising (eg burgers,

TABLE 10: IMAGE STATEMENTS

| | agree % disagree % | |
|---|---|---|
| Accessibility: | 1980 | 1983 |
| 'I would only serve mayonnaise on special occasions' | 25 63 | 13 83 |
| 'Mayonnaise is too expensive to use all the time' | 34 51 | 27 68 |
| 'There's no point in giving mayonnaise to children, they wouldn't enjoy it' | 15 55 | 17 66 |
| | Hellmann's buyer | own-label buyer |
| Versatility: (*not asked in 1980*) 'Mayonnaise is something the family will help themselves to for snacks' | 48 41 | 43 47 |
| 'I think of mayonnaise mainly as an ingredient' | 37 54 | 38 56 |
| 'Mayonnaise has more use than salad cream' | 57 27 | 55 31 |

Source: ICI

TABLE 11: INCREASE IN PENETRATION 1980-83

| AB | C1 | C2 | D | E |
|---|---|---|---|---|
| +3% | +12% | +22% | +117% | +15% |

Source: TGI

potatoes, cheese on toast), while not comparable with 1980, have attained respectable levels. Also, it can be shown that while in 1980 mayonnaise was less versatile than salad cream, the positions are now reversed (Table 13).

A more sophisticated analysis segments mayonnaise users into four categories: traditionalists, combination salad makers, 'new' types of users, and combination plus 'new' users. This indicates that 40 per cent of Hellmann's users are using the product in at least one of the ways shown in the advertising. Interestingly, too, this proportion is significantly higher among Hellmann's users than it is among users of own-label mayonnaise (Table 14).

# THE REPOSITIONING OF HELLMANN'S MAYONNAISE

TABLE 12:   HELLMANN'S USERS: WAYS OF USING MAYONNAISE

|  | (mayonnaise) 1980 % | (mayonnaise) 1983 % | (salad cream) 1983 % |
|---|---|---|---|
| with a lettuce type of salad | N/A | 84 | 97 |
| with tomatoes | N/A | 57 | 69 |
| salad sandwich | 24 | 51 | 63 |
| egg mayonnaise | 52 | 64 | 36 |
| prawn cocktail | 34 | 46 | 30 |
| cold meat without salad | 16 | 19 | 24 |
| chips without salad | 5 | 14 | 18 |
| hot meat without salad | 8 | 14 | 3 |
| fish without salad | 8 | 15 | 11 |
| savoury dip | 8 | 23 | 15 |
| bread & butter without salad | 0 | 12 | 18 |
| with: |  |  |  |
| hamburgers | N/A | 11 | 7 |
| tuna fish | N/A | 34 | 23 |
| cheese on toast | N/A | 10 | 8 |
| jacket potatoes | N/A | 20 | 15 |
| potato salad | 47 | 46 | 43 |
| coleslaw | 42 | 41 | 41 |
| cucumber salad | 10 | 14 | 11 |
| rice salad | 14 | 15 | 8 |
| Russian salad | 8 | 10 | 5 |
| Waldorf salad | 6 | 10 | 4 |
| prawn salad | 1 | 27 | 18 |
| mixed vegetable salad | 2 | 22 | 24 |
| sweetcorn salad | 0 | 11 | 8 |
| other made salad | 9 | 12 | 8 |

Source: 1980–PAS
         1983–ICI

TABLE 13:   AVERAGE NUMBER OF CLAIMED USES PER RESPON-
            DENT

|  | 1980 | 1983 |
|---|---|---|
| salad cream | 3.1 | 6.1 |
| mayonnaise | 2.8 | 6.7 |

Source: 1980–PAS
         1983–ICI

(Note: The increase 1980 to 1983 is considerably exaggerated by a
        longer list of uses: the object of the chart is the relative position
        of salad cream vs. mayonnaise.)

TABLE 14: TYPES OF USE MEASURED

| salad | combination salad | new uses |
|---|---|---|
| lettuce type | cucumber salad | cold meat without salad |
| tomatoes | rice salad | chips without salad |
| salad sandwich | Russian salad | hot meat without salad |
| | Waldorf salad | fish without salad |
| | prawn salad | bread & butter without salad |
| traditional recipe | mixed vegetable salad | hamburgers without salad |
| | sweetcorn salad | cheese on toast without salad |
| egg mayonnaise | savoury dip | jacket potatoes without salad |
| tuna fish | | |
| potato salad | | |
| coleslaw | | |

MAYONNAISE USAGE SEGMENTS

| | all % | Hellmann's users % | own-label users % |
|---|---|---|---|
| 1. salad/traditional only | 31 | 27 | 30 |
| 2. salad/traditional + combination salad | 23 | 23 | 28 |
| 3. salad/traditional + 'new uses' | 17 | 19 | 11 |
| 4. salad/traditional + combination salad + 'new uses' | 27 | 29 | 28 |

Source: ICI

# CONCLUSION

In summary then we can show that the advertising has made an impression; that perceptions of mayonnaise have been changed in the way we intended: that ways of using the product reflect that change. These findings, and the otherwise unexplained acceleration in volume growth from a static distribution base, lead us to conclude that the advertising has been effective in achieving our main objective.

We hope to have shown that the growth we have seen would not have taken place without the advertising. It would be wrong, however, to leave the argument there without admitting that the nature of that growth has not been entirely what we anticipated, and that more remains to be achieved in the future.

We expected growth to come from two sources – from attracting new users to the market, and also from increasing the average weight of purchase which, for most mayonnaise users, has always been very low. In the event, as extensive TCA analyses have shown, the weight of purchase has hardly increased: the brand and market growth has instead largely come from new trialists including, as we have seen, many from social classes hitherto unfamiliar with mayonnaise. Inevitably, not all these trialists will become regular users: hence our strategic focus for the future will be increasingly on creating more weight of purchase.

What, then, have we achieved? We have taken mayonnaise off its pedestal and made it accessible to a whole new market; we have reduced its exclusive association with special occasion salads and encouraged experimentation and a more relaxed attitude towards it. This has increased penetration for the brand: it has also, without a doubt, endorsed the existing behaviour of a core of heavy, versatile users who have always been important to our sales. At the same time, we have not devalued the brand, which retains very high loyalty among its users even at a considerable premium price (TCA shows very little direct switching to own-label or to Heinz).

# 7

# Fulfilling the Potential of St. Ivel Gold

## INTRODUCTION

This case study quantifies the effects on sales of an advertising campaign for a low fat spread – St. Ivel Gold. The brand operates within the yellow-fats market which mainly comprises butter and margarine.

The paper covers the development and initial success of a campaign first aired in January 1981. It further demonstrates the contribution made by this advertising to the brand's sustained growth and profitability over the following three years.

## THE PRODUCT

Labelling regulations in the yellow-fats market stipulate that all products called butter must contain a minimum of 80 per cent fat, and all products called margarine must also contain a minimum of 80 per cent fat. Only the type of fat differs, not the level. St. Ivel Gold contains 40 per cent fat and since neither 'low fat butter' nor 'low fat margarine' are permissible descriptions, Gold is designated a low fat spread. It is in fact a low fat spreading blend of buttermilk and vegetable oil. As such it offers a rich dairy taste together with the health benefits associated with fat reduction. Gold is packed in tubs and spreads straight from the fridge. It is cheaper than butter, but sells at a premium to all margarines. Its main use is as a spread because, unlike butter and margarine, Gold's lower fat level makes it unsuitable for some cooking uses.

## THE ENVIRONMMENT

TCA (see Appendix) shows that the yellow fats market was worth £657.8 million at RSP in 1983. It has traditionally comprised only butter and margarine. Low fat spreads are a relatively recent phenomenon. Overall the market has seen little real growth in the last 10 years; however, its basic structure has changed considerably during this time. A widening price differential between the premium commodity butter and the cheaper margarine has, over the long term, probably contributed to the volume decline of butter and consequent growth of margarine. The volume positions of butter and margarine have more or less reversed since 1975. Then butter held 68 per cent of the yellow-fats market and in 1983 margarines and low fat spreads held 64 per cent.


## GOLD - BACKGROUND

Gold is a relatively young brand. It is priced at a premium over all margarines, but below butter. It was first launched into test market in 1977 and rolled into national distribution in 1979. In 1980, despite considerable advertising support which variously promoted the brand as 'the best thing to come out of the dairy since butter', Gold showed no sign of achieving a profitable sales level. In July 1980, St. Ivel decided to start afresh and appointed J. Walter Thompson.


### Exploratory Research

Qualitative research among non-trialists of Gold was the first step in the evaluation and development of the brand. Here three main problem areas emerged:

1.  Consumers acknowledged only two types of yellow fat – butter and margarine. A low-fat spread was interpreted as a non-yellow-fat product. This description communicated a spread which was more akin to cheese than margarine or butter.
2.  The majority of respondents wrongly believed that margarine, especially soft margarines made from vegetable oils, were lower in fat than butter, because they did not contain rich, dairy ingredients.
3.  In this environment a high level of confusion surrounded Gold. On the one hand, despite its premium price, Gold was similar to margarine. It was packed in tubs, spread from the fridge and was similar in appearance and texture. On the other hand, although considerably cheaper than butter and with a different texture, Gold, like butter, contained dairy ingredients and carried the dairy pedigree of St. Ivel.

It was clearly neither one thing nor the other, so what were its advantages over either of the well-established product types? Its advertising claimed a taste like butter. This was met with a scepticism bred from years of unfulfilled promises by non-butter brands in this area. The pack and advertising also claimed that Gold was low in fat, but this was believed to be true of many margarines, all of which were cheaper than Gold.


### Further Development Research

A second stage of qualitative research was conducted in order to explore the potential of a number of strategic options for Gold. Each of these was presented as an advertising concept. This research isolated an expression of Gold's benefits which consumers found surprising and relevant. It also generated a high level of interest in trial of Gold. This successful concept made no overt claims on taste; instead, emotive clues were used to suggest a rich dairy taste consistent with the imagery of St. Ivel. This was coupled with the statement that Gold contained less than half the fat of butter or margarine. This concept could not and did not refer to Gold as a margarine. Neither did it describe Gold as a low fat spread. The product's appearance and tub packaging were sufficient to position it as a yellow-fat spread, like margarine.

In response to this concept many consumers in fact described Gold as a margarine, but elaborated on this by adding that Gold was a buttery-tasting margarine with half the fat of any other and, as such, was probably healthier.

On the basis of these research findings a new advertising strategy was defined. This remained unchanged throughout the period of analysis: January 1981 to December 1983.

## GOLD - ADVERTISING STRATEGY

### Advertising Objectives

To stimulate and thereafter sustain increased sales for St. Ivel Gold by communicating Gold's dual product benefits of buttery taste with a fat level only half that of butter or any margarine.

To endow the product with a brand status and profile consistent with its premium price and projected user image of modern people who enjoy what they eat but are smart enough to stay fit.

### Target Group

Purchasers of butter who enjoy the taste of that product but who are finding it difficult to justify the premium price on every purchase occasion. In addition, purchasers of premium margarines who value a quality, butter-like taste for spreading. An underlying concern regarding the over-consumption of fats further distinguishes the target consumer irrespective of whether she buys butter and/or margarines.

### Media Selection and Design

Owing to the broad target group, TV was selected as the main medium to increase sales of the St. Ivel Gold brand. A total of £1.6 million was allocated for TV support during 1981, the first year of the campaign, £1.5 million during the second year and £2.3 million in the third year.

Over this period the TV schedule provided short periods of heavyweight support followed by longer periods at a much lower strike rate. This policy of continuous advertising with burst and drip was designed to generate steady demand for the brand, avoiding peaks and troughs which would have caused production and distribution inefficiency of this relatively short shelf-life product.

### The Advertising

'Swimming Pool', the first film in this campaign, was aired in January 1981. It used the visual association of 'butter' sculpture to achieve a buttery-taste response. In a stylish modern presentation this image merged with others representing healthy activity, and combined with overt verbal instruction on the fact that Gold contained only half the fat of butter or margarine.

A second film, 'Squash Court', with a similar structure to the first, was added to the campaign in February 1982. This was followed in February 1983 with a third film, 'Karate', which single-mindedly addressed the fat issue, excluding reference to dairy imagery. The latest film in this series, 'Bowling', was first aired in October 1983.

The first burst in 1981 used a 30-second version of 'Swimming Pool'. This was later cut to 20 seconds. All subsequent films were aired as 20 second treatments in combination with 10-second reminder versions to increase frequency. Each new film has been established with a period of solus exposure followed by rotation with previous films. Storyboard examples appear on pages 109, 111 and 113.

## GOLD SALES SINCE JANUARY 1981

St. Ivel Gold sales appeared to respond immediately to the advertising. Volume sales in the first eight weeks of the campaign were 30 per cent above that of the preceding eight weeks. This growth continued throughout 1981. By the end of that year volume had increased by 33 per cent over the previous year. Volume continued to grow with the development of the campaign. TCA shows that sales in 1982 grew by a further 29 per cent, and in 1983 by another 22 per cent.

Figure 1 illustrates Gold's volume trend since January 1981 in relation to the actual

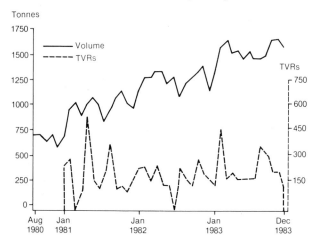

Figure 1. *St. Ivel Gold volume and actual TVRs*
*Source:* (volume) TCA

TVR level throughout the period. The fact that, following many years of poor sales, Gold's growth coincided with the introduction and development of a new advertising campaign is, in itself, insufficient evidence of a causal relationship. So what other factors could have brought about such a reversal of the brand's fortunes?

*Did Gold Simply Benefit from the Market Movement Away from Butter Towards the Relatively Cheaper Margarines and Spreads?*

No! The main movement between these two commodities occurred between 1975 and 1980. As Table 1 shows, it accelerated between 1979 and 1980 when Gold sales were

# ST. IVEL GOLD
## "SWIMMING POOL"          20 SECONDS

St. Ivel Gold is unique

It's made with vegetable oil and real buttermilk.

Yet it contains less than half the fat of butter,

or any margarine.

Think about it

A buttery taste . . .

with less than half the fat.

Gold.

From St. Ivel.

TABLE 1:    BUTTER VS. MARGARINE AND LOW FAT SPREADS – VOLUME

|  | 1975 % | 1976 % | 1977 % | 1978 % | 1979 % | 1980 % | 1981 % | 1982 % | 1983 % |
|---|---|---|---|---|---|---|---|---|---|
| margarine and low fat spread | 32 | 39 | 45 | 47 | 50 | 56 | 60 | 64 | 64 |
| butter | 68 | 61 | 55 | 53 | 50 | 44 | 40 | 36 | 36 |

Source: TCA

particularly low, and has slowed down since 1981 when Gold sales began to forge ahead. Over the last three years, Gold's rate of growth (shown in Table 2) has far outpaced that of its sector. Its brand share has grown from 3 per cent to 6 per cent and it is now the fourth largest brand within margarine and low fat spreads. Gold's growth is therefore not simply the consequence of a shrinking butter market.

TABLE 2:    INDEXED VOLUME GROWTH COMPARISONS

|  | 1980 % | 1981 % | 1982 % | 1983 % |
|---|---|---|---|---|
| total yellow fats | 100 | 101 | 101 | 99 |
| butter | 100 | 92 | 84 | 81 |
| margarine and low-fat spreads | 100 | 108 | 114 | 112 |
| St. Ivel Gold | 100 | 129 | 167 | 204 |

*Is Golds's Growth a Mere Reflection of a Similar Growth in Health Consciousness?*

No! Gold is not the only brand in this market offering a health benefit. Outline and some own-label brands contain the same overall fat level as Gold. Other heavily advertised margarines like Flora contain a high level of polyunsaturated fat and are firmly established within this general 'health' sector. If Gold's growth merely reflected a general trend toward 'health' products, its share of this growing sector would have remained static. Instead, as shown in Figure 2, its share has risen steadily since 1981. Gold's growth is therefore *not* simply a reflection of a growing health trend.

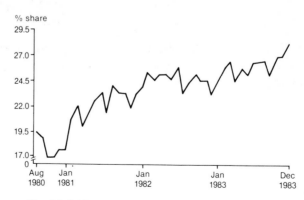

Figure 2. *St. Ivel Gold percentage of health brand volume*
Source: TCA

# ST. IVEL GOLD
## "KARATE"          20 SECONDS

Get your figures straight.

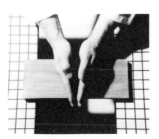

Butter 80% fat.
All margarines 80% fat.

Even polyunsaturated margarines
80% fat.

St. Ivel Gold . . .

. . . 40% fat.

Eat the one with half the fat.

Gold. From St. Ivel.

*Did a Distribution Increase Affect Gold's Growth?*

No! Although success has resulted in marginally broader distribution, Gold's rate of sale where it is distributed has increased much faster than its distribution base. Gold has always been heavily reliant on the multiple trade. Consistently around 80 per cent of its volume is sold through these outlets. Table 3 shows the brand's distribution level in multiples together with its rate of sale per point of effective sterling distribution. Here it is apparent that although some distribution gains have been made, Gold's growth was *not* caused by a growth in distribution.

TABLE 3:    GOLD DISTRIBUTION AND RATE OF SALE – MULTIPLES

| | Aug–Sep 1980 | Oct–Nov | Dec–Jan 1981 | Feb–Mar | Apr–May | Jun–Jul | Aug–Sep | Oct–Nov | Dec–Jan 1982 | Feb–Mar |
|---|---|---|---|---|---|---|---|---|---|---|
| % effective £ distribution | 87 | 90 | 86 | 93 | 90 | 93 | 92 | 92 | 92 | 93 |
| tonnes per % effective distribution | 12 | 11 | 11 | 15 | 16 | 14 | 15 | 16 | 18 | 22 |

| | Apr–May 1982 | Jun–Jul | Aug–Sep | Oct–Nov | Dec–Jan 1983 | Feb–Mar | Apr–May | Jun–Jul | Aug–Sep | Oct–Nov |
|---|---|---|---|---|---|---|---|---|---|---|
| % effective £ distribution | 89 | 92 | 88 | 93 | 90 | 92 | 94 | 93 | 93 | 92 |
| tonnes per % effective distribution | 22 | 20 | 21 | 22 | 22 | 26 | 28 | 29 | 27 | 29 |

Source: Nielsen/Stats MR

*Was Gold's Success the Result of a More Competitive Pricing Policy?*

No! It has been St. Ivel policy to maintain the brand at a premium over all other low fat spreads and margarines. With the exception of occasional periods when Gold's price coincided with that of Flora, this has been achieved. Figure 3 shows Gold price relative to that of the premium brands of margarine, Flora and Krona.

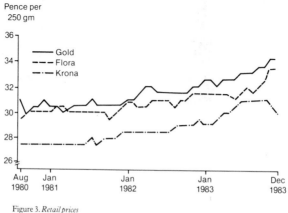

Figure 3. *Retail prices*
Source: TCA

# ST. IVEL GOLD
# "BOWLING"     20 SECONDS

St. Ivel Gold
High on taste

Low on fat.

Just half the fat

of any margarine.

It's made with vegetable oil
and real buttermilk

and it tastes

smashing.

Gold's price differential with butter has remained relatively steady over the period with the exception of December 1982 and January 1983 when EEC intervention depressed the overall butter price.

This maintenance of a price premium therefore suggests that Gold's growth was *not* gained by a more competitive pricing policy.

### Did Gold Advertising Affect Sales?

A simple process of elimination seems to suggest that advertising did affect sales of St. Ivel Gold. It is apparent that Gold sales began to take off in January 1981 and that growth continued at a steady pace thereafter. This does not appear to be the consequence of any natural movement in the market. Nor does it appear to be the result of increased distribution or of an eroded price differential.

Regression and other analyses were carried out in order to isolate those factors affecting volume sales. Here, factors which were quantifiable such as price and distribution were again examined. These analyses also included the TV advertising variable. Empirical analysis showed that this advertising had a lagged effect, not only working in the month of transmission but to a diminishing degree during the following two months. From this analysis it appeared that TV advertising alone, lagged and weighted over a 12-week period, accounted for a considerable part of the brand's volume variance. Figure 4 illustrates this pattern of weighted TVRs in relation to Gold sales.

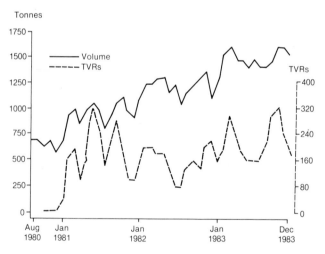

Figure 4. *St. Ivel Gold volume sales + TVRs, lagged & weighted (12 weeks)*
*Source:* (volume) TCA

It also shows that, over and above this short-term effect of the advertising, there was a steady upward trend in sales throughout the period. As an analogue for this trend, we included in our 'model' the cumulative build-up of the weight of TV advertising (TVRs) for Gold. The resulting model accounted for 87 per cent of the variation in the brand's volume sales throughout the period, and its degree of fit to the actual level of sales is illustrated in Figure 5.

The model, full details of which are given in the Appendix, also suggested the analysis

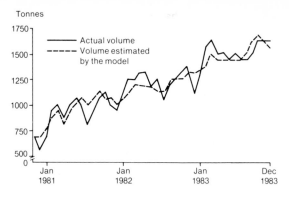

Figure 5. *Gold volume — actual and estimated*
*Source:* (volume) TCA

of the history of Gold's volume sales over the period which is presented in Figure 6. Starting from a 'base level' of just under 700 tonnes per four weeks, sales rose to a level of about 1 600 tonnes. This growth represented additional volume over the whole period of approximately 20 000 tonnes, valued at £25.4 million at consumer prices. Our model directly attributes some 7 000 tonnes of this additional volume (the upper stratum shaded in the diagram) to the short-term effect of the TV advertising. This 7 000 tonnes was valued at £8.9 million at consumer prices, while the total media budget was £5.4 million.

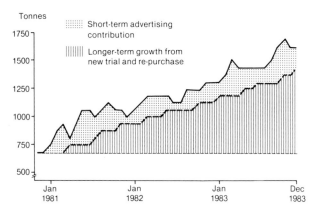

Figure 6. *Gold estimated volume — analysis of the growth*

The contribution of this same advertising to the remainder of the additional volume – 13 000 tonnes valued at £16.5 million cannot be assessed so directly; but since this additional volume was presumably due to increased and satisfactory trial of the brand and to its continued re-purchase, it seems reasonable to conclude that the advertising must have made a substantial contribution to it by providing both stimulus and reinforcement.

In response to this additional demand Gold production has increased to a point where the factory, previously operating well below capacity, has since been extended. As a result of this success the brand's position within St. Ivel has been reversed; from being a drain on resources prior to the new advertising, Gold is now a profit mainstay for the company.

## APPENDIX

The model of consumer purchases of Gold referred to in the main text of this entry was based on an analysis of data derived from AGB's Television Consumer Audit, covering 41 four-weekly periods which began on 9th November 1980 and ended on 31st December 1983.

The quantity which the model was designed to estimate (the 'dependent variable') was the four-weekly volume of consumer purchases of Gold in Great Britain expressed in metric tonnes. The model took the form of a multiple regression equation of the following type:

$$Y = a + b_1 x_1 + b_2 x_2 + b_3 x_3 + b_4 x_4$$

where:

$Y$ = estimated four-weekly consumer purchases of Gold (tonnes)
$a$ = a constant (the 'base level' referred to in the text)
$x_1$ = gross housewife TVRs for Gold in current four-week period
$x_2$ = gross housewife TVRs for Gold 5–8 weeks ago
$x_3$ = gross housewife TVRs for Gold 9–12 weeks ago
$x_4$ = *cumulative* TVRs up to 12 weeks ago used as an analogue of the growth trend

and $b_1$, $b_2$, $b_3$ and $b_4$ are 'regression coefficients', which here represent the average volume of Gold (in tonnes) contributed by each unit of the independent variables. The technical details of the equation are:

|  | coefficient (tonnes) | t-value | mean value of independent variable over whole period |
|---|---|---|---|
| a 'base level' | 718.29 | (17.0) | — |
| independent variables: |  |  |  |
| $x_1$ TVRs, current | 0.202 | (1.4) | 178 |
| $x_2$ TVRs, 5–8 weeks ago | 0.503 | (3.7) | 175 |
| $x_3$ TVRs, 9–12 weeks ago | 0.294 | (2.1) | 170 |
| $x_4$ cumulative TVRs | 0.106 | (12.9) | 2939 |

The adjusted value of $R^2$ (a measure of the proportion of the variance explained by the equation) was 0.875.

The estimate of the total short-term contribution of the TV advertising to Gold volume over the period (7 000 tonnes) quoted in the text was obtained by multiplying each of the coefficients of $x_1$, $x_2$ and $x_3$ in the above table by the mean value of the variable over the whole period (last column), summing, and multiplying the result by 41.

freezer centres in the specific freezer sector, whilst other outlets included independent electrical shops, retail cooperatives, mail-order houses etc.

In 1976 Zanussi established a network of nine independent distributors who agreed to act as exclusive wholesalers of Zanussi appliances, although they carried a wide range of other companies' products where these did not compete with Zanussi. This network, together with central selling to national accounts, gave Zanussi effective distribution in most white-goods outlets by 1979, and this distribution pattern and the levels achieved have not changed significantly since that time.

## The Competition

In 1978 the washing machine market was dominated by Hoover who held some 35 per cent of the volume, followed by Hotpoint with 18 per cent. There were more than a dozen other brands in the market with single figure volume shares, and a number of retailers' own brands. This large number of brands fighting for a share of a single market inevitably led to fierce competition in all of the traditional areas of brand marketing.

Competition in the refrigeration market was scarcely less intense. The market was dominated by Tricity, LEC and Electrolux, with Hotpoint close behind, and a plethora of smaller brands and own-label products struggling for share. The dishwasher market was still in its infancy.

## The Advertising

The most obvious weakness of the branded products in 1978 was the similarity of their advertising and the associated lack of any clearly defined positioning for any of the brands. The advertising at this time could be divided into four broad categories: 'theme' and 'promotional' advertising by individual brands, retailer advertising featuring a brand or brands, and electricity board advertising ultimately intended to promote the consumption of electricity by promoting the purchase of electrical appliances.

The first of these categories, 'theme' advertising by individual brands, was dominated by advertising that concentrated on telling the consumer all about the product and adding a brand name at the end. In other words, it sold primarily the features of the product, and only secondarily the brand name on the product. The cumulative effect, according to our research, of a number of manufacturers pursuing this strategy was to promote knowledge of product features whilst at the same time blurring the differences between brands.

The second category, 'promotional' advertising by the individual brands, compounded this problem still further in that the emphasis was very much on the money-off the particular white box in question, and very little on any values attached to the brand. The third and fourth categories, retailing and electricity board advertising, made an already bad situation still worse for brand values. The retailers' only interest was in announcing to the consumer that he had this or that (or even these) brands in stock at cut price, whilst the electricity boards sometimes ran identical advertisements for three or four different brands and merely changed the brand name at the end of the commercial.

Although it is impossible to directly attribute the one to the other, we do believe that the relatively weak branded-values of the manufacturers' advertising, together with the positive erosion of brand values by the retailers' and electricity board advertising, were significant contributory factors to the consumers' lack of differentiation between the brands.

## CONSUMER ATTITUDES TO ZANUSSI IN 1979

We have already alluded to the fact that, according to both our qualitative and quantitative research, the consumer did not readily differentiate between brands in the white-goods market, and we have expressed our belief that this was in no small measure due to the prevalence of product-feature or price-led advertising (in a market where both the product features and prices were frequently shared by the different brands), rather than advertising that concentrated on brand values.

Exactly the same proved to be true of Zanussi. In 1979 the vast majority of consumers were not spontaneously aware of Zanussi and only half claimed awareness when prompted, despite the company's significant media spend in the previous three years. Amongst those who *had* heard of the brand the associated imagery was limited and confused. We were pleased to find, however, that the majority of those who had actually bought a Zanussi during this distribution-building period were very pleased with it and loyal to the brand.

## HOW THE DECISION-MAKING PROCESS INFLUENCED
## THE ROLE OF ADVERTISING

The decision-making process in Zanussi's prime areas of interest proved to consist of a number of steps undertaken on average over a period of between one and three months, unless it was an 'emergency' replacement of a machine that had broken down irrepairably, in which case the process was much quicker. Generally, the purchase decision was taken in five steps: firstly, the female partner reached the conclusion that a new machine was required or desirable, either because of dissatisfaction with an existing old machine or desire for a first machine.

The second and, as we shall see, crucial step for Zanussi, was the drawing up of a 'mental shortlist' of brands to be considered. Although this was done initially by the female partner this step proved to be equally important to the male when he was involved at a later stage, the rationale behind it being as follows. White goods are significant capital purchases and are expected to last a number of years. They are infrequently purchased and, because they are essentially labour-saving or virtual necessities (eg refrigerators), they are of low interest to the consumer except when purchase is imminent. Thus they represent an area about which consumers know very little and yet they are about to spend a relatively large amount of money on something which they hope will last a long time. This low level of knowledge combined with a relatively high level of spend produces anxiety not to make a mistake, and consumers' solution to this problem is to seek refuge and reassurance in the brand names they feel they 'know'. So familiarity – the irrational feeling of 'I've heard of them so they must be all right' – is a key element of the purchase decision, and the reassurance that it represents can be strong enough to overcome even a persuasive salesman or price offer at point-of-sale.

The third step of the process is the collection of brochures, usually by the female, for brands on the mental shortlist. The fourth stage is detailed consideration of the brochures at home by both partners, with the male generally expressing interest in the mechanical/reliability aspects of the products, the female generally in the ease-of-use aspects. From this consideration a final shortlist of products, sometimes of only one, is drawn up and enquiries are made about prices. The final fifth stage is a visit by both partners to one or more shops to clinch the best deal or method of payment.

We drew two very important conclusions from this decision process: firstly, advertising alone could not sell the product. The process is too drawn out and complex and anyway few consumers are in the market for an appliance at any one time. Secondly, if a brand did not succeed in getting on that original 'mental shortlist' its chances of being bought at the end of the decision process were very much reduced.

We therefore decided, contrary to the rest of the market, that we would use our advertising only to get Zanussi's name on the initial shortlist, and that we would use our brochures to close the sale.

## DEVELOPING AN ADVERTISING IDEA

### A Weakness in the Major Brands

We have noted earlier that the consumer did not readily differentiate between different white-goods' brands. Our research indicated that the major brands held their dominant positions because they were the most familiar rather than through strength of proposition or positioning, in which they were all relatively weak. This of course is entirely consistent with the buying process outlined above: consumers, anxious not to make a mistake and in the absence of any other significant differentiation, shortlisted the brands with which they were most familiar and therefore most emotionally comfortable. Hence, familiarity, built up over time rather than positioning, was a key purchase motivator in 1979.

That appeared to be a weakness in the major brands. They were very familiar, but they didn't really stand for anything in the consumer's mind. We felt that if we could make Zanussi not only very well known, but well known for something that the consumer *wanted* from white-goods products, we would not only get on the shortlist through familiarity but also be in a stronger position once we got there.

### Concept Research

From the knowledge that we had already gained, five concept ideas were now explored in further qualitative research. These were as follows: attractive styling/efficient engineering, low energy costs, personal service, Europe's biggest manufacturer and therefore the most reliable and technological superiority. Of these the most interesting and potentially purchase-motivating proved to be technological superiority because it implied both reliability and also up-to-dateness. Since, as we have seen, the consumer approached the purchase with some anxiety and was concerned that the product purchased would perform reliably for a number of years, both of these elements were very reassuring: from technological superiority consumers derived reliability and also the assumption that they would be buying the most up-to-date machine available at the time, rather than one that might already be a few years out of date and yet would be theirs for several years to come.

*The Advertising Idea*

We now had to translate our learning so far into a sufficiently distinctive advertising idea. It had to be distinctive because we needed Zanussi to become as familiar to the consumer as the major brands in as short a time as possible in order to be included on the initial mental shortlist. And we now knew that it had to position the brand clearly as technically advanced.

We quickly discovered that we had a problem: however we tried to support a 'technically advanced' proposition, we failed to impress the consumer for two apparently insuperable reasons. Firstly, consumers found the whole subject of 'widgets' and other technical support points profoundly uninteresting; and secondly, they didn't believe us. They simply were not prepared to believe that one manufacturer's 'widgets' could be significantly better than another's. So we failed in both of our objectives: we were not going to become familiar quickly with advertising that consumers found uninteresting, and we were not going to establish a strong 'technically advanced' positioning if they simply wouldn't believe us.

The solution, like all good solutions in retrospect, was remarkably simple: *we would make the proposition but not attempt to support it*. And we would do it in a way that would achieve startling standout, so that we would quickly achieve our familiarity objective.

The Appliance of Science was born. The space metaphor was a perfect vehicle for communicating 'technically advanced' and the concept, of a Zanussian planet where unseen advanced beings applied their science to constructing and delivering to earth the most advanced appliances in the universe, whilst rationally ludicrous was emotionally highly enjoyable and strangely reassuring.

We now had an advertising idea which fulfilled the role that we had determined for the advertising: it would get us on the shortlist because consumers found it highly noticeable and enjoyable, and it would give us a strong position once we were there because the nature of the vehicle made them willing to suspend their disbelief and believe an unsupported proposition.


## MEDIA OBJECTIVE AND STRATEGY

Our media objective was to quickly achieve a high level of familiarity for Zanussi by:

— maximising impact of the advertising on the consumer;
— maximising coverage and frequency amongst the target market.

The media strategy was split into two sections:

1. Broad target audience – all adults.
2. Specific target audience – adults interested in kitchen planning.

*Broad Target Audience Strategy*

In order to maximize awareness of the Zanussi 'Appliance of Science' theme, TV was used in three four-week bursts at a high weekly strike rate (circa 150 adult TVRs) in order to dominate the medium while on air.

Given the nature of the objective – awareness building – timing of each burst was based on cost efficiency only, thus enabling Zanussi to achieve the highest share of voice at the lowest possible cost. A minimum of three bursts of activity per year was set.

*Adults Interested in Kitchen Planning*

It was felt that Zanussi's chances of being included on candidate lists when consumers purchased white goods would be improved if the Zanussi name was familiar not only through TV, but also in publications with apparent authority in the kitchen-planning area. It was for this reason that 10 per cent of the total media budget was diverted into key home-interest publications that were seen as authoritative by the consumer.

## MEDIA PLANS

*1979–80*

### TV/POSTERS

A three-week heavyweight 45/30-second TV campaign was purchased December–January at a weekly strike rate of 150/200 adult TVRs. This was backed up by 1 000 posters (48/16/4-sheet). Following this activity three further 15-second bursts on TV were purchased in March–May/June–September. The total national TVR achieved for 1979–80 was 1600 adult TVRs.

### SPECIALIST PRESS

We also purchased double-page spreads in a dozen key home-interest publications such as *Exchange Contracts*, *Good Housekeeping*, *Kitchen Supplement*, *House and Garden*, *Real Life Kitchen Guide*. These publications were chosen on editorial content not coverage.

*1981*

### TV

As in 1980 four bursts of TV activity were purchased on the same planning criteria (150 weekly strike rate, three weeks) in March–May/June–September.

Once again this activity, whilst emphasising various elements of the Zanussi range, was primarily theme and awareness building:

### SPECIALIST PRESS

Given the success of the 1981 activity as measured by reader response the campaign was continued.

# "Zanussi Range"

1½ second silence.

FX (Airport Cargo).

*1st Man* Right. Where's this lot
from then Colin?
*2nd Man* Er — the Planet Zanussi.

*1st Man* Oh yes fine. Zanussi
Freezers — Washing
Machines, Tumble
Driers, Dishwashers . . .
*2nd Man* Er — Brian (Worried).

*1st Man* Now — take this Fridge-
Freezer — How often do
you get craftsmanship
like *that* down here.
*2nd Man* Not very often!

*1st Man* They're all very
reliable.
economical.

Take this dishwasher, no
flying saucers in there eh.
*2nd Man* I don't know how
they do it.

*1st Man* Well you see Colin
its the appliance
of science isn't it.
*2nd Man* Oh — is that what it is?
*1st Man* (condescending) Yes.

Right take it away lads.

SFX: Whirring Sound.

*Announcer V/O* "From the
Planet Zanussi —

The appliance of science."

# "Zanussi Washcraft"

1½ secs silence.
SALESMAN: Of course with
washing machines and
tumble dryers

I'd go for one of the new
Zanussi Washcraft…
(I'm expecting them any minute
now…)

MVO: From Zanussi comes
Washcraft…

engineered for economy,
to save energy,

save powder,
save money,
with every wash.

Built to serve for at least a
decade.

Washcraft from Zanussi.

SFX: Space effects.

SALESMAN: Careful sir, we don't
want to stand…in the way
of progress.

SFX: Space effects.
SFX: Space effects.

MVO: Washcraft.

More appliance of science.
From Zanussi.

*1982/3/4*

The basic strategy of TV and specialist press was continued, with greater emphasis each year placed on cost efficiency with regard to timing. This has led to a three-burst pattern December–January/June/August.

In 1984 we are conducting a number of media tests to see which media buying strategy is the most efficient in maximising awareness for Zanussi. These tests are:

1.   Burst vs. Drip
2.   ITV only – 3 weeks vs. ITV and Channel 4 over 6 weeks.

## COMPETITIVE ACTIVITY

At the beginning of the Zanussi TV campaign it was unusual for large white-goods manufacturers to allocate monies for TV only. The only major advertiser using TV besides the Electricity Council was Creda and this was only a small burst.

Zanussi's launch and subsequent activity produced a major change to competitive manufacturers' media plans. Gradually in 1980 more manufacturers used TV. Table 1 shows that Hoover, Indesit, Tricity and Bendix used TV for the first time. In 1981 Ariston followed suit and in 1982–83 the Electricity Council were advertising at weights far in excess of the original Zanussi TV weights.

TABLE 1:   COMPETITIVE ACTIVITY 1979-83 ADULT TVRS – MAJOR
           MANUFACTURERS

|  | 1979 | 1980 | 1981 | 1982 | 1983 |
|---|---|---|---|---|---|
| Zanussi |  | 1613 | 1600 | 1580 | 1622 |
| Colston | 48 | 107 |  |  |  |
| Creda | 226 |  | 287 | 978 | 807 |
| Bendix |  | 193 | 191 | 148 | 377 |
| Hoover |  | 249 |  | 559 | 633 |
| Indesit |  | 350 | 277 | 587 | 838 |
| Miele |  | 74 |  |  |  |
| Tricity |  | 172 |  | 282 |  |
| Ariston |  |  | 241 |  |  |
| Candy |  |  | 166 | 306 | 70 |
| Electricity Council | 975 | 191 |  | 1990 | 2269 |
| Hotpoint |  |  |  | 934 | 1454 |
| Philips |  |  |  | 266 |  |
| British Gas |  |  |  |  | 1538 |
| Canon |  |  |  |  | 93 |
| Sable |  |  |  | 165 |  |
| Eastern Gas |  |  |  |  | 180 |
| Servis |  |  |  |  | 731 |
| Sharp |  |  |  |  | 309 |
| total | 1249 | 2949 | 2762 | 7795 | 10921 |

Source: AGB

All figures are based on a national equivalent where only regional activity occurred.

Actual white-goods expenditure has not expanded dramatically but Table 2 shows that monies have been switched from press into TV. On all four white-goods sections the percentage of TV expenditure of the total has continued to increase steadily. This we believe is due to the successful use of TV by Zanussi which led to a radical rethink by all major manufacturers of their media plans.

TABLE 2:   TOP LINE TOTAL RESULTS TV PERCENTAGE FIGURES

|  | 1980 | 1981 | 1982 | 1983 |
|---|---|---|---|---|
| cookers | 52.4 | 59.2 | 63.2 | 70.2 |
| refrigeration | 39.9 | 51.7 | 63.8 | 70.2 |
| washing machine and dryer | 43.7 | 54.9 | 78.4 | 87.2 |
| other appliances | 39.2 | 54.3 | 65.1 | 66.8 |

Source: MEAL

## MEASURING THE EFFECTS OF ADVERTISING

### The Measures

We must immediately acknowledge that it is notoriously difficult to separate the contribution which advertising makes to the progress of a brand from all the other elements that constitute the total marketing effort. However, in this case history we do find a very strong correlation between upward movements in awareness and imagery monitors, and actual sales increases. Furthermore, we are able virtually to eliminate two of the other major influences, pricing and distribution, in our efforts to understand cause and effect. By 1979, as we have stated earlier, Zanussi had built its white-goods distribution network and achieved its distribution objectives, and both the levels and channels of distribution have not varied significantly since that time. As far as price is concerned, machine by machine comparisons are very difficult to make across a range of manufacturers because significant variations in specifications are common. However, where direct comparisons can be made Zanussi prices have been comparable with those of their competitors and it has always been the company's policy to pursue parity pricing rather than trading at a premium or undercutting.

We have monitored Zanussi's progress since its relaunch with the Appliance of Science campaign in November 1979 against three parameters – awareness, imagery and actual sales. The awareness and imagery have been evaluated against our advertising objective of getting Zanussi on the consumers' mental shortlist by achieving familiarity and a strong 'technically advanced' positioning, and also against the awareness and imagery of our major competitors. Sales have been evaluated against Zanussi's previous years' performance and the performance of the market as a whole.

### Consumer Awareness

Development in both brand and advertising awareness have been monitored using MAS OmniMAS studies which are based on nationally representative samples of 2000 housewives and heads of households. The first MAS OmniMAS study was conducted in

November 1979 immediately prior to the launch of the Appliance of Science advertising campaign. Awareness levels have been regularly monitored since 1979 and, whilst the number of studies commissioned each year has varied according to our information requirements, we have always conducted a study in January every year since the Appliance of Science campaign began. The January studies have also always followed the December/January advertising bursts, and the questionnaire structure and format has been left largely unchanged in order to minimise any research effect on our results.

TABLE 3:     SPONTANEOUS BRAND AWARENESS

|  | Year* | | | | | | Index | |
|  | 1979 | 1980 | 1981 | 1982 | 1983 | 1984 | 1980–79 | 1984–79 |
|---|---|---|---|---|---|---|---|---|
| Zanussi | 8 | 20 | 20 | 27 | 33 | 39 | 250 | 487 |
| Hoover | 65 | 64 | 62 | 64 | 63 | 66 | 98 | 102 |
| Hotpoint | 42 | 43 | 39 | 38 | 43 | 45 | 102 | 107 |
| Electrolux | 30 | 29 | 27 | 23 | 25 | 24 | 97 | 80 |
| Philips | 22 | 23 | 22 | 19 | 23 | 19 | 105 | 86 |
| Servis | 20 | 21 | 15 | 15 | 16 | 15 | 105 | 75 |
| Indesit | 15 | 16 | 16 | 15 | 17 | 14 | 107 | 93 |

Source: MAS OmniMAS
Base: all housewives/heads of households
* all checks January–November (except 1979)
NB source, base and timing data apply to Tables 3–11 inclusive.

As can be seen from Tables 3 and 4, both spontaneous and total brand awareness of Zanussi have increased dramatically over the period monitored, whilst there has been little or no change for its major competitors. It is reasonable to conclude from these tables that the brand is now significantly more familiar to consumers (and that therefore it is more likely to be included on the 'mental shortlist') in 1984 than it was in 1979. Further evidence for this conclusion can be found in the considerable improvement in Zanussi 'share of mind'. It can be seen from Table 5 that consistently across the period monitored, the consumer could on average spontaneously recall three brands. It is highly probable that these three spontaneously recalled brands would definitely find a place on the con-

TABLE 4:     TOTAL BRAND AWARENESS

|  | 1979 | 1980 | 1981 | 1982 | 1983 | 1984 | Index | |
|  | % | % | % | % | % | % | 1980/79 | 1984/79 |
|---|---|---|---|---|---|---|---|---|
| Zanussi | 50 | 64 | 68 | 77 | 82 | 83 | 128 | 166 |
| Hoover | 95 | 95 | 94 | 95 | 97 | 96 | 100 | 101 |
| Hotpoint | 90 | 92 | 98 | 92 | 94 | 93 | 102 | 103 |
| Electrolux | 85 | 86 | 86 | 88 | 91 | 88 | 101 | 103 |
| Philips | 87 | 87 | 87 | 87 | 88 | 88 | 100 | 101 |
| Servis | 75 | 78 | 78 | 79 | 82 | 80 | 104 | 107 |
| Indesit | 63 | 65 | 69 | 71 | 73 | 73 | 103 | 116 |

Source: see Table 3

TABLE 5:    AVERAGE NUMBER OF BRANDS RECALLED

|  | 1979 | 1980 | 1981 | 1982 | 1983 | 1984 |
|---|---|---|---|---|---|---|
| brand awareness |  |  |  |  |  |  |
| spontaneous | 3 | 3 | 3 | 3 | 3 | 3 |
| total | 8 | 8 | 9 | 9 | 10 | 10 |

Source: see Table 3

sumer's shortlist (given that none of them had any strong negative association) and therefore it is very desirable for a brand to gain a place amongst the three.

Table 6 demonstrates that whereas in 1979 Zanussi was the ninth-best recalled brand, by 1982 it had gained six places to become the third-best recalled, and it has held that position since then. Given that, as we have just seen, on average the consumer can only

TABLE 6:    ZANUSSI – SPONTANEOUS BRAND AWARENESS

|  | 1979 | 1980 | 1981 | 1982 | 1983 | 1984 |
|---|---|---|---|---|---|---|
| rank order of recall | 9th | 6th | 5th | 3rd | 3rd | 3rd |

Source: see Table 3

spontaneously recall three brands and given that, as we saw in the decision-making process, familiarity plays an important part in the construction of the 'mental shortlist' of brands to be considered, we believe that Zanussi's inclusion in these 'top three' will have had a very positive effect on the likelihood of the consumer to buy the brand.

Furthermore, consumers are now not only very much more aware of Zanussi's brand name, they are also very much more aware of its advertising. Tables 7 and 8 demonstrate

TABLE 7:    SPONTANEOUS ADVERTISING AWARENESS

|  | 1980 | 1981 | 1982 | 1983 | 1984 | Index 1984–80 |
|---|---|---|---|---|---|---|
| Zanussi | 15 | 16 | 24 | 29 | 31 | 207 |
| Hoover | 12 | 11 | 15 | 18 | 19 | 158 |
| Hotpoint | 9 | 6 | 10 | 12 | 15 | 167 |
| Philips | 7 | 7 | 7 | 7 | 4 | 57 |
| Electrolux | 3 | 3 | 4 | 4 | 3 | 100 |
| Servis | 2 | 2 | 2 | 1 | 1 | 50 |
| Indesit | 1 | 1 | 3 | 3 | 2 | 200 |

Source: see Table 3

marked increases in Zanussi's proven spontaneous and total advertising awareness which are far in excess of its competitors. Indeed, in 1984, total advertising awareness for Zanussi at 62 per cent is exactly double that of its nearest competitor, Hotpoint, at 31 per cent.

TABLE 8:     TOTAL ADVERTISING AWARENESS

|  | 1979 % | 1980 % | 1981 % | 1982 % | 1983 % | 1984 % | Index 1980-79 | 1984-79 |
|---|---|---|---|---|---|---|---|---|
| Zanussi | 13 | 38 | 40 | 56 | 63 | 62 | 292 | 477 |
| Philips | 27 | 23 | 22 | 23 | 24 | 17 | 85 | 63 |
| Hoover | 25 | 21 | 21 | 27 | 30 | 29 | 84 | 116 |
| Hotpoint | 22 | 19 | 16 | 22 | 26 | 31 | 86 | 141 |
| Electrolux | 14 | 10 | 11 | 13 | 15 | 12 | 71 | 86 |
| Servis | 9 | 7 | 5 | 7 | 9 | 7 | 78 | 78 |
| Indesit | 6 | 4 | 5 | 8 | 10 | 8 | 67 | 133 |

Source: see Table 3

Table 9 illustrates the growth of correct association of the Appliance of Science slogan with Zanussi over time, so that by 1984 75 per cent of the sample make the association correctly. For comparative purposes we have always tracked this dimension against Philips' 'simply years ahead' slogan which cumulatively has had the benefit of exposure to the consumer for a much longer time and at a much higher advertising weight, although it should be said that support for the slogan has recently been withdrawn.

TABLE 9:     SLOGAN ASSOCIATION

|  | 1980 % | 1981 % | 1982 % | 1983 % | 1984 % |
|---|---|---|---|---|---|
| Zanussi – Appliance of Science | 52 | 62 | 71 | 70 | 75 |
| Philips – Simply Years Ahead | 48 | 47 | 45 | 35 | 31 |

Source: see Table 3

*Consumer Imagery*

We have earlier noted that in 1979 it was felt that the major brands were vulnerable, in that although they were well known to many consumers – and therefore qualified on the important 'familiarity' criterion for inclusion on the shortlist – they didn't have a clearly defined positioning in the consumer's mind. At that time it was decided that we would try to achieve both familiarity and positioning for Zanussi, so that it was not only included on the shortlist but was in a stronger position once there. The preceding section demonstrated that a high degree of familiarity has been achieved. This section examines whether or not the selected positioning of 'technically advanced' has also been achieved. As for awareness, our monitoring source has been the regular MAS OmniMAS studies.

Tables 10 and 11 illustrate the relative weakness of Zanussi's imagery in 1979 when compared with the average of five of its major competitors on five key dimensions. The 'make technically advanced products' score at that time was on the average for the market, while other key dimensions concerned with reliability, quality, value for money, and being a big company lagged far behind. By 1984 these last four dimensions have moved much

TABLE 10: DEVELOPMENT OF ZANUSSI IMAGERY

| | 1979 % | 1980 % | 1981 % | 1982 % | 1983 % | 1984 % | Index 1984–1979 |
|---|---|---|---|---|---|---|---|
| make technically advanced products | 20 | 31 | 34 | 39 | 44 | 48 | 240 |
| make reliable products | 14 | 13 | 13 | 22 | 26 | 25 | 179 |
| good reputation for quality products | 12 | 9 | 12 | 18 | 23 | 22 | 183 |
| products good value for money | 10 | 9 | 12 | 14 | 18 | 17 | 170 |
| one of the biggest companies in the market | 6 | 6 | 7 | 8 | 12 | 16 | 267 |

Source: see Table 3

closer to the market average, whilst Zanussi's chosen positioning dimension, 'technically advanced', is now far in excess of the market average. It is also worth noting that the average for the five major competitors has remained static throughout the monitored period on every dimension except 'make technically advanced products' which declined, and we can hypothesise that this may to some extent be in response to Zanussi's strength in this area.

TABLE 11: DEVELOPMENT OF MAJOR COMPETITORS IMAGERY*

| | 1979 % | 1980 % | 1981 % | 1982 % | 1983 % | 1984 % | Index 1984–1979 |
|---|---|---|---|---|---|---|---|
| make technically advanced products | 20 | 17 | 16 | 18 | 20 | 14 | 70 |
| make reliable products | 31 | 30 | 30 | 39 | 42 | 32 | 103 |
| good reputation for quality products | 31 | 30 | 30 | 37 | 38 | 31 | 100 |
| products good value for money | 24 | 24 | 22 | 26 | 29 | 24 | 100 |
| one of the biggest companies in the market | 24 | 23 | 24 | 27 | 27 | 22 | 92 |

Source: see Table 3
* Competitive brands' average based on Hoover, Hotpoint, Philips, Electrolux and Indesit

Recent qualitative research by Consumer Connection conducted in 1983 confirmed the strength of Zanussi's imagery relative to the rest of the market:

> In the laundry and refrigeration markets Zanussi enjoys a pre-eminent position. It is the only real brand possessing both presence and identity. And Zanussi's fame spans both sectors, with most other brands being associated with either laundry or refrigeration.

In the light of the results described above we may reasonably conclude that Zanussi has made very significant progress in achieving the two objectives identified earlier as necessary to increasing the consumer's likelihood to purchase the brand: the Zanussi brand name is now very much more familiar to the consumer than it was in 1979 and the brand is now included in the average of three brands that the consumer can spontaneously recall. Furthermore, the brand is now clearly positioned in the consumer's mind as that from the company which 'makes technically advanced products', and in this respect the brand has a very significant lead over its major competitors. Our original hypothesis was that achievement of these two objectives would through familiarity get us on the consumer's shortlist and through positioning give us a stronger position once there. Zanussi's brochures, which faithfully reflect the advertising idea, would then 'close the sale' and thus Zanussi would improve its sales performance. The next section examines Zanussi's sales performance over the monitored period.

*Sales Performance*

In assessing sales performance we have already said that we can virtually ignore any distribution or price effects since distribution levels and channels have not significantly changed throughout the monitored period and Zanussi have always pursued a parity pricing policy throughout the period. Table 12 illustrates that Zanussi has consistently

TABLE 12: ZANUSSI – SALES PERFORMANCE

| VOLUME | INDEX: 1979 SALES | | = 100 | | |
| | 1979 | 1980 | 1981 | 1982 | 1983 |
|---|---|---|---|---|---|
| *Total* | | | | | |
| total market* | 100 | 93 | 91 | 104 | 113 |
| Zanussi | 100 | 93 | 126 | 138 | 162 |
| *Sector* | | | | | |
| total refrigeration | 100 | 90 | 93 | 106 | 112 |
| Zanussi | 100 | 93 | 109 | 125 | 159 |
| total laundry | 100 | 95 | 89 | 102 | 111 |
| Zanussi | 100 | 93 | 150 | 154 | 330 |
| total dishwashers | 100 | 97 | 102 | 104 | 162 |
| Zanussi | 100 | 91 | 109 | 144 | 191 |

Source: Amdea/IAZ
* total volume sales of sectors/segments Zanussi operates in

out-performed the total market since 1980 and has also achieved significantly better sales in each of the three individual sectors of refrigeration, laundry, and dishwashers. Overall Zanussi achieved a 62 per cent increase in volume over the period 1980–83 against a market increase of only 13 per cent.

## CONCLUSION

Although we remarked earlier in this case history that it is notoriously difficult to separate the contribution which advertising makes to a brand's progress from all of the other elements that constitute the total marketing effort, we do feel that in this case there is an unusually strong association between the achievement of advertising objectives predicted to increase sales performance and the actual achievement of sales performance.

The very significant improvement in Zanussi's sales performance cannot be explained as a function of market growth, since Zanussi's growth out-performed the market by more than 60 per cent. It cannot be explained as a function of increased distribution, since both distribution levels and channels remained effectively static throughout the measured period. And it cannot be explained as a function of pricing, since pricing has effectively remained at parity throughout the period.

In the absence of those explanations it is very tempting to conclude that advertising has made a major contribution to the very significant improvement in Zanussi's sales performance over these years. We believe that to be so. We also believe that we can at least partially explain that contribution in terms of our earlier diagnosis of how advertising might help Zanussi increase its sales: the role of advertising was to get Zanussi on the consumer's mental shortlist, not directly sell the product; familiarity with the brand name was a key element in the reassurance that the consumer needed to include the brand on that shortlist; and a clearly defined positioning – technically advanced – in a market remarkable for the weakness of brand positioning, would put us in a stronger position once we had got on the shortlist.

We have demonstrated that at the beginning of the monitored period Zanussi's name was poorly recalled by the consumer and its imagery was weak. We have demonstrated that the consumer spontaneously recalls only three brands and that Zanussi became one of those brands. We have demonstrated that Zanussi is now strongly associated with a positioning we know to be a key motivator to purchase. We have excluded major influences other than advertising. And we have demonstrated a very significant increase in sales volume well in excess of the market.

# 9

# Cadbury's Fudge: How Advertising has built a Brand

## INTRODUCTION

The purpose of this document is to demonstrate the role of repositioning and advertising in the revitalisation of Cadbury's Fudge since the mid-1970s. The case history shows how even in one of the UK's most crowded and competitive consumer markets, it is the quality of strategic and creative thinking rather than the quantity of marketing support that has been the real determinant of long-term commercial success.

The Fudge example also suggests how effective the asset-based route of 'old brand development' can be as a way of generating incremental business. The statistical likelihood of failure in new product development is well known and this, coupled with the huge financial investment often entailed in this area, makes the successful rehabilitation of existing brands like Cadbury's Fudge especially noteworthy.

This case history also embodies two important advertising principles that are sometimes contentious:

1. Very specific positioning and targetting does not necessarily preclude mass-market appeal. On the contrary, sometimes it facilitates it.
2. It is not always possible to correlate measurable awareness of advertising with its sales effectiveness.

## BACKGROUND

The confectionery market is one of the biggest and most competitive consumer markets in the UK. Market value is around £1200 million with annual adspend of over £80 million. It is increasingly dominated by 'mega' brands of great longevity that are very heavily promoted and have a scale of throughput that is particularly suited to the growing strengths of the grocery trade in this market. It is difficult to make headway against these entrenched brands.

Cadbury's Fudge is a small cigar-shaped bar of fudge covered in milk chocolate. It is individually wrapped and priced at 10p. This compares with the modal price of 17p for all chocolate-coated bars. With minor changes in recipe it has existed for over 40 years.

Up to 1976 Fudge had only ever been advertised tactically with other Cadbury brands in special promotions. Brand volume over the period 1970–75 fluctuated around 2 000–2 500 tonnes with 1975 volume at the lower end of this scale and 19 per cent down on 1974. Before advertising commenced in 1976, Fudge's consumer image was poor; it was felt to be old, recessive, and with no defined place in consumers' repertoires.

## DEVELOPING AN ADVERTISING STRATEGY

Prior to 1976 Cadbury's Fudge had received no solus above-the-line advertising support. Its only 'publicity' was alongside other children's products from Cadbury within a consumer promotion.

Thus our first priority was to examine the overall market position of Fudge in its then current form and package which, in outer appearance, are virtually unchanged in 1984. Qualitative research was undertaken among both mothers and children who were recent eaters of chocolate bars.

### 1974 Qualitative Study: Summary of Results

#### PURCHASING OF FUDGE WAS RARELY A CONSCIOUS CHOICE

Whilst within the groups awareness and purchase were high, few were recent or frequent buyers. Children had been bought Fudge by adults. A considerable number of children and adults had experienced Fudge through Christmas selection boxes, in which context Fudge was thought of as being a 'filler' without its own 'right to belong'.

#### THE POTENTIAL APPEAL OF FUDGE WAS WIDE

Whilst not seen to be either exclusively an adult or child's product, it was suggested that only a minority within any group would eat and buy Fudge.

#### FUDGE'S IMAGE WAS POOR

The product was considered 'old'. It was not seen as a popular product and was not seen to be important enough to be advertised.' It was boring both in appearance and taste, and it was poor value for money in 'eating-time'.

#### HOWEVER, THERE WERE SOME POTENTIAL BENEFITS

Fudge was a neat size – it was filling without being sickly. This was particularly appreciated for mothers of young children – it didn't fill them up before meals – and for mothers themselves who felt that such a product could be a permissible treat free from any taint of over-indulgence. Fudge was an acceptably bland flavour. Thus, it was likely to be palatable to almost anyone.

Importantly, it was seen as a potentially discrete product, unlikely to be duplicated exactly by any other product.

## DIRECTIONS FOR A CREATIVE STRATEGY

### *Defining a Target Market*

#### CHILDREN

Fudge had been historically aimed at children alongside obvious child-sweets such as Cadbury's Supermousse. But Fudge's overt appeal to children was low. Children looked for products they could 'spin-out' or for chewy things, before graduating to have adult chocolate bars as they grew older.

Whilst children did not reject Fudge and positively enjoyed it if given, acceptance of the product tended to be passive rather than active. Children expressed little positive likelihood to buy.

#### ADULTS

Adult purchase for themselves and for children was readily accepted. Children felt adults would buy Fudge as 'cupboard-treats' for home consumption. Mothers felt that Fudge was one of a small number of bars which were suitable in texture, taste, size and shape for a young child to eat.

Most importantly, Fudge was seen by mothers as a nostalgic reminder of the pleasure of eating chocolate bars in their own childhood. Thus our target market was defined as mothers with young children who would both buy Fudge for their children and eat themselves.

### *How Could We Position the Product?*

The problems of Fudge's 'oldness' and its lack of popularity could be addressed by advertising. However, the real task was to establish a discrete and complementary role for Fudge which would expand and give permanence to its place in the confectionery buyers' repertoire. Three factors emerged in assessing this task:

1. Fudge was seen as more wholesome than most confectionery products for children. Its goodness was strongly endorsed by the Cadbury name.
2. Fudge was just the right size for children, and for adults who didn't want anything too filling.
3. Finally, its nostalgic qualities suggested a positioning of eating enjoyment from children to be acceptable to adults. Thus children's enjoyment of Fudge in a warm, light-hearted way fully expressed how adults felt about their own experience of eating Fudge.

## ADVERTISING STRATEGY

### *Target Market*

— Mothers of children aged up to 13 years.
— Children aged 5–13 years.

*Advertising Objectives*

To position Fudge as a wholesome confectionery item of a size ideal for giving to children. To convey to mothers the traditional and wholesome values of Fudge without detracting from children's potential interest in the brand.

*Consumer Proposition*

Cadbury's Fudge is a wholesome and simple little treat to give your children.

*Support*

*Emotionally:* with Cadbury's Fudge you can be sure that you and your children are enjoying something good and wholesome with a little bar that's just enough to be a treat. *Functionally:* It is small and neat, and specially made with good wholesome ingredients to give you and your children its unique smooth, mellow and creamy taste.

*Tone*

Warm; relevant to mothers without alienating children.

## THE CREATIVE SOLUTION: STAGE I

*'Schoolhouse'*

This 30-second TV advertisement depicted an old schoolhouse where a young pupil was staying late to complete an exercise. While completing his exercise he sees his mother arrive and give a Fudge bar to his sister. He attempts to complete his exercise, albeit in a distracted manner, glancing at his sister enjoying her Fudge, until finally on completion he is given permission to run outside and collect his Fudge.

A jingle accompanies the film:

A finger of Fudge is just enough
To give your kids a treat,
A finger of Fudge is just enough
Until it's time to eat.

It's full of Cadbury goodness
And very small and neat,
A finger of Fudge is just enough
To give yourself a treat.

The charm demonstrated in the commercial is depicted on page 138.

*Deployment of 'Schoolhouse' 1976–78*

'Schoolhouse' was deployed nationally as follows:

1976: 1140 TVR
1977: 1241 TVR
1978: 1284 TVR

These TV spend levels helped produce year-on-year sales increases of 38 per cent, 14 per cent and 9 per cent respectively. In comparison, chocolate and chocolate-coated bar market movements were +5 per cent, −2 per cent and +12 per cent respectively.


## CREATIVE PROPOSAL: STAGE II

Two factors led us to look at new creative work:

1.  There had been minor product reformulation to make Fudge less sweet with potentially wider appeal.
2.  Sales increases were slowing down, albeit at a far higher base level.

### New Creative Work

New creative work was qualitatively researched in animatic form. Here we used a new voice-over to emphasise the recipe change:

> Take another look at Cadbury's Finger of Fudge. Now we make it to an original recipe. Take a closer look. It's softer, smoother ... covered creamy-tasting Cadbury's milk chocolate. Cadbury's Fudge, because everyone likes something good to look forward to.

Fading in and out of the background was our now established jingle.

The action of the animatic, later made into a 30-second commercial entitled 'Conkers', ran as follows: It opens on the corridors of a small village school. It is home time and the children rush out to the sound of the school bell. We see two boys playing conkers by the old oak doors. We focus in on the one boy who is holding his conker for the other boy to hit. He tries to hold his conker steady but he notices in the distance his mother arriving with his Fudge, and sees his sister receive hers. It becomes too much for our boy to bear and he rushes off to receive his Fudge, leaving the other boy frustratingly taking a swing at fresh air.

*Research Findings*

### MOTHERS AMBIVALENCE TOWARDS SWEETS WAS HIGHLIGHTED

The idea of wholesome confectionery, the avoidance of 'penny-dreadfuls' helped reduce both their anxiety and guilt towards giving their children sweets.

### FUDGE WAS DEVELOPING POSITIVE BRAND VALUES

Advantages for Fudge cited by respondents were:

— taste
— safety
— ingredients
— advertising
— manufacturer endorsement

Fudge was beginning to position itself through these advantages as a bar bought for children by adults. However, whilst absolute price was a positive attribute, relative to its small size it was thought of as poor value for money.

### FUDGE WAS DEVELOPING A POSITIVE BRAND CHARACTER

Whilst still old-fashioned (not just old), Fudge was taking on the aura of:

A pleasant, fairly serious, solid-reliable but happy type of product, which is lacking dynamism.

### WHILST SPONTANEOUS RECALL OF ADVERTISING WAS LOW, THE DETAIL OF THE RECALL WAS VERY FULL

The jingle and the story-line were fully described by those who remembered the advertisement. The commercial was universally liked, pleasant to watch and conveyed an atmosphere of tradition, nostalgia and warmth.

The message was also clear, namely, 'a treat for children which would not spoil their appetites'. In addition it was felt to be of high quality, 'full of Cadbury goodness'.

### THE VOICE-OVER CREATED CONCERN

Whilst the voice-over was intended to highlight a recipe change, this was either not noticed or produced concern as to what was wrong with the previous recipe. The words 'original recipe' caused particular concern.

Moreover, the jingle had become such a strong and recognisable part of the commercial that fading it out or subordinating it to the background reduced the enjoyment of the commercial for some.

### DISCOVERING NEW POWER IN THE CREATIVE SOLUTION

The most important finding was the realisation that 'Conkers' possessed more *power* than 'Schoolhouse'. Whereas in 'Schoolhouse' the small boy was being kept in against his free will and had to wait until he was given permission to go and receive his reward of a bar of Fudge, in 'Conkers' the boy *freely* chose to go and eat his Fudge bar despite his enjoyment of the conker game and the pressure from the other schoolboy to complete it.

The simple change of emphasis made Cadbury's Fudge into a more desirable/enjoyable product to eat.

## CREATIVE SOLUTION: STAGE II

Thus we made the 30-second TV commercial 'Conkers', using the action as proposed, but we retained the original jingle - now emerging as a component of real potency - and dispensed with the voice-over which was adding little. A still from the commercial is shown below.

*Taking Stock of Fudge's Position in 1981*

QUANTITATIVE RESEARCH

In 1981 a quantitative usage and attitudes study was commissioned. The total sample of 510 women were all regular eaters of chocolate-coated bars. Booster interviews were carried out amongst mothers of children aged 2-8, and also amongst other women eating Fudge. Whilst the findings were lengthy and discursive, two important facts were established to demonstrate that Fudge was successfully competing in the main confectionery market:

*Heavy eaters of confectionery eat fudge*   Fudge buyers buy 60 per cent more than chocolate and chocolate-coated bar buyers generally. Thus Fudge had established itself in the mainstream of the market among heavy chocolate-bar eaters.

Fudge has wide appeal. As shown in Table 1, the proportion of single women buying and eating Fudge was in line with their importance in the population. Whereas the target market in terms of positioning has been specific, the actual source of purchase was more

TABLE 1: AGE PROFILE OF FEMALE BUYERS AND EATERS

|  | Total Sample (510) % | Buy Fudge % | Eat Fudge % |
|---|---|---|---|
| Women aged: |  |  |  |
| 10–14 | 20 | 21 | 26 |
| 25–34 | 25 | 36 | 32 |
| 35–44 | 17 | 19 | 21 |
| 45–64 | 38 | 24 | 21 |

Source: PAS 1981

generalist. Thus specificity in targetting does not necessarily preclude genuine mass-market sales response.

## ADVERTISING INFLUENCE ON SALES

### Methodology and Analysis

In recent years, Cadbury has used a statistical model to provide a more definite explanation of variations in brands' sales share performance and the relative effects of the influencing variables. One of the first stages was to determine what the explanatory variables are and how best to measure them. Suggested variables included:

— Retail selling price
— Relative Price
— Retail Price Index
— TVRs
— Weather data – temperature
— Brand awareness etc.

After inspecting the data by eye, three key variables were highlighted:

1. Brand share of the market
2. Advertising support – expressed as adstock
3. Price – expressed relative to the market

See Appendix for details.

As both sales and price are expressed relatively, general seasonal factors and price rises are eliminated. Figures 1–3 show how the three factors for Fudge varied over the three-year analysis period, January 1981–December 1983. Fudge volume share was then modelled on adstock and relative price. Figure 4 shows actual performance against the model's predictions. The equation and the price and advertising elasticities are reproduced in the Appendix.

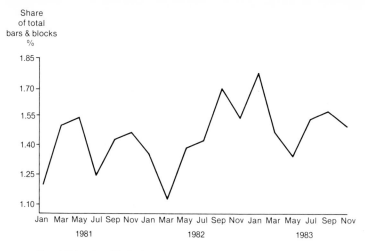

Figure 1. *Volume share of the chocolate and chocolate coated bar market*
*Sources:* AGB, PPI

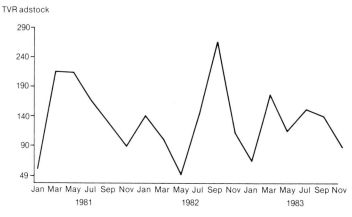

Figure 2. *Six week adstock*
*Source:* AGB

## Results of the Analysis

### ADVERTISING ELASTICITY

The analysis revealed that for every 1 per cent change in 'adstock' a 0.15 per cent increase in sales share will occur. This figure is bound by the parameters within 1981 and 1983, and by the level of spend currently deployed. However, this 0.15 advertising elasticity compares well against an average in the market of 0.09 per cent. For Cadbury during this period, this was the highest advertising elasticity. Furthermore 0.15 is also above the break-even level for Fudge, ie the contribution to profits from the extra sales achieved by an increase in TVRs outweighs the cost of the extra advertising.

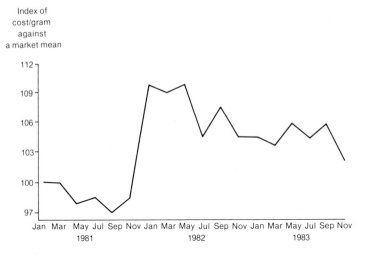

Figure 3. *Price relative to the market*
*Sources:* AGB, PPI

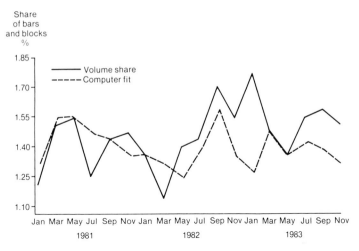

Figure 4. *Brand volume share using relative price and adstock*
*Sources:* AGB, PPI

PRICE ELASTICITY

Price elasticity was low for Fudge, $-0.5$ against an average of $-1.6$. This means for every 1 per cent increase in price, a 0.5 per cent decrease in sales share will occur. Thus Fudge is less price sensitive than other brands. Its price elasticity is also below the break-even; hence cutting price would be unprofitable. This inelasticity may partly be a function of its initial low price and the fairly static actual price it had during the analysis period. Figure 5 shows Fudge volume share modelled on price alone. It is obvious that the

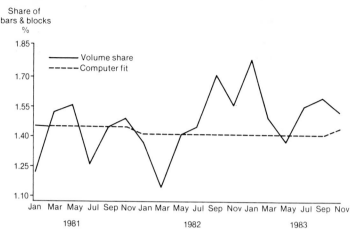

Figure 5. *Brand volume share using price alone*
*Sources:* AGB, PPI

computer is unable to produce a reasonable fit without the use of adstock. Thus, whilst there will be an interaction between price and advertising, price alone does not affect Fudge's brand share markedly, certainly within the parameters of change during 1981–83.

## ADVERTISING AWARENESS: IS IT IMPORTANT FOR FUDGE?

### *Lack of Advertising Awareness – A Possible Flaw*

Whilst sale results have been excellent, advertising awareness has always remained relatively low – not just in terms of total spend but in terms of how much claimed awareness is produced for a certain amount of TVRs.

Cadbury run a continuous monitor of advertising which gives, amongst other variables, a figure for awareness of advertising. Advertising awareness moves generally in line with adstock. Millward Brown, who conduct this continuous monitor, have been able to 'model' the ability of a campaign to produce advertising awareness and, by separating out the long-term residual awareness from current awareness, have computed indices for the ability of a campaign to produce 'current awareness' (see Table 2). Thus, Fudge advertising is less efficient at producing awareness than other Cadbury brands.

TABLE 2:    CURRENT AWARENESS INDEX (1984) OF SOME CONFECTIONERY BRANDS

| | |
|---|---|
| Turkish Delight | 10 |
| Lion Bar | 9 |
| Flake | 6 |
| Crunchie | 6 |
| Mars Bar | 5 |
| Caramel | 5 |
| Fudge | 4 |
| Milky Way | 4 |

Source: Millward Brown

*'Enjoyment' is However Extremely High*

However, in contrast, Fudge's performance against the criterion: 'I enjoy watching it more than most ads' amongst those who remembered the advertising *is* extremely high, as shown in Table 3. The average of all chocolate and chocolate-covered bars is 24 per cent.

TABLE 3:   ENJOYMENT OF ADVERTISING

|  | % |
|---|---|
| Fudge | 51 |
| Flake | 44 |
| Caramel | 35 |
| Turkish Delight | 31 |
| Mars Bar | 29 |
| Milky Way | 23 |
| Crunchie | 21 |
| Lion Bar | 17 |

Source: Millward Brown

*Fudge Advertising Produces Profitable Sales Gains Without High Advertising Awareness*

Thus, Fudge stands in contrast to the traditional view that advertising must produce 'top-of-mind' awareness. In demonstrating the sales effectiveness of Fudge advertising we seem to have a campaign that is highly enjoyable and highly effective without being 'top-of-mind'.

## 1983 DEVELOPMENT

*Addressing the Awareness Issue*

However, despite this proof of sales efficacy, the belief was that if we could achieve greater 'top-of-mind' awareness, results could be even better. In 1983 we set about developing a creative route which would generate greater awareness and yet retain the warmth of the current campaign. This new campaign entitled 'Kids' utilised children's drawings in a very distinctive animated style with what ostensibly seemed great charm.

Alongside this new route we examined two scripts 'Hide and Seek' and 'School Gates' which were straight pool-outs from the current campaign. Once again, we researched the scripts qualitatively amongst mothers. We used a split of both North and South locations, and regular and occasional Fudge eaters.

*Research Results*

### FUDGE WAS A RESPECTED BRAND

In brand-mapping exercised, Fudge was readily placed with other mainstream brands. Its quality and goodness were endorsed. Further, its 'neat' size gave it a unique positioning of 'just right for a nibble', of 'not too much to eat' for adults, and of very suitable wholesomeness for children.

### THE CURRENT ADVERTISING WAS EXTREMELY WELL LIKED

'Conkers' produced an empathetic response across both housewives and young women groups: the 'aah' factor was high. Reactions were consistent and its naturalness and relevance were applauded. Typical responses being:

> It's natural because they're always hungry when they come out of school.
> It's like a true story and the acting is so natural.
> They are real children ... real people. You can see it happening and you can really associate with that. You are immediately in empathy. It tugs at my heartstrings. It's got nostalgia.

Importantly, 'Conkers' was both humorous and involving, with new details and nuances being uncovered every time they watched it.

### THE 'KIDS' CAMPAIGN WAS REJECTED

Despite its impact, the 'Kids' campaign was quickly rejected both by mothers and younger women. Its appeal was felt to be uniquely with children under six. Indeed, it seemed to have lost the nostalgic appeal of 'Conkers' despite the obvious reference to childhood through drawings.

An interpretation of this, given by the researcher was that it represented removal from immediate behaviour. Thus, the drawings were abstractions of childhood behaviour rather than typical and identifiable episodes.

## CREATIVE SOLUTION - STAGE III

In this same research, response to a new creative execution of the existing creative route, 'Hide-and-Seek', was uniformly positive.

'Hide-and-Seek concerns itself with two boys, a mentor and younger boy who hides.

While hiding he spies his mother arriving with his sister with a Fudge bar. We see his sister enjoying her bar, while his seeker seems to get further away from finding him. Unable to wait any longer, he joins his sister and leaves his friend disconsolately kicking a dustbin. This is illustrated on page 146.

TABLE 4:   FUDGE AVERAGE YEARLY IN-STOCK STERLING DISTRIBUTION

|      | Grocers % | CTNs % |
|------|-----------|--------|
| 1976 | 46 | 77 |
| 1977 | 57 | 82 |
| 1978 | 63 | 82 |
| 1979 | 62 | 82 |
| 1980 | 72 | 86 |
| 1981 | 66 | 89 |
| 1982 | 74 | 90 |
| 1983 | 66 | 84 |

Source: Nielsen 1976–82/AGB 1983

TABLE 5:   INDEX OF TOTAL CHOCOLATE AND CHOCOLATE–COVERED BARS[*] AGAINST INDEX OF FUDGE VOLUME SALES[**]

|      | Market * | Fudge ** | |
|------|----------|----------|---|
| 1968 | 100 | 100 | |
| 1969 | 96 | 97 | |
| 1970 | 91 | 91 | |
| 1971 | 98 | 93 | |
| 1972 | 107 | 96 | |
| 1973 | 119 | 102 | |
| 1974 | 111 | 109 | |
| 1975 | 101 | 88 | Fudge |
|      |     |     | Advertising |
| 1976 | 106 | 120 | Starts in |
| 1977 | 104 | 136 | 1976 |
| 1978 | 116 | 149 | |
| 1979 | 117 | 142 | |
| 1980 | 115 | 146 | |
| 1981 | 119 | 161 | |
| 1982 | 132 | 171 | |
| 1983 | 141 | 222 | |

Source: *   CCCA
       ** Cadbury Ltd

## OTHER FACTORS WHICH COULD HAVE AFFECTED SALES GROWTH

### Distribution

Marginal gains in distribution were secured during the period of analysis, although a substantial part of that gain was obtained in the early years of advertising and cannot alone account for such substantial gains in sales, either in the earlier part or the latter part of the period under review (see Table 4).

### Total Market Growth

The total market has grown by 41 per cent from 1968. This is far short of the dramatic pace of Fudge's growth which began its volume gains at the onset of advertising in 1976 and in 1983 stands at 122 per cent above the 1968 levels (see Table 5). Cadbury's total volume during this period has shown some decline.

### Advertising Spend

Since 1977, advertising spend has grown by almost 400 per cent, Fudge's spend by 300 per cent, as shown in Table 6. Table 7 serves to demonstrate the ability of relatively modest exposure levels to produce dramatic sales increases. Also, it shows the indifferent sales performance of Fudge before advertising commences in 1976.

TABLE 6:    ADVERTISING EXPENDITURE ON CHOCOLATE CONFECTIONERY AND ON CADBURY'S FUDGE INDEXED FROM 1977*

|  | Chocolate Confectionery | Cadbury's Fudge |
|---|---|---|
| 1977 | 100 | 100 |
| 1978 | 130 | 135 |
| 1979** | 94 | 73 |
| 1980 | 102 | 67 |
| 1981 | 200 | 177 |
| 1982 | 336 | 262 |
| 1983 | 393 | 294 |

\* First year fully national
\*\* Lower spend due to TV strike late in 1979

## CONCLUSIONS

Consumer research conducted through 1974–75 indicated an opportunity for positioning Fudge as a donor purchase children's treat. By 1983, Fudge had a clear position and was highly regarded as a wholesome and neat product, closely associated with the nostalgia and warmth of childhood.

TABLE 7:   INDEX OF FUDGE SALES AGAINST TV EXPOSURE LEVELS

|  | Index of Fudge Sales | Fudge Network TVRs |
|---|---|---|
| 1968 | 100 | – |
| 1969 | 97 | – |
| 1970 | 91 | – |
| 1971 | 93 | – |
| 1972 | 96 | – |
| 1973 | 102 | – |
| 1974 | 109 | – |
| 1975 | 88 | – |
| 1976 | 120 (100)* | 1140 (100)* |
| 1977 | 136 (113) | 1241 (109) |
| 1978 | 149 (124) | 1284 (113) |
| 1979 | 142 (118) | 355 (31) |
| 1980 | 146 (122) | 515 (45) |
| 1981 | 161 (134) | 1360 (119) |
| 1982 | 171 (143) | 1117 (98) |
| 1983 | 222 (185) | 1108 (97) |

*(Index from 1976)

Advertising has been the only major variable in the period under review. There have been only minor changes in respect of the product, presentation, distribution, and relative pricing. Campaign achievement has been substantial in terms of sales, establishment of a real *bona fide* confectionery brand and, most encouragingly, advertising's contribution has been hugely profitable. Fudge was *the* most advertising-responsive brand in the Cadbury portfolio and one of the most responsive in the market as a whole.

The level of adult consumption also shows that, as intended, its very specific repositioning has not inhibited mass-market appeal and this augurs well for continued sales growth.

The advertising continues to be well liked by the consumer and consistently performs at the top end of enjoyability ratings in quantified tracking data. Coupled with its demonstrable sales effectiveness this means that we will continue to rely on this strategy and creative route to sustain Fudge's growth; with such continuous success we can see no reason to change.

## APPENDIX

1. Fudge's volume share of the total chocolate blocks and bars market as measured by AGB PPI data.

2. Adstock is an expression of the way in which advertising effect builds up and decays over time. The method of calculation assumes that TVRs in Week 1 also have effect in subsequent weeks; the effect diminishing geometrically. The 'decay rate' or 'half-life' (the number of weeks it takes for half the total effect to be felt) has to be chosen. Regressions on total TV advertising awareness and on sales share for a number of brands in the market, using different half-lives, show that an acceptable 'fit' is generally obtained using a six-week half-life. (To be able to make comparisons across

brands/campaigns, all the analyses carried out in this market sector have used the same half-life.) NB TVRs are adult 30-second equivalents.

3.  The following proved to be the best measure of price in terms of explaining volume share variation:

$$\frac{\text{price of brand in £ per kg}}{\text{weighted mean price of market sector in £ per kg}} \times \frac{100}{1}$$

4.  The resulting equation for this model is:

% volume share = 1.9164 + 0.00151 Adstock

(6 week half-life) + 0.00688 Relative Price

The elasticity of a factor, say, adstock, is connected as follows. If:

$$s = \text{constant} + (d \times a) + (c \times p)$$

where  s = sales share (average S)
       a = adstock (average A)
       p = price

Then the adstock elasticity is: dA/S and similarly for price.

# 10
# Paul Masson California Carafes: 'They're really jolly good!'

## INTRODUCTION

The success of Paul Masson California Carafes since their launch in the summer of 1980 in itself provides a fascinating and powerful case history. The purpose of this paper however is to demonstrate advertising effectiveness in a specific phase of that period. That phase is a crucial one for many products, namely the period after initial launch when the original momentum of consumer and trade 'novelty' is no longer sufficient to propel the brand forward, and competitive pressures are building. It is also the case that in a rapidly growing market (such as table wines) no new product stays 'new' for very long. Thus after two years in the market the Paul Masson California Carafe was an established wine product.

This paper is about the re-evaluation of that brand's position in the market – particularly with regard to other branded wine ranges – and the impact that re-evaluation had on advertising. Above all, however, it is about the power of advertising in building brand values that defended the brand from severe generic and own-label competition, and maintained sales growth momentum at a time when other brands had begun to suffer.

## BACKGROUND

Seagram Distillers internationally are the largest wine and spirits company in the world. Very few of their international brands (eg Chivas Regal, Captain Morgan, Mumm, Paul Masson, 100 Pipers etc) carry the Seagram name however. In the UK, the Seagram company is unusual in two respects. Firstly prior to the launch of Paul Masson, its UK turnover was almost entirely (95 per cent) based on spirits. Secondly, unlike most of its competitors, Seagram had no tied distribution either in the on- or off-trade.

Paul Masson Vineyards (California) is a wholly owned subsidiary of Seagram Distillers and Paul Masson is a major brand of wine in the US market – though by no means market leader. Paul Masson himself was a Frenchman who emigrated to California in the 1870s, taking with him vine roots from Burgundy and establishing vineyards some of which, ironically, later provided the cuttings for the replanting of French vineyards in the late 19th century after fungal plagues had destroyed the native French vines.

## THE UK OBJECTIVE

Given Seagram UK's lack of tied distribution, having a strong branded property is critical to be able to sell in effectively to the trade. For the same reason, a product failure, particularly in a growth sector could be extremely damaging to company reputation. Secondly, given the above, and the bias in Seagram's UK business towards spirits (a sector in decline since 1978), it was crucial for Seagram to have a *big* brand – one that would contribute fully to a shift in the company's business base away from spirits and into wine. The criteria for success were therefore long-term rather than short-term; essentially, to establish and maintain a high-volume branded wine property in the UK market.

## THE PRODUCT

A Californian, non-vintage, blended table wine in 1-litre, resealable, non-returnable carafes, available in red, medium sweet white and rosé. A dry white variant was added to the range in the summer of 1983, nationally, although this has had only minor significance to date (less than 20 per cent sterling distribution, less than 7 per cent of sales volume).

## THE UK WINE MARKET

The UK wine market has been growing at between 10–15 per cent per annum since 1975. It is characterised by a plethora of, in effect, unbranded generic wines, a strong own-label sector, and a relatively small though highly profitable branded sector (approximately 15–20 per cent of total). As wines have become more widely available, so they have become more accessible to more people and also cheaper. The traditions of wine have broken down to the extent that the 'new wine majority', though still up-market in bias, are relatively unfettered by the attitudes of their parents. Wine is increasingly an informal drink – both privately and socially. Importantly, however, new drinkers continue to enter the market every year. Volume growth therefore comes from increasing penetration as well as increasing frequency.

## LAUNCH AND ROLL-OUT 1980–82

Initial research conducted prior to the launch had indicated a number of key issues that were to shape our strategic and creative thinking at that time:

1.  Whilst reactions to the wine itself were generally good, the pack (a 'given') aroused some perceived price and disposability problems amongst consumers.
2.  Interest in California origin, however, was high.
3.  Despite the obviously rich creative area of 'the Paul Masson story', research indicated that consumers could find this area boring.
4.  More important was the need for strong branded reassurance especially to less frequent/new drinkers.

In addition we were conscious of the potential presence of a number of 'me-too' competitors waiting in the wings, and hence:

(a)  the implicit danger of focussing on packaging;
(b)  the competitive threat from pursuing a generic or 'origin' route;
(c)  the need to sell the wine itself;
(d)  the need for strong branding.

In order to address these last two points, a presenter route was developed since, with the right person, such a route could give credibility and reassurance on wine values, whilst at the same time offering the opportunity for a unique branded property. The chosen presenter was Ian Carmichael, and a script was developed. Given the desire to use the presenter route to the full and the reduced requirement for informational content, TV was the medium chosen for maximum impact in the key pre-Christmas (1980) period, which is traditionally a highly 'cluttered' time for drink advertising.

Paul Masson California Carafe was launched onto the UK market in the London area in the summer of 1980 and supported with TV advertising at minimal weight (180 TVRs) in that area pre-Christmas 1980. Consumer acceptance was high, and the brand was rolled out nationally during 1981. In the pre-Christmas 1981 period, advertising support was extended into five other areas, at weights of between 200 and 400 TVRs.

As a branded range, Paul Masson California Carafe faced competition from three key directions:

1.  Other branded ranges (e.g. Nicolas, Hirondelle, Don Cortez).

2.  Individual branded wines (e.g. Blue Nun, Mateus, Lutomer, Black Tower).
3.  Own-label and generics.

Whilst these distinctions were less clear-cut in the consumer's mind, it was clear from early post-launch research that Paul Masson California Carafe was most closely compared with the 'other branded ranges' outlined above. Equally clear, was the fact that these branded ranges were themselves the sector most under threat, particularly from the growth of own-label. Such has been the impact of own-label that these ranges were already in decline in 1981. If Paul Masson California Carafe was not to follow the same pattern, it was crucial that the brand should distinguish itself from the field.

It has been a clear objective at the launch stage to brand the product strongly rather than to rely on the generic origin appeal of California. The original advertising had achieved this, but the task was now to protect that branded position. The position at the beginning of 1982 can best be summarised in tabular form (see Table 1). The pre-Christmas period is a crucial one for the wine market and especially for branded wines,

TABLE 1:     PAUL MASSON PERFORMANCE 1980–81

|  | 1980 | 1981 | %± |
|---|---|---|---|
| Paul Masson California Carafe case sales (index) | 100 | 250 | +150 |
| *pre-Christmas period:* | | | |
| total market sales (million units) | 30.1 | 37.4 | + 24 |
| Paul Masson California Carafe brand share | 0.5* | 1.0 | +100 |
| Hirondelle Nicolas Don Cortez } brand share | 10.0 | 8.1 | − 19 |

\* estimate
Source: Seagram UK
         Nielsen (Grocers & Specialists)

TABLE 2:     CONSUMER AWARENESS AND TRIAL 1980–82 (Base: adult wine drinkers)

|  | Jan 1981 | | Jan 1982 | | | |
|---|---|---|---|---|---|---|
|  | London | Southern | London | Southern | Trident | Granada |
| pre-Xmas adult ratings: | 182 | 0 | 270 | 227 | 379 | 0 |
| advertising awareness (prompted): | % 28 | % 3 | % 34 | % 18 | % 42 | % 7 |
| brand awareness (total): | 48 | 21 | 58 | 42 | 71 | 40 |
| trial: | (28)* | (23)* | 28 | 19 | 31 | 17 |
| repeat (% of trialists): | 42 | 38 | 61 | 64 | 55 | 73 |

\* Boosted sample, not comparable with 1982 data.
Source: Gordon Simmons Research Tracking Studies

since the branded sector – normally around 15 per cent of total – increases its share in December to around 17–18 per cent. In the light of this phenomenon, the performance of the other branded ranges was very disappointing.

However, Seagram could take little comfort from their own performance since the majority of the improvement 1980–81 had been as a result of increased distribution for the brand. Whilst the first two years' advertising has been highly effective in terms of consumer awareness, trial and repeat purchase (see Table 2), it was clear that if the Paul Masson California Carafe brand were not, in 1982 and beyond, to go the same way as its competitors, there would have to be a fundamental reassessment of the brand's positioning and advertising.

## THE SITUATION IN 1982

A number of key factors are worth stating at this point since they largely formed the basis for our re-evaluation of the opportunity.

1. Branded ranges were clearly under threat and seemed likely to continue to decline.
2. Individual brands, whilst strong, also appeared to have peaked in share terms.
3. The growth of own-label products was continuing.
4. The launch of the *Le Piat* brand on TV pre-Christmas 1981 seemed to be going very well.
5. Seagram did not have unlimited funds to support the brand, especially in the light of the deteriorating £/$ exchange rate and the need to maintain price at a competitive level.

Our examination of the market at this time was very broad ranging and embraced the following elements.

### Analysis of TGI Data on Brand Repertoires and Usage

Using this data source, we were able to 'map' the wine market on two key dimensions. Firstly, we examined indices of brand share amongst heavier vs. lighter drinkers (the horizontal axis on Figure 1), and secondly the indices of above and below average usage according to most-often usage occasion (the vertical axis on Figure 1). In confirmation of these patterns we were also able to examine the duplication of brand usage (repertoires) amongst all drinkers, thus establishing the degrees of 'overlap' between the different brands. Figure 1, therefore, maps the market in terms of the 'clusters' of brands about the two axes according to usage. Because Paul Masson was not a TGI-listed brand at that time however we had to turn to our own tracking study data to establish the position of our brand within this map.

### Analysis of Tracking Study Data

Analysis of this source with regard to both type of user and usage occasion suggested not only the appeal of the brand to both experienced/heavier and inexperienced/lighter

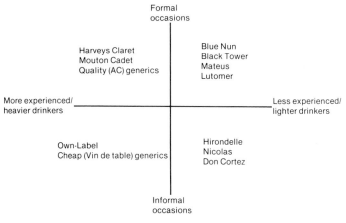

Figure 1. *TGI market map (1982)*
*Source:* TGI

drinkers, but also its ability to fulfil a dual role as an informal occasion brand for the former segment, and as a formal occasion brand for the latter segment (see Table 3).

TABLE 3:     DRINKING OCCASIONS: PAUL MASSON CALIFORNIA CARAFE
             BUYERS 1981

|  | heavier drinkers % | lighter drinkers % |
|---|---|---|
| *formal occasions* | | |
| dinner party | 12 | 21 |
| Xmas/New Year | 5 | 16 |
| *informal occasions* | | |
| drinking at home | 59 | 49 |
| informal party | 17 | 10 |

Source: Gordon Simmons Research 1982 Tracking Study

Thus in positioning terms, and using the same axes as in the TGI analysis, Paul Masson seemed to 'span' the market in a way that no other brand did. Figure 2 indicates diagrammatically the nature of this unique positioning.

## Qualitative Research

The large amount of qualitative research conducted at this time provided us with substantial attitudinal confirmation not only of the usage patterns and repertoires outlined above but also of Paul Masson California Carafe's almost unique position in being capable of appealing to different types of consumer. In so doing, it enabled us to understand the 'critical balance' between on the one hand offering branded reassurance to less experienced drinkers, whilst on the other hand not being patronising, and at the same time providing sufficient wine 'credentials' to make the brand 'legitimate' to the more experienced

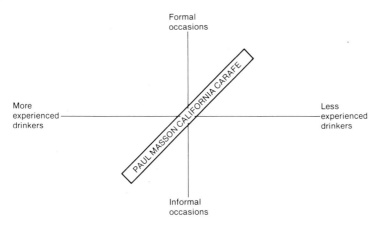

Figure 2. *Masson market positioning*

drinker. This was a balance that we felt most other brands had failed to achieve and hence had accounted for their more narrow appeal and actual usage by segments of consumers within the total market.

## OBJECTIVES AND STRATEGY 1982

### *Market Objectives*

1.  To maintain brand share growth despite the pressures on branded ranges in general.
2.  To reinforce the brand's position *vis-à-vis* own-label.
3.  To make the brand robust in the face of competitive launches/relaunches.
4.  To maintain rate-of-sale increases even when distribution plateaued.

### *Advertising Objectives*

1.  To reflect the balance of formal and informal usage, and hence appeal to both experienced and inexperienced drinkers.
2.  To reinforce the Paul Masson branding.
3.  To build wine 'credentials' for the brand.

In addition, it was an important objective at the time for both the agency and Seagram UK to use advertising cost effectively within a limited budget, but at the same time to be able to demonstrate the differential effectiveness of that advertising.

### *Target Audience*

ABC1 (C2) wine drinkers 25–40, both inexperienced and experienced (though not connoisseurs).

*Brand Positioning*

Paul Masson California Carafes are better-than-average quality, California wines, suitable for both formal and informal occasions.

Although the target audience and brand positioning statements had changed only in their definition of types of drinkers and types of occasions since 1980, the thinking that lay behind this change, out-lined under marketing and advertising objectives above, had moved on significantly.

The role for advertising had in effect been redefined from one primarily concerned with launching the brand (ie building awareness and trial), to one of maintaining the brand through positioning it in such a way that it was less vulnerable to both market forces and competitive threats than any other. It was this redefinition, we believed, that would be crucial to the brand's continued success.

## ADVERTISING DEVELOPMENT AND SUPPORT 1982-84

The original commercial developed for the launch in 1980 had featured Ian Carmichael introducing the wines with a high degree of scepticism. The setting had been a fairly formal one and the featured variant was the red. Our earlier (1980–81) research had confirmed the effectiveness of this commercial in terms of branding and presenter. Our re-evaluation however, had stressed the need for a balance with informal occasions (and hence, more usually, white wine), the need to reinforce the 'Paul Masson' element within the name and to build wine 'credentials' for the brand without boring consumers with detailed product information.

The second film therefore, designed to run in rotation with 'Jolly Good', was 'Grabbed'. Here the setting was an outdoor/informal one, the featured wine was white and Carmichael speaks of Paul Masson having been making wines since 1852. In every respect therefore the two executions are complementary.

The two commercials went on air together for the first time nationally pre-Christmas 1982, at area weights that ranged between 150 and 350 adult ratings. In 1983 support was given to the brand for the first time mid-year in a limited number of areas at low weights (150–400 adult ratings), and pre-Christmas 1983 the brand was again advertised using the same two commercials, but this time only semi-nationally at area weights between 120 and 320 adult ratings.

This period 1982–84, therefore, is the central focus of this evaluation. Let us now go on to examine in detail what the advertising achieved.

## THE RESULTS

In assessing the brand and the contribution of advertising, it has always been recognised that sales and share have been the two key measures. Whilst consumer research on attitudes and behaviour had been valuable in monitoring progress and particularly in shaping strategic direction, as already demonstrated, the focus in this section is on identifying the relative performance of the brand in sales and share terms both vs. other brands, and between advertised and non-advertised areas.

| VISION | SOUND |
|---|---|
| Open on Ian Carmichael in a very British drawing-room. | *Ian Carmichael:* I was first introduced to Paul Masson's California Carafes by some California chaps. |
| On a table stand some carafes, one of which he picks up and shows to camera. We see carafes in CU. | |
| Cut back to presenter. He raises an eyebrow. | Paul Masson I was told have a fruity white that you can really relate to. A rose that's got its act together. And a red that knows where it's coming from .... man. |
| He gives a look of mild disbelief at the words he is using ... which increases in incredulity to the point of distaste. | I decided to try them all the same. |
| He pours himself a glass of wine from the carafe he's holding, then sips some. | |
| He obviously likes what he has tasted. | And I must say – they're really jolly good. |
| Cut to three pack shot and *super: Paul Masson's California Carafes.* | *American VO:* Paul Masson's California Carafes. They're really ... jolly good. |

| VISION | SOUND |
|---|---|
| Open on the harbour of a small fishing port, somewhere on the south west coast of England | |
| | SFX: Motor boat, seagulls and sea sounds. |
| It is late afternoon. | |
| A medium-sized cruiser is slowly making its way into port. | |
| As the camera closes in, we see the skipper at the wheel and another crew member. | |
| Reclining on the after deck with a Carafe is Ian Carmichael. | |
| He talks to camera. | Ian Carmichael: I was chatting to some Californians recently about Paul Masson's California Carafes. |
| Camera closes in on Ian as he gestures towards the Carafe. | Paul Masson, they informed me, has been laying fine wines on people since 1852. |
| As he talks, we close in on his pouring out some wine. | Try a Carafe, they suggested and see how it 'grabs' you, man. |
| Cut to Ian's face registering wry amusement. | Though somewhat wary of being grabbed by a bottle of wine I decided to give it a whirl. |
| Ian takes a non-committal gulp. Then grins to camera. | And I must say, they're really jolly good. |
| Cut back to pack shot of 3 Carafes<br>Super: Paul Masson's California Wines. | Male VO: Paul Masson's California Carafes. They're really jolly good. |

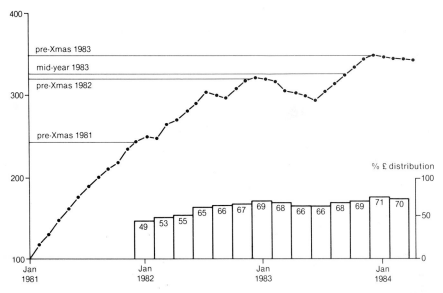

Figure 3. *Index of Paul Masson California Carafe ex-factory case sales (MAT) : year to Jan 1981 = 100*
*Sources:* Seagram UK, Nielsen (Grocers & Specialists)

In the simplest terms, the brand has been a success (see Figure 3). Brand sales have increased consistently across the period even after distribution plateaued in mid 1982.

Particularly impressive have been:

1.  The consistent improvement year-on-year in the pre-Christmas period.
2.  The mid-year achievement in 1983; higher than any previous pre-Christmas peak.

In tandem with this has been the continued development of the brand's consumer franchise. Although tracking study data collected in January 1983 and 1984 was based on a different sample design, and (in 1984) analysed only on a national basis (and hence not comparable with 1981 and 1982), Table 4 indicates quite clearly the development of consumer knowledge and increasing trial of the brand over the 1982–84 period. It also demonstrates increasing frequency of purchase amongst repeat users within the growing overall penetration of the brand and during the peak pre-Christmas period.

TABLE 4:   PAUL MASSON CONSUMER PERFORMANCE 1982–84
(NATIONALLY) (Base: all UK wine drinkers)

|  | Jan 1983 | Jan 1984 |
| --- | --- | --- |
| advertising awareness (prompted) | 31 | 40 |
| brand awareness (total) | 49 | 61 |
| ever bought | 18 | 25 |
| repeat buyers | 10 | 11 |
| (of which) bought in last month | 41 | 47 |

Research: PHD Research Tracking Studies

In addition, qualitative research conducted at regular intervals throughout the period continued to suggest not only advertising's role in the development of a highly distinctive brand personality, but also in positioning the brand as acceptable on a number of usage occasions, and against both sectors of the target audience. This too has been confirmed quantitatively (see Table 5). Within this, however, were the marketing and advertising objectives met?

TABLE 5:    DRINKING OCCASIONS: PAUL MASSON CALIFORNIA CARAFE
            REPEAT BUYERS JAN 1983

|  | heavier drinkers % | lighter drinkers % |
|---|---|---|
| *formal occasions:* | | |
| dinner party at home | 29 | 38 |
| dinner party away from home | 46 | 47 |
| Christmas/New Year | 22 | 22 |
| *informal occasions:* | | |
| drinking, at home without friends/guests | 61 | 43 |
| weekends/meals at home without guests | 11 | 7 |

Source: PHD Research Tracking Study

Table 6 demonstrates that the marketing objective of maintaining share, despite pressures against brands generally, was met. Paul Masson California Carafe share rose in the pre-Christmas 1982 period to 1.4 per cent, making it the sixth biggest brand in the market. More importantly, it maintained this position in 1983 at a time when the other three branded ranges experienced severe decline, and even the individual brands dropped back.

TABLE 6:    BUILDING BRAND SHARE WHEN OTHER BRANDS IN DECLINE

| | Dec–Jan 1980–81 % | Dec–Jan 1981–82 % | Dec–Jan 1982–83 % | Dec–Jan 1983–84 % |
|---|---|---|---|---|
| Paul Masson | 0.5* | 1.0 | 1.4 | 1.4 |
| Hirondelle | 4.8 | 3.9 | 3.3 | 2.1 |
| Nicolas | 2.0 | 1.5 | 1.2 | 0.8 |
| Don Cortez | 3.2 | 2.7 | 2.1 | 1.6 |
| Blue Nun | | | 1.9 | 1.8 |
| Black Tower | | | 1.1 | 0.9 |
| Lutomer | | | 3.6 | 3.3 |
| Mateus | | | 1.4 | 1.2 |

* estimate
Source: Nielsen (Grocers & Specialists)

TABLE 7: ADVERTISED VS. NON-ADVERTISED AREAS

| | Dec–Jan 1982–83 | | Dec–Jan 1983–84 | |
| brand shares: | national | Wales, West, Westward | national | Wales, West, Westward |
| --- | --- | --- | --- | --- |
| Paul Masson | 1.4 | 1.2 | 1.4 | 0.8 |
| Hirondelle | 3.3 | 3.6 | 2.1 | 1.7 |
| Blue Nun | 1.9 | 1.9 | 1.8 | 1.7 |

Source: Nielsen (Grocers & Specialists)

Whilst competitive price differentials across the period 1982–83 were almost entirely consistent, and distribution between the two periods relatively static for all brands, advertising support for Paul Masson however was not. One area (Wales, West, Westward) received no support in 1983 although it had received support in 1982. If brand performance in Wales, West, Westward is compared to the national performance, the picture in Table 7 emerges. From this analysis it can be seen that Paul Masson California Carafe performed significantly worse in the non-advertised area than in the rest of the country. With all other factors remaining constant, advertising was the only variable within the mix that changed. Furthermore, if one examines all four identifiably separate Nielsen areas* and compares sales performance for the full year 1983 vs. 1982, Table 8 emerges. This relationship is shown graphically in Figure 4. Together with the share data described earlier it provides clear evidence of the role and effectiveness of advertising in sustaining and building the brand in both share and sales terms across the period.

TABLE 8:     1983 VS. 1982 (YEAR TO FEB–MAR FOLLOWING)

| | Sales ±% | TVRs ±% |
| --- | --- | --- |
| London | +13 | + 50 |
| Southern | +28 | +122 |
| Wales, West, Westward | − 6 | −100 (ie no support in 1983) |
| Lancashire | − 8 | − 22 |

Source: Nielsen (Grocers & Specialists)
        AGB

Turning to the second and third marketing objectives, Table 9 illustrates further the 'robustness' of the Masson brand – not only did it maintain share, but it did so in the face of further severe encroachment on the branded sector by own-label and the continued success of Le Piat. Here, too, this was not the case in Wales, West and Westward, where Le Piat share reached only 1.6 per cent in December–January 1983–84, yet as we have seen, Masson share dropped back from 1.2 per cent to 0.8 per cent. Once again, therefore, in the context of contrast price differentials and a static distribution position, Masson's 'robustness' can really only be explained in terms of advertising support and strategic/creative 'edge' over the competition.

---

*Nielsen tables combine Midlands & Anglia, Yorkshire & Tyne Tees, Scottish & Grampian TV areas, all of which received differential levels of support.

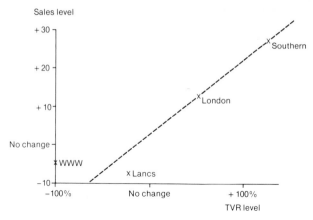

Figure 4. *1983 vs. 1982 year to Feb–Mar following*

TABLE 9:    ROBUSTNESS IN THE FACE OF COMPETITIVE LAUNCHES AND THE GROWTH OF OWN LABEL

|  | Dec–Jan 1982–83 % | Dec–Jan 1983–84 % | Brand Share %± |
|---|---|---|---|
| Paul Masson | 1.4 | 1.4 | n.c. |
| other branded ranges* | 6.6 | 4.5 | −2.1 |
| individual brands** | 8.0 | 7.2 | −0.8 |
| Le Piat | 2.0 | 2.7 | +0.7 |
| All others (generics & own label) | 81.9 | 83.9 | +2.0 |

\* Nicolas, Hirondelle, Don Cortez
\*\* Blue Nun, Black Tower, Lutomer, Mateus
Source: Nielsen (Grocers & Specialists)


Finally, what about rate of sale? From an examination of the sales performance, effective sterling distribution and, hence, rate of sale, across the period 1982 vs. 1983, quite clear comparisons can be made between the major competitive brands. From this analysis, it can be demonstrated that in 'real' terms, rate of sale for Paul Masson California Carafe increased by 10 per cent across the period. This performance was significantly better than the other branded ranges (which declined between 16 and 33 per cent), and better even than any other individual brand except Blue Nun, whose rate of sale increased by 24 per cent largely because distribution for that brand fell back 10 points. As a measure of consumer offtake, this is yet another indicator of the strength of the Masson franchise vs. the competition.

Once again, it is worth pointing out that in the only identifiable non-advertised area in 1983, Wales, West and Westward, not only did Paul Masson California Carafes' effective distribution actually fall by 2 per cent but rate of sale even through that reduced base dropped by 19 per cent, on a par with the other branded ranges.

It will be recalled that the advertising objectives for the brand, as well as relating to content (already addressed), also included the proviso that the advertising should be cost effective within a limited budget, while at the same time being capable of demonstrating differential effectiveness. Taking differential effect first, we have referred already to the 'special case' of Wales, West and Westward having received no support in 1983. In addition, Granada was the only identifiable area to receive support pre-Christmas 1983 but not mid-year. To compare performance between these we also need to examine an area which received support in both periods. We have selected Southern as that area, on the basis of comparable total market sales, distribution and population levels. Figure 5 illustrates the relative performance of the three areas over the 1983 period. From this it

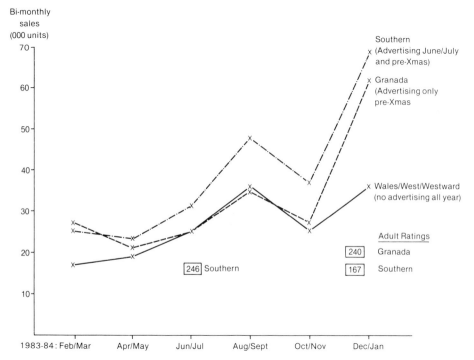

Figure 5. *Relative performance in advertising areas and control*

*Source:* Nielsen (Grocers and Specialists)

can be seen that whilst all three areas start roughly on a par in sales terms in February–March, the situation changes significantly across the year. Granada (advertised only pre-Christmas) follows the same sales pattern as Wales, West and Westward for every period until December–January, when it pulls ahead dramatically. Southern, on the other hand, appears to respond well to advertising in the June–July period and that improvement is maintained across the rest of the year, effectively 'distancing' Southern from the other two areas for the second half of the year. This then is the clearest possible illustration of discernible and differential advertising effectiveness between different levels of support in three comparable areas.

Turning now to cost effectiveness of advertising, Table 10 examines the adspend of the four major TV spenders amongst the established brands in 1983. Taking ratecard

TABLE 10:   COST-EFFECTIVE ADVERTISING EXPENDITURE VS. COMPETITION 1983 (YEAR TO FEB–MAR 1984)

|  | TV and press £000 spend (ratecard) | £ million sales | advertising as % of sales |
|---|---|---|---|
| Paul Masson | 614 | 6.34 | 9.7 |
| Hirondelle | 1069 | 10.41 | 10.3 |
| Mateus | 952 | 5.43 | 17.5 |
| Black Tower | 1000 | 4.52 | 22.1 |

Source: MEAL
       Nielsen (Grocers & Specialists)

expenditure on TV and press and comparing this with sterling sales of the brands it can be seen that not only was Paul Masson California Carafe advertising effective, it was also *cost effective* vs. other brands.

The true expenditure picture is even more interesting. Taking the whole period of the brand's existence (1980–84) the *actual* expenditure behind the brand has yet to exceed £1 million in total. Yet over that period the brand's sales have been well in excess of one million cases (12 million bottles). Advertising support therefore has amounted to less than £1 per case (7–8p per bottle) which at current prices represents less than $2\frac{1}{2}$ per cent of retail value.

Finally, it is perhaps worth restating that the advertising achievement has been one not only of distinctive branding, but of effective *positioning*. It is through its achievement of the 'critical balance' referred to earlier (neither too patronising nor too 'product story' – based for inexperienced drinkers; not too lightweight in wine credentials for the experienced drinker), that the advertising has positioned the brand desirably to both sectors of the market.

The final table (Table 11) illustrates precisely the nature of that achievement. From the most recently available TGI data it can be seen that Paul Masson California Carafe has established itself not only amongst a more even spread of users, but also across a broader spectrum of usage occasions than any of its mainstream competitors.

TABLE 11:   BRAND PROFILES (1984) BY DRINKER TYPE AND USUAL DRINKING OCCASIONS

|  | Paul Masson % | Black Tower % | Blue Nun % | Nicolas % | Don Cortez % | Hirondelle % | Sainsbury's % |
|---|---|---|---|---|---|---|---|
| *drinker:* | | | | | | | |
| heavy | 32 | 20 | 9 | 25 | 15 | 15 | 18 |
| medium | 46 | 46 | 36 | 38 | 35 | 36 | 38 |
| light | 21 | 30 | 52 | 34 | 48 | 46 | 41 |
| *occasion:* | | | | | | | |
| at home | 86 | 69 | 60 | 83 | 72 | 68 | 72 |
| at other people's home | 25 | 26 | 21 | 21 | 19 | 22 | 22 |
| in restaurant | 29 | 33 | 39 | 40 | 24 | 27 | 25 |

Source: TGI 1984

## EVALUATING THE ACHIEVEMENT

Undoubtedly, in the first two years of the brand's life, advertising played a key role in building awareness and trial of the product as well as trade acceptance. Without a tied distribution network this would have been very difficult without advertising. But what of the period under discussion here: the third and fourth years of the brand's life?

The preceding analysis has demonstrated the importance of the re-evaluation of the brand and the role of its advertising in 1982. What was summarised briefly in the way of research (see pages 155–157) was in fact a highly intensive exercise covering many months.

The results however appear to have justified that effort. By comparing the performance of Paul Masson California Carafe to other brands (especially other branded ranges) and, where possible, between advertised and non-advertised areas, it has been demonstrated that against a background of consistent competitive price differentials and distribution strengths, advertising has achieved the following:

1.  Maintenance of brand share and hence sales growth when other brands (including those advertised at heavier weights) were declining in the face of a growing own-label sector and a significant competitive launch (Le Piat). This 'robustness' has been shown not to have been the case in a non-advertised area over the same period.
2.  Maintenance of rate-of-sale growth when a distribution plateau had been reached. Again, not the case in the non-advertised area.
3.  Clearly differentiable sales effect across a full year in three areas; one receiving no advertising at all, one receiving advertising pre-Christmas only, one receiving advertising mid-year and pre-Christmas.
4.  Cost-effective support for the brand compared to levels of support for competitive brands and cost-effective support for the brand in real terms, amounting to an advertising to sales value ratio of less than $2\frac{1}{2}$ per cent.

For Seagram (UK) Ltd, the success of Paul Masson California Carafe has been a major achievement. Wine products now account for over 40 per cent of company turnover compared to less than 5 per cent in 1979. With the continued decline of spirits this has had a significant impact on company profitability. Not only is Paul Masson California Carafe now still the number six brand in the UK market, it is actually brand leader in the in-litre-size sector and second only to Mateus in rosés. Furthermore, the credibility gained with the trade as a result of the success of Paul Masson California Carafe ensures a sympathetic response to Seagram wine products in the future.

For Paul Masson in California, the UK now represents the biggest export market for Carafes in the world, in fact only some 100,000 cases less than US sales. It also represents a firm foundation for both themselves and Seagram UK to launch other Paul Masson products into the UK in the future.

# 11
# Curly Wurly: The Effect of an Advertising Relaunch

## MARKET BACKGROUND

Curly Wurly was launched in 1971 as part of a new product development programme jointly carried out by Cadbury Ltd and one of their advertising agencies, Leo Burnett Ltd. The product is a squiggly bar of toffee enrobed in Cadbury's milk chocolate. It was positioned in the self-purchase kids confectionery market with a primary target market of children aged 5–11 years old.

Up to five years of age the majority of confectionery purchasing is supervised and paid for by an adult, usually the mother. When the child is aged 5–8 adult influence decreases and older children aged 9–11 have virtual total freedom as to what items they buy. Confectionery, savoury snacks and soft drinks all compete for pocket money spending. Within confectionery the brand is in competition with a diverse range of products from Mars bars to 'penny tray' items.

## ADVERTISING BACKGROUND

The launch advertising had featured Terry Scott as a schoolboy with the theme 'Outchews everything for $2\frac{1}{2}$p'. This advertising was very successful in generating awareness and trial. We found, however, that mothers somewhat disapproved of the product because they perceived it as being messy: bits of chocolate fell off the bar when it was bitten into. Therefore, we were in danger of having a Cadbury product which mothers positively discouraged their children from purchasing and consuming.

The product was changed slightly to alleviate this problem and this change was communicated to children and mums, again using Terry Scott and retaining the launch commercials humour and fun. We found subsequently that the 'apology' nature of this advertising had not motivated mums to condone children's purchasing and children felt that their Curly Wurly which they had known and loved had changed, not necessarily for the better.

## THE PROBLEM

After five years without much marketing activity and without advertising, a review of Curly Wurly was conducted in 1981. Although sales were steady, they were at a very low level. Also the competitive environment had changed. Other chewy bars were more prominent: Toffo and Texan, the latter's manufacturer was spending money behind the brand.

It was decided to conduct some qualitative research amongst our target market to find out the current status of Curly Wurly. The findings of this research highlighted our problem.

Curly Wurly was seen as a very low-status confectionery product rather than a higher profile countline alongside products such as Mars etc. It also had numerous other problems:

— low level of awareness;
— often a countline substitute;
— descriptive vocabulary of the product had declined;
— lack of image which led to lack of competitive edge;
— mums rather than kids were buying: there was no strong appeal to children;
— there was virtually no advertising recall.

It was hypothesised that these problems arose because of a lack of advertising support. Advertising had, and could again, communicate the nature of the product and its highly competitive price. Of our target market now aged 5-11 the vast majority would not have been aware of our last advertising.

We noted, however, that the brand was still selling moderately well with all these problems and no advertising support. This meant that a relaunch should be able to inject new life into Curly Wurly by motivating our new target market.

## THE RELAUNCH

### The Strategy

After extensive work on Curly Wurly it was decided to leave the advertising strategy virtually unchanged from the launch strategy.

#### THE ROLE OF ADVERTISING

To make our prime target market aware of Curly Wurly.

#### ADVERTISING TASK

To re-establish Curly Wurly as the long-lasting chocolate-covered bar for kids which offers real value for money.

## TARGET AUDIENCE

Again defined as 5–11 year olds with a bias to 5–8 year olds. Our secondary target market was their mothers.

## ADVERTISING BRIEF

The brief can be summarised as to create advertising which would be involving and humorous to kids but which would not alienate mothers.

## COMPETITIVE POSITIONING

The best-value chewy bar you can buy.

## RATIONALE

1. Children perceive the main benefits as value and long-lastingness, ie length of chew.
2. Curly Wurly is covered in Cadbury's milk chocolate.
3. Curly Wurly costs only 10p.

## PROPOSITION

Curly Wurly is so chewy that it lasts and lasts and it only costs 10p.

## EXECUTIONAL GUIDELINES

— ensure long-lastingness is communicated;
— ensure price is included;
— Cadbury name to be included.

Communication of delicious has not been included because to children all confectionery, especially chocolate confectionery, is delicious.

## Media Choice

Funds were made available for a relaunch in 1982. The media budget was small by confectionery market standards: including production the advertising spend was less than £500000. Our media objectives were defined as follows:

1. To advertise the brand nationally and re-establish it as a major children's sweet.
2. To commence advertising early in 1982 and to maintain effective presence as long as affordable.

Based on these criteria, TV and cinema were selected as the most appropriate media to relaunch the brand. TV would enable us to quickly re-establish Curly Wurly as part of children's confectionery repertoire and cinema would allow us to add impact and to provide continuity of presence at key times of the year such as school holidays etc.

TV: Burst:   February–March, 175 TVRs
      Drip:   April–June, 250 TVRs
Cinema: April–December (school holidays only)

*Advertising Development*

The development of children's advertising is fraught with problems, particularly when humour is intended. What appeals to a five-year-old can be seen as being very childish and thus a turn-off for a nine-year-old.

The creative group came up with two executions based on the idea that if a Curly Wurly was straightened out it would be 21 inches long and provide a much longer chew for 10p. In one execution 'Going Metric' a comparison was made between a 21-inch long Curly Wurly and a 533 mm long Curly Wurly, both obviously being the same length. The other execution 'Scared Stiff' was based on the idea of frightening the Curly Wurly so it would straighten out to 21 inches.

These ideas were put into qualitative research in animatic form and exposed to children aged 6–11 years old. Five-year-olds were excluded because they are a little too young to use in research.

It was found that both executions had strong appeal and involvement across the whole sample of children. They responded straight away to the humour, both verbal and physical. We found, however, that there was a major problem using product length as our USP (unique selling proposition). The children we spoke to had a poor grasp of numbers and length measurement and very little familiarity with inches. Also, Curly Wurly was seen by them as a bar with holes punched in it rather than a squiggled-up strip. This was also consonant with the way they ate the product which bore no relation to the length idea.

The creative group were rebriefed and came up with a new idea based on the thought that a Curly Wurly was so chewy and lasted so long that when you were eating it you could not talk for ages. The execution consisted of a moose and a young boy sitting on a bench. The moose is trying to get the boy to tell everybody about Curly Wurly – that it is chewy, long-lasting and only costs 10p. The boy cannot talk because he is chewing his Curly Wurly. The idea is Curly Wurly is 'too chewy for words'.

The idea in animatic form was again researched among our target market. We were well aware that it was all too easy to get it wrong, therefore further research was felt to be necessary.

The idea researched very well indeed and we found that the moose was potentially a very strong and original branding device for Curly Wurly. He evoked a very positive response among children and his character was sufficiently complex and engaging to provide the basis for extensive use in relation to the product. He had appeal across a broad age range which was very important. We learnt also that, because of the static scenario, the right kind of body-landuage between the moose and the boy was crucial and this was where the appeal to children lay. Following this research minor changes were made to the script which was then shot and aired in 1982.

'Sorry about this. Tom is supposed to be telling you about Cadbury's Curly Wurly.'

'Aren't you?'

'Tell them about the thick Cadbury chocolate and smooth chewy caramel, Tom.'

'Mmmmm'

'Hurry up, Tom. We've only got a few more seconds.'

'What a long chew for 10p. It's amazing.'

'He can talk! I made him talk!'

CADBURY'S CURLY WURLY.
TOO CHEWY FOR WORDS.

## EVALUATION OF THE RELAUNCH

We had two types of measures to evaluate the effects of the relaunch. These were:

1. AGB Personal Purchasing Index (PPI), a weekly diary panel of 10 000 individuals aged 5–65 years old.
2. A specially designed tracking study conducted by Cocks Williamson Associates in three stages. The sample for each stage was 200 boys and girls aged 7–11 years old, BC1C2, split North and South. The three stages were:

| pre-advertising: | 18–30 January 1982 |
|---|---|
| post-burst: | 22–31 March 1982 |
| post-burst & drip: | 8–17 June 1982 |

### Sales

PPI showed a dramatic sales effect. Throughout 1981 sales had been fairly steady, at about 3.4 million units per bi-month. In the first bi-month we advertised, the sales rise was 70 per cent, in the next: 100 per cent and for the rest of the year: 120 per cent. Overall, sales more than doubled (see Table 1). Ex-factory data confirmed these figures. The increase among children was nearly 70 per cent. It was larger, 150 per cent, among adults, who mostly bought multi-packs of four bars.

TABLE 1:   SALES (million units)

|  | Jan–Feb | Mar–Apr | May–Jun | July–Aug | Sept–Oct | Nov–Dec |
|---|---|---|---|---|---|---|
| 1981 | 3.1 | 3.6 | 3.3 | 3.8 | 3.6 | 3.3 |
| 1982 | 5.3 | 7.4 | 8.2 | 7.6 | 7.2 | 7.9 |

Source: PPI

### Purchasers

Penetration was also examined separately for children aged 5–12, and adults. The advertising started in February 1982. Table 2 shows this information. Not only had we persuaded more children to buy the brand but we had motivated adults to buy for their children.

TABLE 2:   PENETRATION (per cent)

|  | Jan–Feb % | Mar–Apr % | May–Jun % | Jul–Aug % | Sept–Oct % | Nov–Dec % |
|---|---|---|---|---|---|---|
| 1981 |  |  |  |  |  |  |
| children | 12.1 | 12.8 | 10.8 | 16.1 | 13.8 | 14.5 |
| adults | 1.1 | 1.2 | 1.3 | 1.8 | 1.6 | 1.3 |
| 1982 |  |  |  |  |  |  |
| children | 15.5 | 20.8 | 23.8 | 20.0 | 20.8 | 20.3 |
| adults | 2.0 | 3.1 | 3.8 | 2.6 | 2.3 | 2.0 |

Source: PPI

*Tracking Study*

The three stages of the children's tracking study gave the following results, which make it clear how the advertising worked.

(a)  Spontaneous awareness of Curly Wurly increased throughout the three stages of the survey, (see Table 3). 99 per cent of the sample claimed to have heard of Curly Wurly on prompting at the final stage of the survey.

TABLE 3:   SPONTANEOUS AWARENESS

|  | *Curly Wurly* % |
|---|---|
| pre-advertising | 7 |
| post–burst | 15 |
| post–burst and drip | 24 |

(b)  Curly Wurly was rated the second most-liked product by children by the final stage. At the pre-stage it was rated in seventh position, (see Table 4).

TABLE 4:   LIKED MOST

|  | *Curly Wurly* % |
|---|---|
| pre-advertising | 9 |
| post–burst | 15 |
| post–burst and drip | 16 |

(c)  Curly Wurly was rated the most fun and exciting brand by 45 per cent of the sample. This was higher than for any other brand.

(d)  Curly Wurly is now rated top as being the most long-lasting brand, as in Table 5. Prior to the advertising, Toffo and Mars were regarded as being more long-lasting products than Curly Wurly.

TABLE 5:   LONGLASTINGNESS

|  | *Curly Wurly* % |
|---|---|
| pre-advertising | 28 |
| post–burst | 33 |
| post–burst and drip | 49 |

(e)  Curly Wurly is the current leader in terms of being value for money. (Mars used to be regarded as the best value for money brand.) 69 per cent of the sample say the brand is good value. Curly Wurly has risen steadily on this measure across the three parts of the research (see Table 6). The spontaneous reasons played back for best value for money is its long-lastingness, its size, chewiness and price of 10p.

TABLE 6:   VALUE FOR MONEY

| | |
|---|---|
| pre-advertising | 47% |
| post-burst | 54% |
| post-burst and drip | 69% |

(f)   76 per cent of the sample spontaneously claimed that they had seen TV advertising for Curly Wurly. On further prompting this figure rose to 90 per cent. (see Table 7).

TABLE 7:   TV ADVERTISING AWARENESS

| | spontaneous % | spontaneous and prompted % |
|---|---|---|
| pre-advertising | 7 | 7 |
| post-burst | 52 | 70 |
| post-burst and drip | 76 | 90 |

The moose and the boy were the most frequently mentioned aspects of the commercial. 78 per cent of children mentioned the moose and the same proportion mentioned the boy. 39 per cent of the sample mentioned good value.

In terms of appeal the moose and humour were the most frequently mentioned aspects which were liked. There were no major dislikes about the advertising. The major preference attributed to Curly Wurly itself was the chewiness. Mentions of this attribute increased over the three stages of the research.

All in all the advertising had considerable impact. In particular there were increases in positive attributes with decreases in negative attributes about the product. Awareness of and knowledge about the advertising was exceptionally high.

*Factors Affecting Sales*

Since there was no change in the product, we have to look for possible causes of these successes during 1982 in pricing or distribution (the only other major factors), in addition to advertising.

1.   In 1982 there was considerable activity in confectionery *pricing*. Larger bars, money off and other attractions resulted in an actual drop in countline average prices of 4 per cent. This was against general retail price rises that year of over 8 per cent. Thus the background was that countlines looked considerably cheaper.

Curly Wurly did not take part in this activity. Its bar price of 10p was unchanged. In 1981 this had been somewhat reduced – by 7 per cent in fact – by some promotional pricing. The cut was less in 1982 – the average retail price was only 2 per cent below list. Thus price cannot have played a part in the sales rise.

2.   Certainly *distribution* rose in 1982 in grocers as well as confectioners, tobacconists and newsagents (CTNs). The only data available are shown in tables 8 and 9. The rise was at best, from the data available, from 34 per cent (average September–December 1981) to 49 per cent (maximum observed) in 1982, or +44 per cent, in grocers; it

TABLE 8:    IN-STOCK STERLING-WEIGHTED DISTRIBUTION – PER CENT

| | Jan–Feb % | Mar–Apr % | Grocers May–Jun % | Jul–Aug % | Sept–Oct % | Nov–Dec % |
|---|---|---|---|---|---|---|
| 1981 | N/A | N/A | N/A | N/A | 36 | 32 |
| 1982 | 42 | 46 | 49 | N/A | N/A | N/A |

Source: Nielsen

was from 48 per cent to 66 per cent or +38 per cent, in CTNs. These are clearly less than the sales increases: throughput per outlet went up more than 50 per cent.

It must be arguable whether the distribution increase is a cause of sales, which is independent of advertising. It is our view that the gain in distribution was achieved with the help of advertising. It is one of the ways advertising works, to motivate and enthuse salesmen and retailers. The two work together and cannot be totally separated.

TABLE 9:    IN-STOCK STERLING-WEIGHTED DISTRIBUTION – PER CENT

| | Jan–Feb | Mar–Apr | CTNS May–Jun | Jul–Aug | Sept–Oct | Nov–Dec |
|---|---|---|---|---|---|---|
| 1981 | N/A | N/A | N/A | N/A | 50 | 46 |
| 1982 | 52 | 61 | 66 | N/A | N/A | N/A |

Source: Nielsen

3.  Profit figures cannot be revealed in detail, but it can be stated that this advertising definitely paid for itself. The way the calculations are done can be indicated by the following argument which uses conventional factors (ie not exact, but not misleading).

PPI shows sales in 1982 increased by 22.9 million units, reaching a peak in the second bi-month after the relaunch but continuing at a high level for the next three (and actually for longer). We attribute this annual increase to the advertising. Since the pickup of PPI is about 70 per cent, the actual increase was 32.7 million units (this order of size is confirmed by ex-factory sales).

As already stated, the retail price of 10p was very little reduced in practice. Taking off a conventional 30 per cent for retailer margin, the extra cash received was £2.29 million.

Costs of production and distribution of the extra units sold have to be allowed for, but overheads like machinery, office staff and so on are hardly affected by such changes in volume. Suppose we conventionally allow 60 per cent of the manufacturer's selling price for the marginal costs, or £1.37 million. This leaves £920,000 from which advertising costs have to be deducted before an additional profit is left. Since the advertising cost about half this it is clear that its investment was very sound.

## CONCLUSION

The advertising was very successful in creating awareness and generating trial, by communicating to a new target market the existence of the brand and its positive attributes.

There is no doubt in our minds, or the client's, that advertising caused the sales increase in 1982. This increase raised more than enough additional profit to pay for the advertising.

The main conclusion has to be, however, that even with a small number of OTS (opportunities to see), a brand can be restored to prominence, provided the advertising is striking and relevant.

# 12

# Defence Proves the Best Form of Attack for Cuprinol

## THE MARKET BACKGROUND

### The Product and the Company

Seventy-five years ago a Dane called OP Christensen discovered that by dissolving copper salts in a spirit solvent he could make a preservative which was insoluble in water. He sold it originally in Scandinavia to protect fishing nets. This original product was first marketed in Britain fifty years ago as a wood preservative under the name 'Cuprinol', and rapidly became the dominant brand in the market. Further technical development by the Cuprinol company led to the production of an extensive range of wood preservatives to suit varied professional and DIY requirements, all sold under the Cuprinol name. Although the company (now a subsidiary of the Berger Nicholson Group, and hence of Hoechst in West Germany) has diversified into other DIY areas, the range of Cuprinol wood preservatives remains the core of its business.

Wood preservatives can be defined as products for treating wood, containing chemicals that kill and resist further attack from insects and rot. But the consumer sees the problem primarily as one caused by 'damp' rather than by the insects and fungi which infect the wood. Accordingly, the main uses are for exterior doors and windows, fences, sheds, greenhouses and garden furniture, and internal structural timber such as roof joists, ceiling beams or flooring.

For many years the Cuprinol company has been acknowledged as one of the world's leading authorities in the development of wood preservative products, with a high reputation for successful technical research and development. Nevertheless wood preservatives have generally been seen as a 'stress purchase', with a correspondingly low consumer interest, offering very limited opportunities for market expansion.

### The 'Mature Market' Concept

The concept of the 'mature market' is now well established in marketing theory. It describes a market where, for whatever reason, the limits of overall expansion appear to have been reached – either temporarily or permanently – and therefore the objectives of marketing have become limited to retaining or increasing brand share. The classic example in the UK is the confectionery market.

The wood preservative market was regarded as essentially such a market. Although there has been some volume growth, it has been related chiefly to the increase in home ownership and the spread of DIY. Cuprinol's brand share was more than 60 per cent by volume, and it stood virtually alone as the scientific, high-margin product in the market. The chief competitor was not another brand, but the cheap low-margin commodity, creosote. The total market size was estimated in 1982 to be about £15 million at retail prices.

Although Cuprinol has advertised consistently for the past 20 years, in an effort to extend product usage and to keep projecting the name as the generic for wood preserva-tives the advertising budget from 1973 to 1977 (see Table 1) reflects the static nature of

TABLE 1:    ANNUAL ADVERTISING SPEND

| year | current prices £000 | constant 1983 prices £000 |
|------|------|------|
| 1973 | 52 | 269 |
| 1974 | 54 | 253 |
| 1975 | 79 | 292 |
| 1976 | 70 | 212 |
| 1977 | 79 | 202 |
| 1978 | 220 | 490 |
| 1979 | 156 | 301 |
| 1980 | 182 | 282 |
| 1981 | 144 | 190 |
| 1982 | 203 | 232 |
| 1983 | 1005 | 1005 |

Source: MEAL
Advertising Association Index of Media Rates

the market. In constant prices after allowing for media inflation the advertising expendi-ture tended to be around £2–300000 in 1983 terms. This, and its small volume and fragmented distributed structure, has meant that there is very little hard data published in the market.

### Change and Competition

During the late 1970s, the major change that occurred in the DIY market was related to distribution rather than product development. Following the earlier 'retail revolution' in food and household goods marketing, the nature of the DIY business began to change equally dramatically.

The traditional 'hardware' shops, with their emphasis on personal service and com-modities rather than brands, began to be superseded, first by the grocery chains (Tesco, Asda, Sainsbury etc) seeking higher-margin products to add to their inventory, and then by the purpose-built DIY superstores – Texas, B & Q etc. As had happened with grocery brands, the manufacturers' objectives shifted, from retaining the goodwill of shop assist-ants and owners by pre-selling their customers, to obtaining the all-important 'facings' in the self-service environment. Cuprinol responded to this change with more in-store pro-motional activity, and a higher advertising investment (Table 1).

In 1982, however, a new situation faced the Cuprinol company and their advertising agency, Everett's. Two major competitors – ICI Dulux and Sterling Roncraft – moved into the wood preservative market with every sign of serious intent. Both companies had heavily advertised brand names in the more competitive decorative sectors of the DIY market, and although it would be presumptuous to guess their reasons for this development, their entry was probably due in part to the greater marketing opportunity afforded by the concentration of market share in the new retail outlets.

Whatever the causes, the threat of such competition – ICI had already announced an advertising budget of £700 000 in 1983 – had to be met with a new marketing approach for Cuprinol at once.

## CONSTRUCTING THE MARKETING PLAN

### First Stage: Qualitative Research

A continuous programme of consumer research including 'usage and attitude' surveys and group discussions had in the past given the vital knowledge necessary for developing advertising to extend the preservative market. However, facing the new competitive threat, which took a platform based on 'decoration' as well as 'preservation', it was necessary to examine afresh consumer attitudes to Cuprinol in this new scenario. Everett's therefore undertook a series of group discussions to provide a framework for planning. In spite of the acknowledged limitations of the technique, the findings that emerged were sufficiently consistent to allow agency and client to move confidently into the planning stage. The principal findings were:

1.  The typical Cuprinol user is a man with a practical outlook, and one who likes to do things the right way – a conscientious but not a pernickety worker.
2.  He is not interested in the technicalities of wood preservation, only in the results. He sees the problem as essentially protection against 'damp'.
3.  Cuprinol is not seen as competing with creosote in specific situations – creosote is a crude product, only suitable for cheap wood and where finish is unimportant.
4.  The name Cuprinol is seen as virtually synonymous with wood preservation, but more as a generic than a brand; the consumer wouldn't search it out if an alternative was more readily available.

### Second Stage: Creating the Strategy

The marketing objective was deceptively simple: to protect Cuprinol's dominant share of the wood-preserver market against new competition, primarily from ICI Dulux and Sterling Roncraft.

Out of this, however, came a complete change of strategy. As the overwhelming brand leader Cuprinol had in the past concentrated on reinforcing its generic status, educating its users and potential users, and relying on good distribution to maintain its sales.

What was now resolved upon was a very strong promotion of the name Cuprinol as a *brand*. The budget was increased to approximately £¾ million for advertising which made possible the use of TV, at least in selected areas, supported by some specialist press.

Apart from promoting the TV campaign to the trade, no other changes in the marketing programme were envisaged. This, incidentally, simplified evaluation of the campaign.

The advertising proposition was equally simple: '*Cuprinol is the only real choice in wood preservers*'. As the research indicated that this was pretty close to what a majority of consumers believed anyway, the advertising had to concentrate on reinforcing the message, without the need for any elaborate rational demonstration or justification.

At the heart of the creative strategy which developed from this were the communication objectives; the consumer should:

—  *know* that Cuprinol works by lodging protection against damp and decay in the grain of the wood;
—  *think* of Cuprinol as the supreme preserver, uniquely formulated to keep wood in good condition;
—  *feel* that using Cuprinol gives the satisfaction of a constructive job well done.

These objectives became the brief for the creative department. The approach to the key question of advertising effectiveness was deliberately thorough to ensure that the maximum understanding would be gleaned from this strategically fundamental advertising 'experiment'. This required both an assessment of the impact of the campaign on the target audience using conventional consumer research, as well as a careful analysis of the sales response through the development of computer-based models of market behaviour.

## CAMPAIGN EXECUTION

### The Campaign in Outline

The total advertising budget for the year was £750000 (see Table 2). Two major TV bursts were scheduled, for April–May and August–September, using a mixture of 30-second and 10-second spots. Specialist press was used during the campaign period, which began with the peak spring user-period, and ended with the secondary autumn peak. One commercial, with a 10-second adaptation, was used. Storyboard and press proofs are shown on page 186.

### Media Strategy

Previous Cuprinol advertising had used colour magazines and specialist press. The decision to devote 90 per cent of the budget in 1983 to TV was determined by the need to achieve dominance and to promote a strong branding message.

Posters had been considered as an alternative, but they were felt to lack the impact required for initial branding, and to be too heavily town-biased. TV had the advantages not only of impact and colour, but of speed of communication, and of providing a powerful story for the trade. In order to achieve dominance for the product in the medium, it was decided to concentrate on areas of highest potential, and to make use of the opportunities offered by the opening of Channel 4.

Regional sales data were converted to TV regions, and TGI information employed to refine demographic targeting in terms of TV areas (see Table 3). The prime target

TABLE 2:    BUDGET SUMMARY

| | | £ |
|---|---|---|
| *Media* | | |
| TV | 621 000 | |
| consumer press | 36 000 | |
| trade press | 22 585 | |
| total planned media expenditure | | 679 585 |
| *Production* | | |
| TV | 47 000 | |
| consumer press | 7 000 | |
| trade press | 6 000 | |
| total production allowance | | 60 000 |
| total planned 1983 advertising budget | | £739 585 |

market was defined as ABC1 men of 35 +, but an important objective was to widen the market to take in younger men and C2s.

Areas selected for TV were: London, Central, HTV, TVS, Anglia and Granada. The Central area was dropped in the second burst, and this provided a further control for research. The target was 500 adult TVRs in the first burst and 400 TVRs in the second. High rating peak-time spots on ITV were chosen, with selected programmes from Channel 4 to provide added frequency above the 4 + OTS level and to extend coverage of the market, particularly in the younger age groups.

TABLE 3:    SALES BY TV REGION

| ITV Area | sales profile (%) | Index (100) |
|---|---|---|
| London | 20 | 103 |
| South | 10 | 119 |
| Midlands | 13 | 85 |
| North West | 12 | 93 |
| Yorkshire | 7 | 74 |
| North East | 3 | 67 |
| Wales and West | 10 | 129 |
| South West | 5 | 176 |
| East | 8 | 121 |
| Central Scotland | 5 | 91 |
| North Scotland | 2 | 170 |
| Border | 2 | 89 |
| Channel | – | 159 |
| Northern Ireland | 2 | 79 |

*TV Performance*

Because of the regional nature of the campaign, rating targets were deliberately set high. Desired coverage and frequency of the proposed bursts were established, based on projected levels of impact, and the results (summarised in Figure 1) show that on a delivery of 980 TVRs the cover of all adults was 91 per cent, with a 4+ cover of 75 per cent, and 8+ of 53 per cent. Overall delivery exceeded targets by 9 per cent.

Figure 2 shows coverage build-up by week and Figure 3, network rating by week. The use of daytime was not part of the buying strategy, as it was considered that Channel 4, used selectively, offered much better value, especially against ABC1C2 men. Table 4 shows spend by daypart (the term given to the partitioning of the day into different cost bands).

The value of Channel 4 varied by area, and Figure 4 shows expenditure and rating achievement by channel across both bursts. All areas showed an over-delivery with the exception of TVS, where there was a 4 per cent shortfall.

TABLE 4:   PERCENTAGE SPEND BY DAYPART ITV AND CHANNEL 4 –
           TOTAL

|  | % of total spend |
|---|---|
| daytime | – |
| pre-peak | 16 |
| peak | 73 |
| post-peak | 11 |
| | |
| total | 100 |

*Key to daypart*

| | |
|---|---|
| daytime | Up to 16.00 (Mon–Fri) |
| pre-peak | 16.01–17.40 (Sat–Sun up to 17.40) |
| peak | 17.41–22.40 |
| post-peak | 22.41–Close |

This is a general classification which will vary slightly by area.

*Creative Strategy*

The initial creative idea was researched in storyboard and narrative tape form to ensure communication effectiveness and credibility against the key target consumers. Group discussions were held with both existing users and potential users to establish the comprehension and acceptance of the main message.

The findings indicated that the creative expression was very powerful with only minor changes in the voice-over being required. One such change was the replacement of the expression 'special treatment' with the term 'special formula,' which overcame the concerns expressed by some consumers about being required to understand how to 'treat' wood.

Because of the wide range of varieties of Cuprinol and the differing pack designs and sizes, Everett's felt that any attempt to show the packs would be confusing., In the light

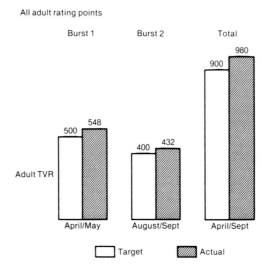

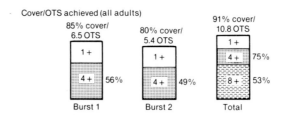

Figure 1. *Campaign summary*
*Source:* C.R.A.F.T.

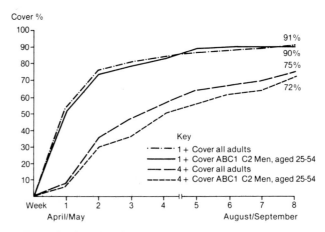

Figure 2. *Cover build-up by week*
*Source:* C.R.A.F.T.

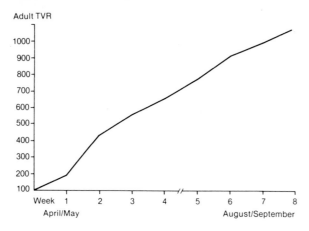

Figure 3. *Network ratings achieved by week*
*Source:* AGB

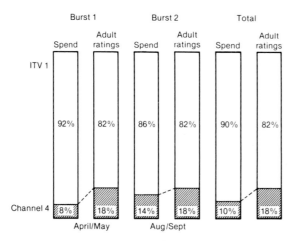

Figure 4. *Spend and rating achievement by channel*

of the initial research, it was clear that consumers were not much interested in the technical aspects of the range. Instead, attention was concentrated entirely on the brand name itself, in the form of large wooden letters. As the camera panned along the letters, they were subjected to the worst assaults of the seasonal elements, from driving rain and snow to intense summer heat. At the letter *I*, this sequence was briefly interrupted while the letter itself was dipped in Cuprinol to show the process of penetration. In the final spring sequence, a cat in pursuit of a butterfly leapt up on the letters, and the words 'wood preservers' were spelt out in primroses in the foreground. The voice-over ended with the words which summed up the theme of the campaign: '*The Cuprinol range of wood preservers – they're in the wood for good.*'

The creative treatment, which was closely followed in press adaptations, not only acted

THE WOOD AROUND YOUR HOME...

NEEDS CONSTANT PROTECTION FROM THE
PERILS OF NATURE...

ONE SPECIAL FORMULA...

PENETRATES DEEP INTO WOOD...

TO PROTECT AND PRESERVE ITS LIVING BEAUTY  ·
YEAR IN AND YEAR OUT...

THE CUPRINOL RANGE OF WOOD PRESERVERS.
THEY'RE IN THE WOOD FOR GOOD.

as a powerful branding vehicle – with the name never off the screen – but also had the advantage that, since it avoided the use of actors, it allowed the commercial to be shown unamended on Channel 4 without compromising the agency or client in the IPA/Equity dispute. The storyboard of the final commercial is given on page 186.

## CAMPAIGN EVALUATION

### Competitive Activity

In the event, little or no promotional activity was detected on behalf of Ronseal Wood Preserver, though expenditure on Ronseal Varnish was at a very high level and this appears to have influenced our research finding.

The two competing Dulux products, however, did receive support, particularly Wood-sheen. Between the first and second post-advertising consumer surveys Dulux Woodsheen expenditure was £480000, all on TV, and the Dulux Timber Colour recorded spend was £73000, all in the press.

The weight of TV spend used for Cuprinol advertising within the regions is shown in Table 5.

TABLE 5:   COMPETITORS' TV ADVERTISING SPEND

|  | pre-survey to 1st post-survey £000 | 1st post–survey to 2nd post–survey £000 |
|---|---|---|
| Ronseal Wood Preserver | 11 | – |
| (Ronseal Varnish) | (244) | (350) |
| Dulux Woodsheen | – | 324 |
| Cuprinol | 581 | 407 |

Source: MEAL

Detailed MEAL figures for Cuprinol and the major competing brands are given in Table 6.

### Research Findings

The wood preservative market lacks the sophistication of major markets in which detailed audit figures relating to consumer off-take and retailer purchases can be presented. Furthermore, since Cuprinol is sold exclusively through wholesalers and the major retail chains, there is virtually no available information about the direct level of consumer off-take, or about the regional distribution of sales over the short term.

The only information relating to sales was in overall national ex-factory terms, and the detailed analysis of this data is covered in the next section. Because of the intrinsic difficulties of using total ex-factory sales, it was essential at the outset to complement this work with consumer research. This was designed to provide measures of the direct advertising impact on target consumers in terms of brand and advertising awareness levels, advertising content, recall etc. In this way a comprehensive evaluation package was

TABLE 6:    THE COMPETITIVE ADVERTISING CONTEXT (£000)

| | 1982 total | Jan 1983 to pre-survey | pre to 1st post-survey | | | 1st to 2nd post-survey | | |
|---|---|---|---|---|---|---|---|---|
| | | | TV* | press | total | TV** | press | total |
| Cuprinol Wood Preserver | 203 | – | 581 | 4 | 584 | 407 | 16 | 423 |
| Dulux Timber Colour | 90 | – | – | – | – | – | 73 | 73 |
| Dulux Woodsheen | 90 | – | – | – | – | 480 | – | 480 |
| Ronseal Wood Preserver | – | – | 11 | 16 | 27 | 17 | 16 | 33 |
| (Ronseal Varnish) | (1291) | (279) | (439) | (40) | (479) | (550) | (52) | (702) |
| PBI Bio Woody | – | 61 | – | 43 | 43 | – | 30 | 30 |
| Sadolins | – | – | 20 | 3 | 23 | – | – | – |
| Solignum | 160 | – | – | – | – | – | – | – |

Source: MEAL
 * Regions used:
   Cuprinol – London, Central, Granada HTV, TVS, Anglia
   Sadolins – Ulster only
   Ronseal Wood Preserver – 2 spots only, 1 in Central, 1 in London (possibly a MEAL error)
   Ronseal Varnish – national
 ** Regions used:
   Cuprinol – London, Granada, HTV, TVS, Anglia
   Dulux Woodsheen – national
   Ronseal Wood Preserver – London
   Ronseal Varnish – national

created to enable a thorough assessment to be made of the effectiveness of the advertising. In the event, the ex-factory sales analysis proved to be extremely successful in establishing and quantifying the effect of the advertising.

CONSUMER RESEARCH RESULTS

Questions were placed in the Gallup omnibus survey immediately preceding and following the April–May advertising burst, and again following the second burst in August–September. Each survey was conducted on a nationally representative sample of adults. Fieldwork dates and sample sizes are shown in Table 7. The fact that the advertising was not national allowed the non-advertised areas to be used as a further control for research purposes.

TABLE 7:    CONSUMER SURVEY DETAILS 1983 (SAMPLE SIZES)

| | fieldwork dates | | |
|---|---|---|---|
| | pre-advertising 14–19 April | 1st post-advertising 25–30 May | 2nd post-advertising 21–16 September |
| advertising (test areas) | 710 | 702 | 607 |
| non-advertised (control) areas | 258 | 265 | 395 |

Five questions were asked: on spontaneous and prompted brand awareness, spontaneous and prompted advertising awareness, and on the content of the advertisements. The results given below are for all adults questioned, except where stated.

Spontaneous brand awareness rose from 23 per cent to 35 per cent after the first burst, and again marginally to 36 per cent after the second burst in the test areas. These results are for the areas common to both Cuprinol advertising bursts for true comparative purposes. In Central, which had advertising in the first burst only, awareness doubled from 16 per cent to 32 per cent before falling back to 23 per cent. Despite the relatively small sample base for this one area, these results provide added confirmation of the advertising effects. Although there was an increase from 13 per cent to 19 per cent in the non-advertised areas, due probably to seasonal factors, this fell after the second burst to 15 per cent.

Apart from the generic creosote, with a spontaneous awareness of around 15 per cent throughout the surveys, Ronseal was the only brand to show significant awareness. A comparison of Cuprinol and Ronseal performance is given in Figure 5. Clearly the general Ronseal advertising contributed to the awareness levels for Ronseal Wood Preserver, but the dominant position achieved by Cuprinol after the advertising is clear.

The achievement against the target demographic groups is shown in Table 8. This is available only for the national analysis, combining both advertised and non-advertised areas, but the greater penetration amongst C2s and the youngest age group is obvious.

TABLE 8:    SPONTANEOUS CUPRINOL AWARENESS

|  | national % | 16–24 % | 35–44 % | ABC1 % | C2 % |
|---|---|---|---|---|---|
| pre-survey | 21 | 8 | 25 | 29 | 22 |
| 1st post-survey | 29 | 19 | 40 | 34 | 31 |
| 2nd post-survey | 28 | 18 | 41 | 36 | 39 |

Prompted brand awareness showed a slightly different pattern, with almost all brands showing an increase after the first burst, but falling back somewhat after the second; as this was true also of the commodity creosote it may be presumed to be evidence of seasonal interest levels. But whereas in the non-advertised areas Cuprinol showed a fall back to the level of the pre-survey after the second burst, in the advertised areas awareness remained at 62 per cent compared with the pre-survey 55 per cent after peaking at 68 per cent following the first burst. Comparison with Ronseal is shown in Figure 6, and this further demonstrates the impact of the Cuprinol advertising. Interestingly, Dulux Wood-sheen also showed a fall in prompted awareness at the second survey, from 17 per cent to 12 per cent nationally despite the heavy advertising.

Advertising awareness confirmed the effectiveness of the Cuprinol campaign with spontaneous awareness of the advertising rising from 3 per cent to 18 per cent in the advertised areas after the first burst and still further to 20 per cent following the second burst. This compared with 2 per cent to 6 per cent to 3 per cent in the non-advertised areas. Conversely, awareness of Ronseal advertising fell over the period and was significantly below Cuprinol in both post-surveys despite being well above in the pre-survey, (see Figure 7). There was virtually no awareness of any other brand advertising.

In terms of *prompted* advertising awareness, Cuprinol moved from 7 per cent to 26 per cent to 30 per cent in the advertised areas (see Figure 8), marginally overtaking Ronseal. In the non-advertised areas the results were 8 per cent to 10 per cent to 6 per cent.

More significant, however, were the findings from the communication question. Asked

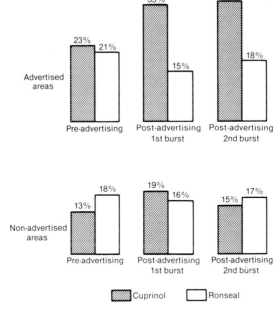

Figure 5. *Spontaneous brand awareness*

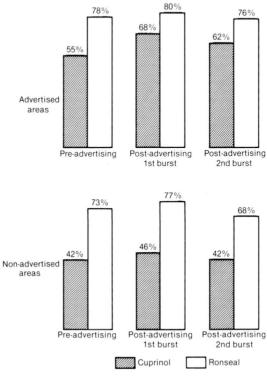

Figure 6. *Prompted brand awareness*

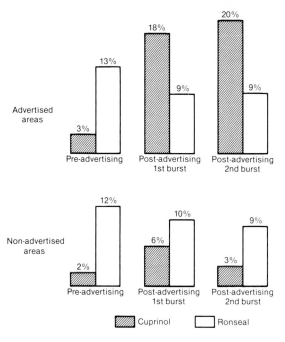

Figure 7. *Spontaneous advertising awareness*

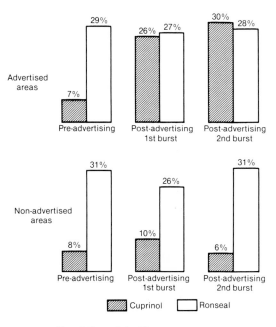

Figure 8. *Prompted advertising awareness*

what they thought the advertising was trying to say about the product, those who claimed to have seen the advertising gave the replies shown in Table 9.

TABLE 9:    CONSUMERS' RECALL OF CUPRINOL ADVERTISEMENT

|  | post 1 | post 2 |
|---|---|---|
| preserves wood | 40 | 45 |
| best on market | 18 | 17 |
| soaks into wood | 11 | 12 |
| cat/fence/etc | 5 | 11 |

No other comments were made by more than 5 per cent of respondents. These findings confirm that the objectives outlined by the creative strategy were being achieved.

*The Sales Analysis*

The examination of the sales response was undertaken to establish in strict statistical terms the proof that advertising had been a significant factor in generating sales, to quantify the magnitude of that effect, and thereby to aid future advertising planning.

In simple terms, the fact that there had been a considerable volume increase in 1983 was very clear (Table 10). Volume sales were 17.5 per cent up on the previous year in the context of a broadly static picture over the previous 10 years. Part of this increase can be accounted for by the promotion to the trade of the forthcoming TV campaign, resulting in a sell-in during February 60 per cent above the previous year. Restocking in the secondary September–November season averaged an increase of 38 per cent over 1982, implying strongly that the advertising had indeed succeeded in stimulating consumer demand. In the opinion of the Cuprinol company, though some of these sales represent increased distribution and an improvement in brand share, the sale of the increase coupled with the increased efforts of competitors can only be explained on the assumption that the total market also expanded, at least in the short term.

TABLE 10:    CUPRINOL ANNUAL VOLUME SALES INDEX

| 1974 | 100 |
|---|---|
| 1975 | 103 |
| 1976 | 103 |
| 1977 | 100 |
| 1978 | 112 |
| 1979 | 116 |
| 1980 | 102 |
| 1981 | 108 |
| 1982 | 106 |
| 1983 | 125 |
| 1984 (Jan–Jun) | 143 |

The most recent evidence – for the first half of 1984 – confirms this rejuvenation in response to a maintenance of the high level of advertising spend employed in 1983. This conclusively shows that the sales effect was not simply a stocking-up by the trade but represented a massive stimulus to the demand for Cuprinol.

To quantify the extent to which advertising had contributed to this success within the overall mix of economic and marketing forces on the brand, computer-based mathematical models of Cuprinol sales performance were developed. This work was performed in conjunction with Chase Econometrics Interactive Data Corporation and involved both pure statistical and econometric approaches to the evaluation.

The lack of long-term monthly sales series dictated that the econometric model be based on the annual data from 1974. Detailed data existed, however, from 1980 and this was used to develop a short-term forecasting model for producing an alternative, simple statistical view of the magnitude of the advertising influence in 1983.

### THE SHORT-TERM SALES FORECASTING MODEL

The monthly sales data from 1980–82 was used to develop a simple forecasting model based on the seasonal and trend factors derived from a State-Space statistical analysis. This technical procedure automatically analysed the past data to establish the best statistical model underlying the sales pattern, and this was then used to forecast monthly sales in 1983. No other factors were used in these forecasts other than the past sales data.

A comparison of the resulting overall forecast for 1983 with the actual volume achieved enabled a simple estimate to be made of the excess volume generated in 1983 over that expected on the basis of the broad parameters prevailing in 1980–82. The actual monthly sales pattern for 1980–82 and the resulting forecasts for 1983 together with the actual sales achieved in 1983 are shown in Figure 9.

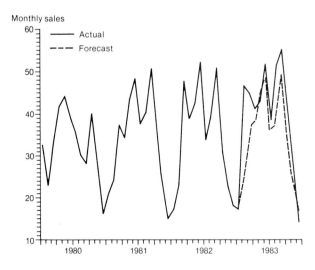

Figure 9. *The short-term forecasting model*

The resulting annual picture is shown in Table 11 with the estimates from the model for 1980–82 serving as a guide to the accuracy of the model. Thus the model forecast a slight increase in 1983 compared to 1982, against an actual increase considerably greater than this.

This simplistic approach ignores specific external factors and estimates sales solely on the basis of the sales picture in 1980–82. It shows the magnitude of the additional volume

TABLE 11:    CUPRINOL VOLUMES (1980-83)
(INDEXED TO 1980 ACTUAL = 100)

|                | 1980 | 1981 | 1982 | 1983 |
|----------------|------|------|------|------|
| actual         | 100  | 106  | 104  | 122  |
| model estimate | 106  | 106  | 104  | 105 (forecast) |
| 1983 actual vs. forecast: + 16% | | | | |

generated in 1983 above what would otherwise have been expected, the model suggesting the former to be 16 per cent. This is the difference between the actual sales and the statistical forecast. Essentially, Cuprinol was growing very slowly in sales terms according to this model, and the majority of the actual 17.5 per cent increase over 1982 was therefore due to the changed activity in 1983. As only the advertising changed materially in this year it is strong circumstantial evidence for a significant advertising effect. This is proven in detailed terms in the next section, where the magnitude of the specific advertising influence is estimated.

THE ECONOMETRIC MODEL

As stated earlier, this analysis was restricted to annual data. However, there are considerable advantages in using annual data for a product like Cuprinol which has very marked seasonality both in sales and correspondingly in advertising. Spurious correlations can often be obtained with such seasonality and great statistical care needs to be employed in developing valid models of a quarterly or monthly nature in these circumstances. Furthermore, the treatment of the advertising variable is also more complex, necessitating account to be taken of the carry-over effect from one period to another. In annual models it is usually possible to ignore carry-over effects, as they have been in this exercise. The disadvantage is simply that there may be insufficient observations of insufficient precision to enable a statistically meaningful analysis to be completed. On this occasion the data was such that a very satisfactory model was achieved that explained a high level (86 per cent) of the sales movements over the ten year period in terms of a few key economic and marketing variables.

In general, the simpler the model the better, and the Cuprinol model was simple, but effective. Annual volume changes were related in a regression model to three consumer influences on consumption, namely:

1.   The real price of Cuprinol, ie the price relative to the Consumer Price Index.
2.   Total real personal consumer expenditure in the country.
3.   The real annual Cuprinol advertising spend, ie after allowing for media inflation.

The exact form of the model is given in the Appendix.

The movement of these variables over the ten year period and the corresponding variation in Cuprinol sales (indexed to 1974) are shown in Figure 10. All three variables were statistically significant in explaining sales movements. Other variables, such as a time trend, were tried but found to be not statistically significant. The model was examined for robustness with regard to different mathematical formulations and different time periods, and was seen to be satisfactory.

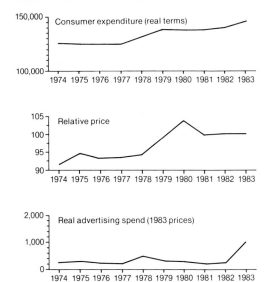

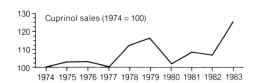

Figure 10. *The econometric model: Cuprinol regression variables*

The model was very sound on all the usual statistical criteria, and the extent to which it explained sales movements can be seen in Figure 11 where the model estimated sales (fitted) are plotted with the actual.

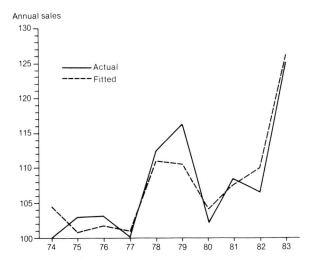

Figure 11. *The econometric model: Cuprinol actual and fitted (1974 = 100)*

To understand the importance of each factor in marketing terms the sensitivity of sales changes to the three influencing factors was calculated in terms of 'elasticities'. These express the percentage change in sales caused by a 1 per cent change in the factors and are summarised in Table 12. This means that a 1 per cent increase in the price of Cuprinol relative to general inflation reduces volume by 1.01 per cent, whereas a 1 per cent increase in total real consumer expenditure in the country raises volume by 1.35 per cent. Similarly a 1 per cent increase in real advertising spend raises volume by 0.06 per cent. Although this may seem small, because of the relative magnitudes of advertising and sales over the ten year period advertising can be seen to have more than paid for itself and to have been a major factor in the expansion of sales in 1983.

TABLE 12:    CUPRINOL VOLUME ELASTICITIES

| | |
|---|---|
| price | −1.01 |
| consumer expenditure | +1.35 |
| advertising | +0.06 |

Using the model to simulate the effect of different advertising spends it was possible to quantify the impact of the additional advertising in 1983. This showed that the increase in spend in 1983 over 1982 of approximately £0.8 million gave an estimated 10 per cent volume gain, purely from the advertising. This represented a revenue figure well in excess of the cost of the advertising.

In overall volume growth terms the model estimate and actual changes were in broad agreement, namely:

*1983 Growth Comparison*
actual:              +17.5%
model estimate:   +15%    – 5% from consumer expenditure
                            – 10% from advertising
                            – nil from price effect (real price constant 1982 vs. 1983)

Interestingly the overall 15 per cent growth predicted by the econometric model in 1983 is close to the 16 per cent 'excess' growth estimated from the purely statistical approach, and this provides added confirmation of the change brought about by the advertising.

Further analysis suggests that the heavy advertising in 1983 reduced the average advertising impact per £, which is likely to be partly due to diminishing returns as advertising spend is increased and partly to consumers only partially 'adjusting' to their new demand expectations. The latter suggests that there is likely to be some carry-over of the advertising impact into 1984. This is borne out by the first half-year sales results which are somewhat above the levels predicted by the model, despite allowing for the continued heavy advertising into 1984.

The overall conclusion from the econometric work is that the advertising played a major part in the rapid growth in Cuprinol sales in 1983 and that the increases more than paid for the cost of the advertising. The greater understanding of the brand dynamics with regard to price, advertising and the external economic forces will play a significant role in leading to more profitable brand management in the future.

## APPENDIX

*The Econometric Model*

The linear form of the demand model is given by:

$$S_t = c_o + c_1 E_t + c_2 P_t + c_3 A_t$$

where:

$S_t$      = Cuprinol volume (ex-factory litres) in year t, indexed to 1974 = 100
$c_o$      = a constant
$E_t$      = real aggregate consumer expenditure (in constant 1980 prices)
$P_t$      = relative price of Cuprinol, ie Cuprinol price deflated by the retail price index
$A_t$      = real Cuprinol advertising expenditure, ie total press and TV expenditure (MEAL) deflated by the AA index of media rates
$c_1, c_2, c_3$ = coefficients of the demand equation representing the impact of each factor on volume

This equation was also estimated in log form (each of the variables $S_t$, $E_t$, $P_t$ and $A_t$ expressed in logs), which produced slightly more statistically significant results for each of the individual factors, but very similar overall conclusions. As a result the log form was principally used in the advertising evaluation work.

The two sets of results are shown below, where for comparative purposes the elasticities of demand are presented, and the close agreement between the two approaches is evident.

*Equation Statistics (1974–83 data)*

|                       | linear | log  |
|-----------------------|--------|------|
| Corrected $R^2$       | 0.80   | 0.80 |
| Durbin-Watson         | 2.05   | 2.36 |

| coefficient         | elasticity | | t-statistic | |
|---------------------|--------|--------|--------|--------|
|                     | linear | log    | linear | log    |
| $C_1$ (expenditure) | +1.33  | +1.35  | 2.5    | 2.7    |
| $C_2$ (price)       | −1.00  | −1.01  | −1.6   | −1.7   |
| $C_3$ (advertising) | +0.04  | +0.06  | 1.9    | 2.0    |

# 13

# Kraft Dairylea: The Transformation of a Brand's Fortunes

## BUSINESS BACKGROUND

### The Company

Kraft Foods Ltd. is the UK operating division of one of the largest food manufacturing companies in the USA. They have substantial international businesses in most major markets. In the UK, Kraft market a range of cheeses (including Dairylea, Philadelphia, Singles and Slices), margarines, salad dressings and frozen foods.

### The Brand

Since its launch in 1950, Dairylea has been the leading brand of processed cheese spread in the UK. It has always been sold in its distinctive presentation of six triangular cheeses in a round box. A tub presentation was launched in 1977. The product is a distinctive, mild, creamy cheese, much enjoyed by children and adults alike. Dairylea is Kraft UK's biggest brand and major profit earner.

### The Market and Competition

The market for processed cheese spreads was estimated to be £50 million at retail selling price in 1983. The main branded competition to Kraft comes from Primula, a range of

TABLE 1:  PROCESSED CHEESE HOUSEHOLD
CONSUMPTION

|  | *oz. per person per week* |
|---|---|
| 1975 | 0.28 |
| 1976 | 0.29 |
| 1977 | 0.24 |
| 1978 | 0.23 |
| 1979 | 0.23 |
| 1980 | 0.23 |
| 1981 | 0.24 |
| 1982 | 0.25 |
| 1983 | 0.24 |

Source: National Food Survey

products in tubes. Other manufacturer brands represented are Rowntree Mackintosh, Kerrygold and Gold Spinner from St. Ivel. More recently many own-label and imported brands, all under-cutting Dairylea on price, have been introduced.

The National Food Survey shows processed cheese consumption in gradual decline, stabilising in the late 1970s (see Table 1).

There are two further sources of competition for processed cheese spreads in general and Dairylea in particular:

1.  Natural cheeses – consumption of which grew by 10 per cent between 1975 and 1983, in particular the non-cheddar varieties such as Edam and soft white cheeses.
2.  All other spreads such as meat and fish pastes, pâtés, Bovril and Marmite, vegetable spreads and jam. There is no evidence of any growth in this area since 1975.

## THE PROBLEM

### *Business*

From 1973 to 1980, sales of Dairylea were in consistent long-term decline. Every year ex-factory sales showed a fall, until in 1980 ex-factory tonnage was 64.3% of the 1973 level. Consequently the historical margins on the brand were being squeezed, and increasingly trade dealing was further undermining the brand's profitability. Figure 1 shows Dairylea sales over the period 1975–80.

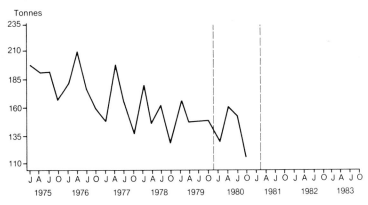

Figure 1. *Quarterly ex-factory sales all Dairylea (tonnes) — actual (indexed)*

A number of factors were at work. Mathematical analysis indicated that two key factors affecting Dairylea sales were:

#### DECLINING BREAD SALES

The bulk of Dairylea consumed is spread on bread. Bread consumption, on the basis again of the National Food Survey, showed a consistent decline from 1973–78 before stabilising. In 1980 consumption was 93% of the 1973 level. Figure 2 shows the trend in bread consumption over the period 1975–83.

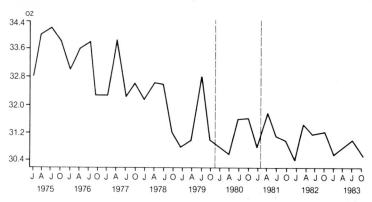

Figure 2. *Quarterly domestic bread consumption: ounces per person per week*

*Source:* National Food Survey

The jump in 1979 is related, we believe, to the increase of one million children switching to packed lunches as the prices of school meals rose. The subsequent period of stabilisation was heralded by the generic advertising campaign for bread reported on in *Advertising Works 2*.

### LOWER REAL ADVERTISING EXPENDITURE

By 1979–80 Dairylea's level of real advertising expenditure had slipped back markedly (see Table 2). Within the processed cheese spread sector, considerable in-roads were made into Dairylea's market share by price-based competition, particularly St. Ivel Gold-spinner and the many stores' own-label brands introduced.

TABLE 2: 'REAL' DAIRYLEA ADVERTISING EX-PENDITURE AT CARD RATES (MEAL) – DEFLATED BY RPI (ALL ITEMS) 1980 = 100

| year | index |
| --- | --- |
| 1975 | 120 |
| 1976 | 146 |
| 1977 | 131 |
| 1978 | 160 |
| 1979 | 90 |
| 1980 | 100 |

### Identifying the Consumer Problem

Over the period of falling sales Dairylea's penetration had remained remarkably consistent. TGI indicated that the proportion of housewives claiming to buy in the previous six months had remained unchanged at around 42 per cent (see Table 3). Dairylea has remained a brand more likely to be brought by housewives from the C1C2 social grades with children. In 1980, 47 per cent of 'triangles' users and 56 per cent of tubs' buyers were housewives with children, and it was estimated that 66 per cent of total brand

TABLE 3:   DAIRYLEA PENETRATION 1973–80

(Base: all housewives)

|      | %<br>either | %<br>triangle | %<br>tub |
|------|-------------|---------------|----------|
| 1973 | 41.8        |               |          |
| 1974 | 42.4        |               |          |
| 1978 | 41.6        | 38.0          | 6.7      |
| 1980 | 41.4        | 36.4          | 7.2      |

Source: TGI

volume was accounted for by members of households with children in them; 46 per cent of Dairylea servings are to children.

All the qualitative research conducted over this period indicated that Dairylea remained a highly regarded brand. Mothers considered its taste unique, and both attitudinally and in paired comparison product tests it was rated superior to any competitive brand. There was no clear evidence in any of this research that provided a direct indication of what was wrong with Dairylea – the brand was 'drifting' slowly, losing share in a declining market.

There were hints of two further factors recurring in qualitative research:

1.  Saturation in ownership of fridges was completed by the late 1970s and accompanying this was a move towards 'fresher' foods. Fresh, natural cheeses had become cheaper relative to Dairylea. Thus the easy storage of Dairylea ceased to be such an advantage, and its 'processed' quality increasingly a problem, and source of concern.
2.  In the purchase of cheese spreads it seemed that mothers were more prepared to skimp and buy a cheaper brand when the purchase was primarily for the children. 'They'll not notice the difference'.

Other factors of note were:

### THE PRODUCT

Minor formulation problems had taken place over the 1970s. The most significant product change was the introduction of the tub in 1977. This grew to account for 30 per cent of the brand's tonnage by 1980. But it failed to reverse the overall downward trend on the brand.

### PREVIOUS DAIRYLEA ADVERTISING

Dairylea had been advertised throughout the 1970s with a number of different advertising campaigns and a variety of strategies. The period 1974–76 saw the use of TV with two campaigns majoring on the brand's appeal to children. 'Children's Drawings' preceded one set on a stage at a school. A campaign featuring Stratford Johns followed this, and endeavoured to broaden adult consumption of the brand in a change of strategy.

From 1978–80, with budgets under pressure on several Kraft brands, a new approach was adopted for Kraft the company. The campaign used women's magazines primarily,

and featured most Kraft brands in one overall campaign. Dairylea was featured promi-
nently and the brand's budget funded one-third of the campaign. Over and above this a
TV commercial, 'Drum and Triangle', was tested regionally over this period, but with
disappointing results in those areas supported.

## MARKETING STRATEGY

By 1980, Dairylea was at the crossroads. Kraft had to take a decision about Dairylea's
future as a major advertised brand. A complete reappraisal of the brand's performance
and potential was undertaken. A considerable body of qualitative and quantitative research
was reviewed.

The conclusion reached was that Dairylea still had considerable strength and relevance.
Its basic product quality was recognised. Children expressed an overwhelming preference
for it. The brand's history was another strength, for today's mothers remembered the
brand fondly as part of their own childhoods. Its main weakness was that it was seen as
processed, a little artificial in some way, and hence not real food. Nutritionally, mothers
expressed doubts about Dairylea.

The decision was taken to re-present Dairylea in such a way as to capitalise on the
brand's strengths and modify consumers' preceptions so that its mild, pure, dairy-based
virtues and child-appeal predominated over concerns about its processed nature and
perceived artificiality. There were three basic elements involved in this re-presentation:

1. New advertising.
2. A commitment to a higher level of advertising expenditure.
3. A minor revision of the packaging graphics to make them brighter, clearer and more
   impactful.

The marketing objectives were:

— to maintain brand leadership and the price premium, with modest growth in tonnage;
— to achieve growth in sales of the tub in order to compensate for further expected
   decline in triangles' sales.

## ADVERTISING STRATEGY

The advertising strategy developed took the following form:

### Advertising Objectives

1. To increase the frequency of purchase of Dairylea among existing occasional buyers.
2. To build an image for Dairylea as delicious, nutritious, creamy cheese made from
   natural ingredients, which children love.

### Role for Advertising

To remind mothers how much children enjoy Dairylea and to build their impression of
its natural goodness.

## Target Group

Every mother with at least one child between the ages of two and twelve. She is concerned, or likes to think she is concerned, about giving her children the right kind of foods to make them grow up healthy and strong. At the same time, however, it is 'anything for a quiet life' and she will prefer to buy things they ask for, or she knows they like.

## Target Responses

### NOTICE

— Dairylea looks really appetising spread like that. It comes in a tub as well as triangles.

### BELIEVE

— I will be doing the children some good if I give them Dairylea because it is made of good dairy ingredients (butter, milk, cheese).
— If I get some Dairylea in, I can be sure it will get eaten. It is really popular with the kids.
— The tub is a convenient way of serving Dairylea, particularly when they (the kids) are all in together.

### FEEL

— I know that I am giving the children the right sort of food if I give them Dairylea. It is nice to see them tucking into it.

Two commercials have been developed to this strategy. 'On the Farm' ran in 1981 and 1982, and 'Mural', its successor which features the tub, ran in 1983. Storyboards for the two commercials are shown on pages 204–205. Both commercials have key elements in common:

— bright, robust, healthy, lively children enjoying Dairylea together;
— strong links with the farm, cows and outdoor activity;
— illustration of the natural ingredients (butter, milk and cheese) from which Dairylea is made;
— the Dairylea tune and song;
— the Dairylea cow graphic linking with the greater prominence given to this on the revised packs;
— The line 'Kids will eat it till the cows come home', linking with store promotion and displays.

## Media Selection

The final strand of the re-presentation involved increasing the impact and salience of the brand. The advertising set out to be more memorable and intrusive than any previous

# KRAFT dairylea

## "On The Farm"

We are the kids who love our cheese.
And we all love Kraft Dairylea.

So every lunchbox in the land has
its triangle.

And if you've ever wondered how you
get triangles from a cow . . .

Well, you need butter, milk and
cheese and a little bit of time.

For spreading butter, milk and
cheese you can't do better than
choose these.

They taste just great and are good
for you.

That's the triangle!!

MVO:  Kraft Dairylea.  Kids will
eat it till the cows come home.

# KRAFT dairylea
## "Mural"

My tummy says it's time for tea
So let's down tools for Dairylea.

There's enough for him and me and me
A taste of the country.

I like the taste of butter, I like the taste
of cheese, I like the taste of milk.

They're all in Dairylea.

Straight from the tub, our mums have
found there's so much more to spread
around.

It tastes just great
It's good for you

A taste of the country.

MVO:  Kraft Dairylea
Kids will eat it till the cows come home.

Dairylea advertising in order to meet the objective of halting the decline in frequency of purchase among existing users.

TV was the only medium felt to provide this impact, and from 1981–83 has been the sole medium employed. There have been six periods of TV advertising over this period using the new commercials. The results can be seen in Table 4.

TABLE 4: ADVERTISING SCHEDULE

|  | Network TVRs |
| --- | --- |
| 'On the Farm' | |
| April–May 1981 | 786* |
| September–October 1981 | 388* |
| April–June 1982 | 613 |
| September–October 1982 | 382* |
|  | |
| 'Mural' | |
| June–July 1983 | 491 |
| August–October 1983 | 473 |

*These bursts are regional to the extent that they covered only the 70-80 per cent of the country where per capita sales and the penetration of Dairylea buyers were higher, and better media value could be obtained this way.

## RESPONSES TO THE ADVERTISING

### *Qualitative research*

Two major programmes of qualitative research have been undertaken into the new Dairylea campaign. In January 1981, the Consumer Connection conducted eight group discussions with mothers into all elements of the re-presentation of the brand. Their findings relating to an animatic of 'On the Farm' were summarised as:

> Overall this is well received. It was conveying a suitable message and image for Dairylea.

More detailed respondent quotes illustrate this:

> 'That one shows it's good for you, it's the farm aspect – it's natural.'
> 'The dairy product thing is coming through – the cow, the farm.'
> 'They are tough kids, so it doesn't look as if it's for softies.'
> 'That's more what you'd associate Dairylea with – cows, and a little bit of sunshine ... out of doors ... good fresh air.'

And a further four group discussions were conducted by The Qualitative Consultancy into the animatic of 'Mural' in March 1983. Their summary concluded:

> The animatic 'Mural' creates a strong interest among current users and non-users of Kraft Tubs. The healthy children and outdoor setting mean that the product can support an image of healthy good food values and nourishing wholesome ingredients.

Respondents comments were again favourable:

> 'It's made from milk and butter and cheese. Very catchy. It grows on you.'
> 'Fresh and natural and good for you. It appeals to me. It is happy and healthy, everybody's idea of being in the country.'

'I think it's a good advert, very cheerful and entertaining. My children would love that, munching around, fresh air.'

These two pieces of qualitative research into animatics provided invaluable guidance in executing the finished commercials.

### Quantitative Research

Just as the 'Mural' commercial went on air a quantified test was conducted by the market research company RBL, using their pre-testing technique. This involved testing the effectiveness and communication of 'Mural' using comparisons between a test sample of 150 exposed to the commercial, and a similarly sized control sample exposed to the pack only. The findings endorsed the qualitative research. All key measures of the commercial's likely effect – propensity to buy, overall opinion and brand associations – were direction-ally higher among the sample exposed to the commercial. But because of the very high scores recorded among the control sample few differences were statistically significant.

The commercial was found to enhance mothers' image of Dairylea as a dairy product that is liked by and good for children. The research also provided further important reassurance about the tub presentation and the wisdom of featuring only this pack in the new Dairylea commercial.

## EFFECTS ON SALES

The new Dairylea advertising and re-presentation of the brand has had a dramatic effect on sales of the brand. The long-term decline has been reversed. Ex-factory tonnage has grown each year (see Table 5). Ex-factory despatches in 1983 were 21.4 per cent above the low level of 1980. All the additional volume has come from the tub presentation with the rate of decline of the triangle slowed considerably. The issue is whether any factors other than the revised advertising could account for the brand's growth. Distribution and price can be discounted.

TABLE 5:    DAIRYLEA: VOLUME SALES GROWTH

| | |
|---|---|
| 1981 | +10.5% |
| 1982 | + 4.5% |
| 1983 | + 5.1% |

Source: Kraft

1.  Distribution has remained constant. Sterling-weighted distribution of triangles and tubs has not changed (see Table 6).

TABLE 6:    DAIRYLEA: STERLING DISTRIBUTION

| | 1978 | 1982 |
|---|---|---|
| Triangles | 95% | 94% |
| Tubs | 69% | 72% |

Source: Kraft

2. Since 1980, the 'real' ex-factory price of Dairylea has risen much faster than wholesale food prices in general as Figure 3 shows. This is a further significant indication of the increased 'strength' of the brand. Trade dealing and price cutting have been largely eliminated. This increased net sales value of each tonne has been a major contributor to the increased profitability of the brand.

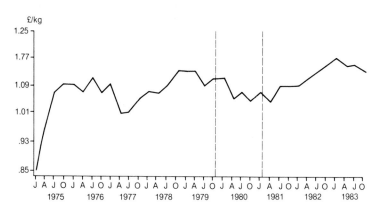

Figure 3. *'Real' ex-factory price of Dairylea (all pack sizes) in £ per kg.*
(= actual current price <u>deflated</u> by Index of Wholesale Prices, Output of Food Manufacturing Industries: Mar 1975 = 100)

## CONSUMER BEHAVIOUR

TGI indicates that six-monthly purchase penetration of the triangles has remained consistent but that of the tub has grown (see Table 7). In consumer terms the increased volume has clearly come from an increased frequency of purchase from existing users, reversing the trend of the 1970s.

TABLE 7:     DAIRYLEA PENETRATION: 1980-83

|      | Triangles %| Tubs % |
|------|-----------|--------|
| 1980 | 36.4 | 7.2 |
| 1981 | 37.9 | 8.9 |
| 1982 | 38.1 | 10.5 |
| 1983 | 36.2 | 10.3 |

Source: BMRB/TGI

## THE VALUE OF THE ADVERTISING

Mathematical modelling has been undertaken to establish the likely level of Dairylea sales, in the absence of the repositioning and change of advertising strategy. The model constructed is explained fully in the Appendix. It suggests that the two key variables determining Dairylea's ex-factory sales are bread consumption and advertising expendi-

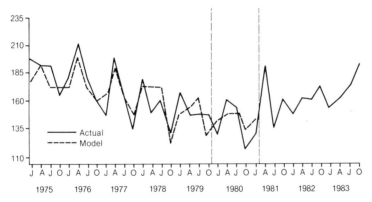

Figure 4. *Quarterly ex-factory sales, all Dairylea (tonnes) indexed*

ture. The model explains 64 per cent of the variance in the Dairylea sales trend over the period 1975–80. Figure 4 shows the fit of the model against actual sales.

From this work, forecasts have been prepared for the period 1981–83 of what Dairylea sales would have been, given the level of bread consumption monitored, and had advertising support been continued at the average real cost level pertaining in 1979–80 and deployed in the same way. These projections indicate that Dairylea sales would have continued to decline, albeit at a slower rate than previously.

In fact Dairylea sales began to rise from the first regional burst in 1981. In all the extra sales (the difference between the projection and those achieved) totalled 13.5 per cent more than those projected over the full period. That tonnage is indicated by the shaded area in Figure 5.

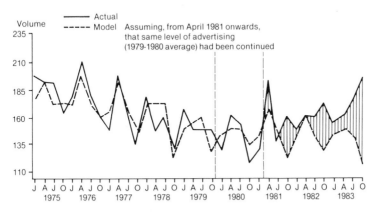

Figure 5. *Quarterly ex-factory sales, all Dairylea (tonnes) indexed*

Over the eleven quarters, the *profits* on that extra tonnage exceeded the total additional advertising cost (above the 1979–80 average level) by a margin of 66 per cent. Thus, the increased advertising investment yielded immediate and substantial extra profits.

Profit levels to Kraft on the brand have increased markedly. Economies of scale of production have been recovered. The increasing strength of the brand has enabled trade discounting and dealing to be cut back. The extra tonnage has been highly profitable

TABLE 8:     DAIRYLEA: 'REAL' PROFITS (1980 = 100)

| | |
|---|---|
| 1979 | 110 |
| 1980 | 100 |
| 1981 | 49 |
| 1982 | 104 |
| 1983 | 185 |

Source: Kraft

tonnage to Kraft for these reasons. Indeed an index of the profits (in 'real' terms) gained from Dairylea by Kraft shows the following trend (see Table 8). As a result of the re-presentation Dairylea has been transformed in three years, and should now continue to be Kraft's major brand and profit earner for the rest of the decade. In 1979 this seemed unlikely.

### The Future

It is planned to continue this successful strategy on Dairylea. Two national waves of advertising are envisaged each year. A first burst in 1984 has resulted in a further sales uplift of 12 per cent, in March and April, over 1983 levels.

A third commercial developing the successful key elements of 'On the Farm' and 'Mural' is planned for 1985 to avoid any problem with wear-out resulting from over-exposure.

## CONCLUSIONS

1.  A number of key elements in the advertising and marketing mix have worked together. The new creative approach has worked in combination with the higher level of support, the solus use of TV, and the revised pack graphics. In our view the transformation of the brand's fortunes would not have been possible without the new advertising content.
2.  It is also our view that advertising was the only variable in the marketing mix which could both reverse the long-term sales decline *and* at the same time translate the additional investment into a significant improvement in the brand's profits in three years.
3.  More importantly the new advertising approach has achieved three years of sustained growth for a brand which in 1980 appeared to be in a state of terminal decline. At that time Dairylea was in danger of suffering further cut-backs in support and being 'milked' for profits. In this respect, and at a broader level, this study calls into question any over-ready acceptance of brand life-cycle theories.

## APPENDIX

The model of Dairylea ex-factory sales volume referred to in the text was based on a multiple regression analysis of data from 25 quarterly periods beginning with January, 1975 and ending in March, 1981.

The equation was of the form:

$$Y = a + b_1 X_1 + b_2 X_2 + b_3 X_3 + b_4 X_4 + b_5 X_5$$

where:

$Y$ (the 'dependent' variable) = quarterly ex-factory sales of Dairylea (all pack sizes), in tonnes.

$X_1$ = domestic bread consumption, in ounces per person per week (source: National Food Survey).

$X_2$ = quarterly advertising expenditure for Dairylea in £000 at card rates (source: MEAL), *deflated* by the Index of Retail Prices (all items), January 1984 = 100.

$X_3$, $X_4$ $X_5$ were 'dummy' variables for the first, second and third quarters of each year respectively. (Each of these variables had the value of 1 in the relevant quarter and 0 in other quarters).

'a' was a constant derived from the analysis and $b_1$ $b_2$ ... $b_5$ were 'regression co-efficients' expressing (in tonnes) the average volume of Dairylea associated with each unit of the variable concerned.

The technical details of the equation are as follows:

| variable | coefficient (tonnes indexed) | t-value |
|---|---|---|
| $X_1$ bread consumption | 139.8 | 5.2 |
| $X_2$ real ad-expenditure | 1.267 | 2.0 |
| $X_3$ 1st quarter | 216.8 | 2.7 |
| $X_4$ 2nd quarter | 177.5 | 2.0 |
| $X_5$ 3rd quarter | 71.7 | 0.8 |
| a (constant term) | −3106.9 | −3.6 |

The adjusted value of $R^2$ (the proportion of the variance 'explained' by the equation) was 0.64.

In using the model to 'predict' the levels which Dairylea sales *would* have taken in each quarter from April 1981 to December 1983 if the new campaign launched in April 1981 had *not* been undertaken, the assumption was made that throughout this period 'real' advertising expenditure (at January 1974 prices) in each quarter was at the average levels which it had reached in 1979–80, namely: 1st quarter, £23 000; 2nd quarter, £101 000; 3rd quarter, £71 000; 4th quarter, £15 000. The levels of bread consumption used in the prediction were the actual levels, taken from the National Food Survey.

# 14

# Kellogg's Coco Pops:
# A 'Storybook' Success

## BACKGROUND

Kellogg's Coco Pops was launched in 1960 into the ready-to-eat (RTE) cereal market, as a speciality-appeal brand for children. Like many children's cereals, Coco Pops is a 'pre-sweetened' cereal containing added sugar. These 'pre-sweetened' cereals are a valuable market sector, accounting in 1983 for 11.4 per cent of the £350 million RTE market. Large brand franchises have been built in this sector, namely: Kellogg's Frosties and Quaker's Sugar Puffs. In addition to Frosties and Coco Pops, Kellogg's have three other children's 'pre-sweetened' brands: Ricicles, Smacks and Puffa Puffa Rice.

During the first ten years of Coco Pops' life, the child appeal cereals enjoyed volume increases which maintained their share of an expanding market. By the 1970s however, all cereals appealing to children were vulnerable to the negative pressure of a falling child population and hence a decline in children's consumption of cereals. During the 1970s, cereals with added sugar had been under even greater pressure as consumption studies conducted amongst all age groups indicated a slight shifting of consumer preference towards *un*sweetened cereals.

Throughout this period, it was Frosties that occupied the major part of the Kellogg Company attention in this sector and the brand was supported over the years with high levels of TV advertising. Other large children's brands from both Kellogg's and their major competitors also enjoyed strong TV support and traditionally it has always been a very 'noisy' market. By contrast, Coco Pops and two of the three other Kellogg 'pre-sweetened' cereals saw activity in a much lower key. Too small to be able to afford TV budgets, they were supported over many years by shared pack promotions advertised intermittently in children's press.

Children are known to be a notoriously fickle target group: 'faddish' about food, they can be strongly motivated to ask for a particular product through involving advertising. It is not surprising therefore that in a period of adverse pressure, and with little exposure, it was these smaller 'pre-sweetened' brands which diminished in their importance to consumers.

And not only to consumers: there were major problems too on the trade front, as retailers were faced with a proliferation of new cereal products and were continually forced to rationalise the number of brands vying for shelf space. Time after time the casualty list included one or more of the three smallest, virtually unsupported, brands.

Ricicles, being a slightly larger brand, held its position, but, in short, the three smallest brands were falling from consumer consciousness and becoming less available as distribution became patchy.

### The Marketing Decision

By 1981 their position was causing increasing concern and the prognosis was pessimistic unless major action was taken to reverse the downward trend. (By the beginning of 1981, the GB sterling distribution of Coco Pops, for example, had dropped to only 50 per cent against an average level of 79 per cent for most major cereal brands - NIELSEN).

At that time, several pieces of strategic and qualitative research conducted across Kellogg's brands were suggesting that a change in parental attitude appeared to be underway. It seemed that parents were demonstrating a greater readiness to indulge their children by paying a bit extra for food and snacks regarded by their children as 'treats'. Parents appeared more willing to provide the cereals their children asked for - including relatively more expensive, 'pre-sweetened' brands.

This encouraged us to believe that consumer demand could be rekindled for this type of product if only availability could be improved. With distribution falling as de-stocking became more widespread, the moment for activating this market sector had arrived.

### The Marketing Objectives

The objectives for this action were defined as follows:
1. To stimulate consumer demand in order to build a significant 'pre-sweetened' child brand which would underpin the successful Frosties franchise.
2. To reverse the trend of distribution loss by demonstrating the Kellogg Company commitment to the smaller pre-sweetened cereals, thereby encouraging the trade to restock.

Both objectives were to be achieved without loss of profitability to the reactivated brand or brands.

## STRATEGIC PLANNING

We believed the most efficient use of new investment in this sector to be the strong support of *one* of the range rather than diffusing effort over three brands. The question was, which one?

In each case the potential for volume growth through distribution gains was clear: all three brands had considerable ground to be regained, whilst retaining a sufficient base from which to rebuild.

One brand, Smacks, was rejected because its product characteristics were similar to an already well-established, competitive brand. The possibility of creating the necessary level of product interest amongst both trade and consumers was considered to be severely reduced without very large levels of investment.

Of the two remaining brands, Coco Pops held sterling distribution at a marginally higher level and, more importantly, had maintained a higher rate of sale than its companion brand. Despite the pressure on distribution, Coco Pops clearly held an intrinsic attraction for some consumers. The product itself was the most distinctive and motivating advantage for Coco Pops. Cereals made from sweetened puffed rice, such as this, were much enjoyed by children, but this was toasted, puffed rice with an important difference – it was chocolate-flavoured! We knew children found its chocolatey flavour delicious and the product great fun. Together with the noise and play qualities of the much more famous Rice Krispies, Coco Pops turned milk a light brown, chocolatey colour.

So Coco Pops' product difference was judged to offer the greatest potential for building Kellogg's business in this sector. It also provided the opportunity for advertising which was capable of stimulating interest and demand from both the child target audience and the retail trade.

*Media Selection*

Kellogg's and J. Walter Thompson knew that the effort needed to change the fortunes of the brand would be considerable in every way. There were two layers within our target group: Coco Pops' appeal was strongest among *children* under nine years, and this meant we would need the tacit approval of their *mothers* who, of course, actually *buy* the cereals. Of major importance too was the need for the trade to see the level of Kellogg's commitment to the brand and respond appropriately in widening distribution and building stocks. Without strong impact behind the advertising against these two very different groups (children and mothers), we could not expect to achieve our objectives.

Quite simply, we needed the impact of TV. This was chosen because it provided a unified stimulus of words and pictures – necessary to motivate children to remember and ask for Coco Pops. They would often view with their mothers who would also see the advertising and this medium had already proved its effectiveness for other child cereal brands. TV would also benefit us by providing the strongest possible evidence to the trade that the Kellogg Company was prepared to make a serious investment for growth in this market sector.

## ADVERTISING STRATEGY AND EXECUTION

We defined the role of the advertising as needing to tell children (and their mothers) that Coco Pops are delicious and fun. We knew that we should communicate this in an inventive, playful way that could develop Coco Pops as a child-like personality.

Qualitative testing of two different advertising approaches with children, in the summer of 1981, led to production of 'Storybook'. The film was executed with simple and colourful animated graphics throughout, accompanied by a cheerful rhyming tune. The entire 30-second commercial played with rhymes based upon the brand name so that 'Storybook' became an involving game – in a learning idiom familiar to children (see page 216 and 217).

It is worth noting that, although launched in 1960 as Coco Pops, the brand was renamed Coco Krispies in 1966 and remained so until our decision to revert to the original name for the 1981 relaunch. Our reasons were two-fold:

1.  We wished to establish a separate identity for this brand, distinct from the established puffed-rice product – Rice Krispies.

2. 'Pops' would communicate the 'explosive', fun qualities of the product more effectively.

This change of name and a new pack were designed to strengthen Coco Pops' appeal and it is likely that they did so, although we could not have expected to quantify their effect.

In order to test consumer and trade responses to renewed investment in Coco Pops without investing funds at the high level needed for national support, we decided initially to advertise the brand in just two areas. This would enable the campaign performance to be evaluated in terms of rate of sale, distribution and volume sales. Volume and profit forecasts could then be made for the longer-term potential.

If these projections were favourable, we planned to roll out the advertising into a further area or areas, and ultimately it was hoped that Coco Pops' performance would warrant national advertising support.

### Area Choice

The areas selected to test the brand's potential were London and Anglia.

London was chosen principally because its size allowed for readings built upon a large base. As such, it also demanded high investment which demonstrated to the grocery trade the Kellogg intention to build this market sector. In addition to this, the nature of the grocery trade in London and Anglia included a stronger-than-average representation of own-label cereals. As a unique product, with no own-label equivalent, Coco Pops could contribute to total Kellogg Company success in these strongly competitive areas.

'Storybook' went on air in London and Anglia in mid-October 1981 for six weeks, followed by a further six weeks in early 1982 (Figure 1).

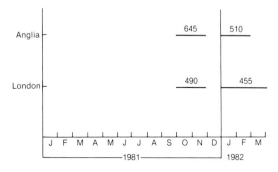

Figure 1. *Television advertising first six months (30 second child TVRs)*

## EVALUATING THE EFFECT

### The First Six Months

The effect on trade distribution was immediate in the two test areas. The grocery trade appeared to be impressed with Kellogg's evident determination to rebuild brand sales and responded accordingly. The Kellogg sales force reported an 'outstanding' response to the advertising activity and the Nielsen audit of bi-monthly regional sterling distribution bore

# KELLOGG'S COCO POPS
## "STORYBOOK"
### 30 seconds
© 1981 Kellogg Co.

| | | |
|---|---|---|
| **1** Coco Pops | **2** Spinning Tops | **3** Coco Pops |
| **4** Pit Stops | **5** Snow Drops | **6** Chocolate flavour ... Coco Pops |
| **7** Clippety Clops | **8** Bunny Hops | **9** Balloon ...... |

# KELLOGG'S COCO POPS
## "STORYBOOK"

*(continued)*

**10** Pops

**11** Milk Drops ... on ... **12** Coco Pops

**13** Jack in the Box

**14** Mrs Mops

**15** Mr Spocks

**16** Keystone Kops

**17** But nothing tops

**18** Kellogg's Coco Pops

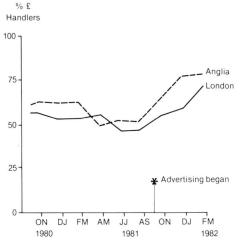

Figure 2. *Coco Pops regional distribution*
*Source:* Nielsen

this out. London and Anglia recorded distribution levels and volume sales significantly higher than the national pattern. In the period preceding advertising, August–September 1981, Coco Pops held 48 per cent sterling distribution in the London area. Six months after advertising began, in February–March 1982, this level had risen to 73 per cent. The same rate of distribution increase was seen in Anglia, where it rose from 52 per cent to 79 per cent. (Figure 2).

Figure 3 demonstrates that, as hypothesised, the intrinsic consumer appeal of Coco Pops did show itself during the year before advertising - particularly in London. However, when advertising began and distribution widened, sales in both the test areas rose dramatically.

During the first six months of TV advertising, Nielsen's bi-monthly audit of the tonnage sold by region reported sudden increases. London showed a 79 per cent increase

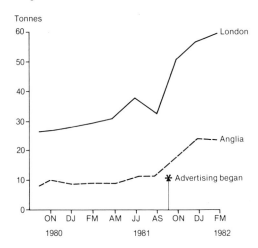

Figure 3. *Coco Pops volume sales*
*Source:* Nielsen

from 120 000 packets just before advertising, to 210 000 packets in February–March 1982. The rise in Anglia was even higher at 92 per cent, from 43 000 to 82 000 packets.

### Rolling Out

At this stage, the results provided strong encouragement to extend the advertising into a third area and we chose Yorkshire, developing a large area in the North.

Yet again the sales force reported a positive response from the grocery trade and strong in-store displays for Coco Pops. Just prior to the start of advertising, the brand's distribution level was 58 per cent in Yorkshire. Six months and two bursts (12 weeks) of TV advertising later, it had risen to 72 per cent (Figure 4).

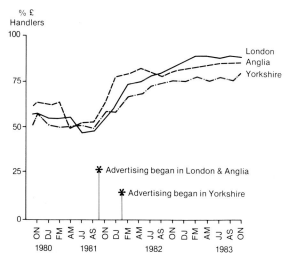

Figure 4. *Coco Pops regional distribution*
*Source:* Nielsen

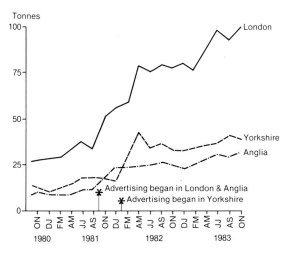

Figure 5. *Coco Pops volume sales*
*Source:* Nielsen

In Yorkshire, consumer response to 'Storybook' and to the increased distribution was even greater than it had been in London and Anglia during their first six months of activity. Yorkshire showed a 119 per cent increase in volume sales (Figure 5).

London and Anglia continued to show encouraging results: with London still gaining in distribution and volume sales, and Anglia maintaining its growth. In July and August 1982 all three areas were given a further burst of TV advertising to continue the growth momentum (Figure 6).

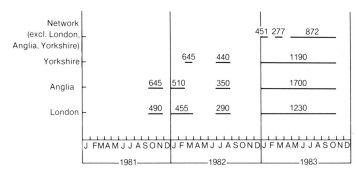

Figure 6. *Television advertising 1981 — 83 (30 second child TVRs)*

## First Year Evaluation

### RATE OF SALE

In Coco Pops' first year of advertising, the London and Anglia distribution drive successfully brought about by the Kellogg sales team translated into a strong consumer response.

Comparison of the monthly tonnage sold per point of sterling distribution for the years before and after advertising had begun, showed that monthly sales rose by 66 per cent and 50 per cent in London and Anglia respectively. This provided strong evidence that the advertising appeared to be working and in the same period, even Yorkshire (which began its advertising later) showed a 33 per cent increase (Table 1).

TABLE 1:   REGIONAL RATE OF SALE

| | | year ending | |
| Coco Pops average monthly sales: | Aug–Sep 1981 | Aug–Sep 1982 (tonnes per %£ handling) | Aug–Sep 1983 |
| --- | --- | --- | --- |
| London | 0.6 | 1.0 | 1.0 |
| Anglia | 0.2 | 0.3 | 0.3 |
| Yorkshire | 0.3 | 0.4 | 0.5 |

Source: Nielsen

*National Extension*

This 1982 growth convinced Kellogg's and JWT that Coco Pops' TV support should be extended nationally in 1983. We established 'Storybook' in all the new areas with two introductory bursts in January and March 1983, at a higher rate than in the first three areas. Following that, the newly advertised areas joined London, Anglia and Yorkshire in a pattern of continuous airtime support until the end of October (Figure 6). For the originally advertised areas we produced a 30-second follow-up film to 'Storybook', in the same style, called 'Chapter 2'.

The result of this investment was strong distribution and sales volume growth in every area of the country. By the end of 1983, national distribution of Coco Pops had reached 75 per cent (a 34-point increase on the period prior to regional advertising). Volume sales for Great Britain had very nearly trebled and the GB rate of sale – the hard test of consumer response – increased as Table 2 shows.

TABLE 2:   COCO POPS AVERAGE MONTHLY SALES (GB)

|  | | year ending: | |
| --- | --- | --- | --- |
|  | Aug–Sep 1981 | Aug–Sep 1982 | Aug–Sep 1983 |
| tonnes per %£ handling | 2.5 | 3.6 | 4.4 |

Source: Nielsen

Between 1981 and 1983, Coco Pops' volume share of the RTE cereal market rose from 0.4 per cent to 1.0 per cent, in a total market growth of 8.7 per cent and its sterling share rose from 1.0 per cent to 1.7 per cent – NIELSEN.

## HAD THE ADVERTISING CAUSED COCO POPS' SUCCESS?

Naturally, we were delighted with this performance. But could we be sure that the advertising was the significant factor in Coco Pops' success? Certainly the results were very marked and coincided with the objectives and timing of our activity. Nevertheless, could we be sure:

— that these results were unique to Coco Pops and not simply the effect of a wider trend in consumer preference back to the more specialised 'pre-sweetened' brands?
— that if they were unique, they were not wholly cannibalistic of other Kellogg brands?
— that this increase in brand popularity was not caused by other factors, such as a relative price reduction for Coco Pops?

Having examined these possibilities, we were sure. The other small 'pre-sweetened' brands started 1981 in similar circumstances to Coco Pops. When their performances were examined over the same period (as in Figures 7 & 8), it was clear that Coco Pops' sales and distribution success had taken place against the downward trend of the unsupported brands.

Importantly, as Table 3 indicates, Coco Pops' rate of sale increased from 1981 to 1983,

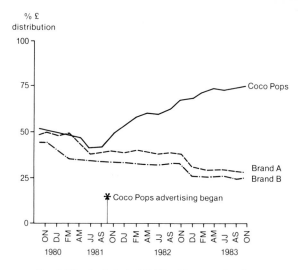

Figure 7. *GB sterling distribution 1980- 83 'small' pre-sweetened brands*
*Source:* Nielsen

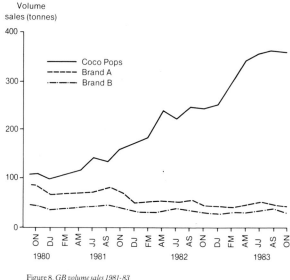

Figure 8. *GB volume sales 1981-83*
*Source:* Nielsen

while those of brand *A* and *B* remained relatively constant. That they remained fairly constant and that they continued losing distribution only as they had done prior to Coco Pops' activity demonstrated that Coco Pops was not cannibalising heavily on them. Of the larger children's 'pre-sweetened' brands, Frosties showed volume growth, whilst Quaker's Sugar Puffs declined in volume. Coco Pops' success did not harm other Kellogg brands.

TABLE 3:   GB RATE OF SALE

| year ending | Coco Pops | Brand *A* | Brand *B* |
|---|---|---|---|
| Aug–Sep 1981 | 2.5 | 1.7 | 1.2 |
| Aug–Sep 1982 | 3.6 | 1.5 | 1.1 |
| Aug–Sep 1983 | 4.4 | 1.5 | 1.2 |

Source: Nielsen

Reviewing the retail pricing levels of Coco Pops and the other brands in the 'pre-sweetened' category, we concluded that Coco Pops did *not* become a relatively less expensive brand. Table 4 demonstrates that between 1981 and 1983 Coco Pops and the other smaller children's 'pre-sweetened' brands (brands 1, 2 and 3) maintained their relative price relationship with each other. The larger 'pre-sweetened' brands became, comparatively, even less expensive over this period which was, in fact, to Coco Pops' *dis*advantage.

TABLE 4:   CHILDREN'S 'PRE-SWEETENED' CEREALS

| | annual average pence/kg indexed on all RTE* | | |
|---|---|---|---|
| | *1981* | *1982* | *1983* |
| brand 1 | 213 | 218 | 219 |
| Coco Pops | 179 | 179 | 182 |
| brand 2 | 158 | 161 | 162 |
| brand 3 | 153 | 156 | 160 |
| brand 4 | 130 | 130 | 131 |
| brand 5 | 117 | 124 | 115 |

Source: TCA
*RTE = 100

So, Coco Pops' success contrasted with the performance of the most similar brands and could be explained by no other reason than its advertising support. The campaign had run in two, then three areas – the trade restocked Coco Pops and consumers purchased it more. The brand developed so we extended it nationally: trade distribution and consumer purchasing grew still further. The advertising *worked*. As good as this performance was, it was a fairly conventional story of before-and-after success, exactly as we had intended it should be. Or was it?

As with all good children's tales, there was the surprise of the unexpected for Coco Pops' 'Storybook'. For when the advertising originally went on air in those two, then three areas, it was responsible for a great deal more than the direct growth results in those areas alone.

When Coco Pops went on air in London and Anglia, the grocery trade was so impressed with Kellogg's commitment to rebuilding brand sales that they also reintroduced it into stores in *all* other areas. (Figure 4 shows some indication of this where distribution in Yorkshire rose before the advertising broke in that area.) The overall results were increases in consumer off-take throughout the whole of Great Britain and an increased rate of sale far beyond the regions of London, Anglia, Yorkshire and their immediate TV overlap areas. The fact that Coco Pops grew strongly in these other areas was not a direct result of consumers seeing the advertising, for at that time they had had no opportunity to do so. The increases in volume sales were brought about indirectly – and yet simply – by making the product more available to consumers. We had earlier speculated that demand could be stimulated if availability were to be increased – and we had been right.

Against a previously declining trend, we believe that we can be confident that the increase in distribution in *un*advertised areas was primarily a trade side-effect of the decision to advertise in the three original areas. The increase in consumer off-take resulting from this increase in distribution is therefore part of the indirect effect of the advertising on sales. However, as has been implied, increased distribution in the unadvertised areas was also accompanied by an increased rate of sale per distribution point. Although it seems likely that a large part of this increase is also attributable to an indirect effect of advertising, our argument here must necessarily be more guarded. In so far as this increase in rate of sale is attributable to better quality in the new distribution or better facings in the old, this too may be reasonably aggregated into the indirect effect – neither would have been likely without the catalyst of advertising in the original areas. But it is impossible to quantify the contribution of factors such as these to rate of sale over and against other possible influences.

Thus, although it seems certain that the *full* effect of advertising in the three original areas was much larger than the increase in sales in those areas themselves, it is more difficult to put a *precise* figure on what that full effect was. What we can conclude is that the *direct* effect in the three original areas was proportionately much larger than the *in*direct effect in the rest of Great Britain.

Tables 5 and 6 show the distribution and sales volume growth in the three originally advertised areas and in the remaining six areas, which began their support later on. (The sales volume figures in Table 6 have been rounded off, for simplicity.) In both tables we have looked at the growth over three periods:

1.   In the year prior to TV activity.
2.   In the period of TV activity in London, Anglia and Yorkshire only.
3.   In the period of national TV support.

From these tables, we can calculate the increase in rate of sale per distribution point. The comparison in Table 7, between the test areas and the rest of GB in period 1–2, demonstrates conclusively that increased sales in London, Anglia, Yorkshire were due not only to substantially larger gains in distribution than in the unadvertised areas, but also to substantially larger increases in rate of sale. The fact that this increase was at least three times larger in the test areas than in the rest of Great Britain, offers a very good estimate of the relative power of the *direct* effect of the advertising.

The effect of the introduction of the advertising into the rest of Great Britain (period 2–3) is entirely consistent with the earlier results. The increase in rate of sale in the rest of Great Britain is three times greater than the previous increase in the unadvertised period (period 1–2). Of course, in this case (unlike the original test areas) a purist interpretation would point to the existence of an underlying upward trend established in the previous unadvertised period but, even if we make full allowance for this, the increase in the direct effect on rate of sale must still be very substantial. Furthermore, part of the increase which we have discounted will itself be, in large (though not precisely quantifiable) measure, a carry-over from the indirect effect in the earlier period.

TABLE 5:   COCO POPS DISTRIBUTION GROWTH

| | Period 1 Oct–Nov 1980– Aug–Sep 1981 % | | Period 2 Oct–Nov 1981– Dec–Jan 1983 % | | Period 3 Feb–Mar 1983– Dec–Jan 1984 % |
|---|---|---|---|---|---|
| sterling handlers (average) | | | | | |
| London | 53 | | 74 | | 88 |
| Anglia | 57 | TV airtime | 78 | | 85 |
| Yorkshire | 51 | | 72* | | 78 |
| 3-area average | 54 | | 75 | TV airtime | 84 |
| rest of GB | 42 | | 51 | | 66 |

* Feb–Mar 1982–Dec–Jan 1983 (for Yorkshire we made a very slight time adjustment in period 2 to allow for its later TV launch)
Source: Nielsen

TABLE 6:   COCO POPS VOLUME SALES GROWTH

| | Period 1 Oct–Nov 1980– Aug–Sep 1981 | | Period 2 Oct–Nov 1981– Dec–Jan 1983 | | Period 3 Feb–Mar 1983– Dec–Jan 1984 |
|---|---|---|---|---|---|
| *bi-monthly* average tonnage (indexed on period 1) | | | | | |
| London | 100 | | 220 | | 290 |
| Anglia | 100 | TV airtime | 240 | | 300 |
| Yorkshire | 100 | | 250* | | 270 |
| 3-area average | 100 | | 240 | TV airtime | 290. |
| rest of GB | 100 | | 145 | | 300 |

* Feb–Mar 1982–Dec–Jan 1983 (for Yorkshire we made a very slight time adjustment in period 2 to allow for its later TV launch)
Source: Nielsen

TABLE 7:   COCO POPS: COMPONENTS OF GROWTH

| annual growth | period 1–2 increase in: | | | period 2–3 increase in: | | |
|---|---|---|---|---|---|---|
| | total volume % | ÷ distribution = % | rate of sale % | total volume % | ÷ distribution = % | rate of sale % |
| London | +123 | +40 | +59 | + 32 | +19 | +11 |
| Anglia | +138 | +37 | +74 | + 25 | + 9 | +15 |
| Yorkshire | +148 | +41 | +76 | + 9 | + 8 | + 1 |
| 3-area average | +136 | +39 | +70 | + 22 | +12 | + 9 |
| rest of GB | + 45 | +21 | +20 | +107 | +29 | +60 |

Source: Nielsen

## CONCLUSIONS

Overall, we can summarise the effects of Coco Pops' first year of TV advertising as having caused increased volume sales in the initial three advertised areas, through distribution and rate of sale increases. Over the same period the advertising encouraged distribution increases throughout the rest of Great Britain which in turn resulted in an increased sales volume.

When support was extended nationally, it continued the growth in distribution and rate of sale in the initial areas (albeit at a slowing rate) and in the rest of the country it encouraged distribution which resulted in even higher volume growth.

Before extending support nationally, we had predicted in September 1982 that on the basis of distribution and rate of sale analysis in the test areas, national TV support in 1983 would yield a sterling distribution of 77 per cent and consumer sales of 1990 tonnes. In the event, 1983 brought us an average GB distribution of 73 per cent and sales of *1987* tonnes.

It was part of our objective that the advertising investment should pay for itself. In the three years 1981–83, the Kellogg Company spent a total of £1.5 million advertising Coco Pops through JWT. Over that same period the gross sales value of the brand totalled approximately £10.5 million which was judged a strong and profitable return on that investment.

It is frequent practice in econometric analysis to treat distribution as an independent variable – a separate and unrelated factor affecting sales. Yet distribution can itself be legitimately influenced by marketing action. This paper demonstrates a case in which one of the objectives of *consumer* advertising was to increase *trade* stocking, ie distribution was turned into a dependent – or, at least, intermediate – variable. Therefore, when the trade increased distribution (and hence sales) in areas *without advertising*, that too was an advertising effect. Advertising works – and sometimes it works even where it does not appear!

# Section Three

*Small Budgets*

# 15

# The Relaunch of
# Cow & Gate Babymeals

## INTRODUCTION

This paper describes a genuine sales success story for Cow & Gate babymeals. Against a background of disappointing sales and an absence from consumer advertising of over two and a half years, the brand reacted strongly to advertising in support of a relaunch in summer 1983.

The case for advertising's contribution to this success is demonstrated by isolating the effect of other brand and market variables. This examination leads us to conclude that the placing of a persuasive advertising message in carefully selected media was the major contributor to Cow & Gate's sales growth.

The sales effect of the advertising is all the more interesting in that the media spend was at a low level throughout the campaign.

## BACKGROUND

### The Company

Charles Gate founded a dairy in Guildford in 1850, and in 1910 began producing baby-milks. Cow & Gate expanded to produce other babyfoods, with babymeals produced from 1965. Today, Cow & Gate is exclusively a babyfeeding company and is now the largest manufacturer of babyfoods in the UK. It produces products in all sectors – milks, meals, rusks and juices, as well as specialist foods for the treatment of infant feeding disorders – to meet all a baby's feeding needs up to the age of one year.

### The Brand

Cow & Gate babymeals are packed in jars and are produced in two stages. Stage 1 is for babies beginning mixed feeding from about three months; it is a very smooth product with no lumps, and it is presented in 78 g jars. Stage 2 is for babies aged from about six months; it has a thicker texture and contains small pieces, and is sold in 113 g jars. Both stages are produced in a range of breakfast, dinner and dessert varieties. In addition, Cow & Gate produce a single-stage range of baby yogurt desserts in 113 g jars.

*The Market*

The babymeals market was worth £52 million in 1982. However, the market had declined in real terms since 1974 to only 90 per cent of its value, as Table 1 shows.

TABLE 1:    BABYMEALS MARKET VALUE (RSP)

|                     | 1974 | 1976 | 1978 | 1980 | 1982 |
|---------------------|------|------|------|------|------|
| £m                  | 18   | 27   | 31   | 45   | 52   |
| Index               | 100  | 150  | 172  | 250  | 289  |
| Index at 1974 prices| 100  | 95   | 87   | 95   | 90   |

Source: EIU/trade estimates

The size of the babymeals market and its potential for growth are closely related to the annual birth rate. In 1983, for the first time since 1980, the decline in the birth rate stopped (see Figure 1). The birth rate, and hence the market, shows no seasonal differences.

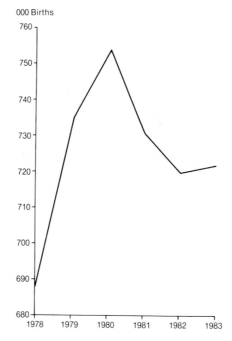

Figure 1: *The annual birth rate*
*Source:* Office of Population, Censuses and Surveys (England and Wales),
Scottish Office, Northern Ireland Office

The babymeals market consists of two basic product sectors: 'wet' meals, which are sold in jars and cans ready to heat and serve, and 'dehydrated' meals, which are sold in a powder or granulated form and are reconstituted by adding water or milk. From 1979, the dehydrated sector of the babymeals market grew at the expense of the wet.

Because the various brands of babymeals are available in widely differing sizes, the shift in balance between wet and dehydrated is best shown on a servings basis. Table 2 shows that in independent chemists by the end of 1982 dehydrated babymeals accounted for seven out of ten of all manufactured meals served compared with five out of ten in 1978.

TABLE 2: INDEPENDENT CHEMISTS: SHARE OF SERVINGS BY WET AND DEHYDRATED BABYMEALS

|  | 1978 % | 1979 % | 1980 % | 1981 % | 1982 % |
|---|---|---|---|---|---|
| wet | 47 | 37 | 32 | 31 | 30 |
| dehydrated | 53 | 63 | 68 | 69 | 70 |

Assumptions:    One pack Cow & Gate, Heinz and Gerber    = one serving
                      One pack Robinsons and Heinz weaning    = three servings
                      One pack Milupa    = twelve servings
Source: Nielsen/AMV estimates

## Competitive Situation

Prior to the relaunch, Cow & Gate were in a weak position competitively. The position as shown in Table 3 represented a loss of one share point in volume and two share points in value for Cow & Gate since the beginning of 1982.

TABLE 3:    BABYMEALS BRAND SHARE

|  | Volume % | Value % |
|---|---|---|
| Cow & Gate | 9 | 7 |
| Heinz cans | 54 | 37 |
| Heinz jars | 9 | 8 |
| Gallia jars | 1 | 1 |
| *Total wet meals* | 73 | 53 |
| Milupa | 8 | 18 |
| Robinsons | 11 | 17 |
| Heinz weaning food | 2 | 2 |
| Boots own label | 6 | 10 |
| *Total dehydrated meals* | 27 | 47 |

Source: RSGB Baby Panel, 12 weeks ending 18th June 1983

## STATE OF THE BRAND PRIOR TO RELAUNCH

### The Trend to Dehydrated Products

Cow & Gate is a wet brand and was therefore suffering in the trend in the market towards dehydrated products.

Qualitative research conducted by AMV in 1981 revealed that mothers saw real product benefits in dehydrated babymeals, which accounted for their popularity. Like all manufactured babymeals, they were seen as being convenient, but they were also seen to have additional benefits over wet meals: they could be made up in small quantities and various textures to suit each baby's individual needs.

## Distribution

Although Cow & Gate were building distribution in the grocery trade, sales opportunities were being missed through very low distribution in this sector (see Table 4).

TABLE 4:     STERLING PROFILE BY SOURCE OF PURCHASE

|  | total market | | Cow & Gate | |
|---|---|---|---|---|
|  | 1982 % | 1983 % | 1982 % | 1983 % |
| grocers | 37 | 35 | 5 | 9 |
| Boots | 42 | 42 | 62 | 63 |
| other chemists | 20 | 21 | 33 | 26 |
| other outlets | 1 | 2 | – | 2 |

Source: RSGB Baby Panel, 12 weeks ending 16th June 1982 and 18th June 1983

## Price

The brand leader, Heinz cans, is seen to be the definitive brand in the wet meals market, with the definitive price against which other brands are compared on a unit-by-unit basis (not price per gram).

Cow & Gate was perceived by mothers as being the most highly priced brand. Twenty-seven per cent of mothers felt that Cow & Gate babymeals were highly priced, as compared with only 12 per cent for Heinz (PHL, May 1983).

In fact, in spring 1983 Cow & Gate jars were up to 30 per cent per unit more expensive than Heinz cans (Table 5).

TABLE 5:     INDEX OF AVERAGE RSP PER UNIT

|  | Index |
|---|---|
| Heinz cans (128 g) | 100 |
| Cow & Gate 1 (78 g) | 118 |
| Cow & Gate 2 (113 g) | 129 |
| Cow & Gate yogurt (113 g) | 121 |
| Heinz jars (128 + 170 g)* | 135 |

*Nielsen reports two sizes together as average
Source: Chemist Nielsen, March–April 1983

*Lack of Support*

Cow & Gate received no advertising support from January 1981 until the relaunch in August 1983. In contrast there was significant activity from competitors, especially in the dehydrated sector. Heinz weaning food was launched in May 1981 with national advertising support on TV, and in July 1982 Robinsons relaunched their product with new packaging and heavy advertising support. Then in June 1983 Heinz launched their Pure Fruit range, again with significant spend on TV.

Milupa, who had successfully launched their range in the early 1970s, continued to build their franchise by extensive sampling through clinics, health visitors and the 'Bounty Bag' (sampling of mother and baby products to mothers in hospitals). Then, in summer 1982, Boots repackaged their dehydrated product and significantly extended the range of varieties offered. Table 6 summaries competitive activity.

TABLE 6:    SUMMARY OF COMPETITIVE ACTIVITY

| | Year ending | | | | | |
|---|---|---|---|---|---|---|
| | Dec 1981 | | Dec 1982 | | Jun 1983 | |
| | £000 | % | £000 | % | £000 | % |
| Total | 1010 | 100 | 1926 | 100 | 2546 | 100 |
| Heinz | 856 | 85 | 970 | 50 | 1565 | 62 |
| Robinsons | 74 | 7 | 908 | 47 | 954 | 37 |
| Others | 80 | 8 | 48 | 3 | 27 | 1 |

Source: MEAL (TV and Press Expenditure)

*Product Formulation Problems*

Following product placement (PHL 1983), it was found that Cow & Gate's texture was being criticised for being too thin and runny; texture problems were likely to be adding to the brand's sales deficiencies.

## THE CONSUMER AND BRAND DECISION-MAKER: USAGE AND ATTITUDES

*The Consumer*

The ultimate consumer is, of course, the baby, and the success or failure of a brand will depend on his or her acceptance of it. The mother, though, is the brand decision-maker, and there are important differences between first-time and subsequent mothers' attitudes to feeding their babies (AMV Qualitative).

First-time mothers are generally less confident about how to feed their babies, especially babies under six months. They are driven by an underlying concern that their baby should behave normally, yet they have no real benchmark of their own by which to judge what is normal. Therefore they will turn to others for advice: to their mothers, their peers, the clinic and the health visitor.

The subsequent mother tends to take a more pragmatic approach to feeding, as she has been through it all before and so can rely on her own experience more than on the advice of others. She will often replicate the brand choices established with previous babies.

### Attitudes to Manufactured Babymeals

Manufactured babymeals are generally considered to be second best to real food, but because they are so convenient their use is heavily rationalised, and almost all mothers use them to some extent. There is also a very clear underlying belief that all babyfoods will be safe, as manufacturers are totally trusted to produce appropriate products.

Mothers stressed the need for variety in babies diets, for several reasons: so that babies can be educated to different tastes, so that they don't become faddy eaters, so that they get a nutritionally balanced diet, and so that they do not become either flavour dependent or brand dependent. This results in an almost total absence of solus brand usage in the market, and a pattern of brand choice influenced by availability of varieties.

### Cow & Gate Strengths and Weaknesses

Prior to the relaunch, awareness of Cow & Gate was lower than that of Heinz, Robinsons and Milupa.

Qualitative research (AMV 1983) revealed that competitive brands had developed strong images. Heinz was viewed very positively as expert in all manufactured foods, including babymeals. Robinsons was seen as a reliable, long-established company, and Milupa, although relatively new to the UK market, had already built up a reputation as a producer of delicious products.

Cow & Gate's brand imagery was almost entirely generic. Apart from some positive values gained from the use of Cow & Gate babymeals, positive imagery tended to emanate from the benefits of the glass jars which were considered the preferred mode of packaging for wet meals (clean, hygienic, easy to open, resealable) (PHL 1983). There was some praise for Cow & Gate as a user of natural ingredients, but generally the brand had no real benefits, as all manufactured babyfood has to be reliable. Thus there was felt to be no real reason to purchase.

Cow & Gate's user profile had become progressively more upmarket until 1983; usage was biased towards ABs (see Table 7).

TABLE 7:    CLASS PROFILE

|  | housewives % | babymeals all users % | Cow & Gate users % |
|---|---|---|---|
| AB | 16 | 18 | 24 |
| C1 | 23 | 22 | 18 |
| C2 | 28 | 31 | 33 |
| DE | 33 | 29 | 25 |

Source: TGI 1983

*Product Usage Problems*

Babymeals are recommended to be served from the age of three months. Stage 1, or strained meals, are served from this age, and Stage 2, or Junior meals, are introduced from age six to eight months. Table 8 shows that Cow & Gate usage was disproportionately concentrated among younger babies.

TABLE 8:    USAGE OF WET BRANDS BY AGE OF BABY

|  | total wet % | total Cow & Gate % | total Heinz cans and jars % |
|---|---|---|---|
| under 3 months | 3 | 7 | 2 |
| 3– 6 months | 22 | 27 | 21 |
| 6– 9 months | 31 | 34 | 31 |
| 9–12 months | 22 | 18 | 22 |
| 12–18 months | 18 | 11 | 19 |
| 18–23 months | 5 | 3 | 4 |

Source: RSGB Baby Panel, 12 weeks ending 18th June 1983

Table 9 shows that the problem was prevalent in both stages of the brand. Looking at the Stage 1/strained products, nearly twice as much of Cow & Gate's product volume is served up to six months old compared with the brand leader, Heinz. And whereas 40 per cent of Heinz Junior is served to babies over one year old, only 33 per cent of Cow & Gate's Stage 2 reaches older babies.

TABLE 9:    USAGE OF STAGES OF WET BRANDS BY AGE OF BABY

|  | Cow & Gate Stage 1 % | Heinz Strained jar % | Heinz Strained can % | Cow & Gate Stage 2 % | Heinz Junior jar % | Heinz Junior can % |
|---|---|---|---|---|---|---|
| Under 3 months | 18 | 3 | 4 | – | – | – |
| 3–6 months | 60 | 43 | 38 | 10 | 4 | 4 |
| 6–9 months | 17 | 27 | 38 | 44 | 18 | 27 |
| 9–12 months | 3 | 9 | 14 | 25 | 33 | 29 |
| 12–18 months | 3 | 19 | 6 | 17 | 42 | 31 |
| 18–24 months | – | – | 1 | 5 | 2 | 9 |

Source: RSGB Baby Panel 12 weeks ending 18th June 1984

## SUMMARY OF COW & GATE'S POSITION PRIOR TO RELAUNCH

1.  Cow & Gate was suffering in the trend towards dehydrated babymeals.
2.  There were missed sales opportunities due to low distribution in the grocery trade.
3.  Cow & Gate was significantly more expensive than Heinz cans, the definitive wet brand.

4. Cow & Gate had received no advertising support since 1980, compared with significant activity by competitors.
5. There were product texture problems.
6. There was a lack of brand awareness and brand values, so no reason to purchase Cow & Gate.
7. Usage of Cow & Gate was disproportionately concentrated among younger babies.

## THE RELAUNCH: PROBLEMS ADDRESSED

Four problem areas were identified to be addressed prior to the relaunch: the product formulation and range, chemist-only distribution, Cow & Gate's price, and the low levels of consumer awareness and interest in the brand. These were the only areas that were addressed in the relaunch: all other aspects of the marketing mix remained static.

## THE RELAUNCH: MARKETING ACTIVITY

### Product Formulation and Range

The product was reformulated to address the criticisms on consistency that had been made by mothers. Both the Stage 1 product and the Stage 2 product were made thicker. The range of varieties offered was rationalised, with the withdrawal of the less popular varieties and the introduction of new varieties. Whereas before, some varieties were available in one stage only, several were now produced in both stages. Prior to the relaunch the range consisted of 45 main meals/desserts and five yogurts; after it there were 46 main meals/desserts and five yogurts, with a further four yogurts added in February 1984.

The improved products were introduced in their existing packaging with no indication that the recipes had been improved. Since the target market of mothers is constantly changing and experiencing the product for the first time, there was no need to alert them to the change.

The products are now continually re-evaluated and will be improved as required.

### Chemist-Only Distribution

Prior to the relaunch, Cow & Gate had a single sales force which dealt with hospitals as well as with the chemist and grocery trade. The sales force was restructured to split the medical (hospital) sales force from the retail sales force, so that each could develop its own special area of expertise. In addition, the national account team was strengthened in order to capitalise on the growing importance of the grocery multiple.

### Price

While it was recognised that the premium price over Heinz cans which existed prior to the relaunch was too high to encourage sales, it was considered important to maintain some price premium to add value to the product.

After an initial price reduction in May 1983, the price was held in the face of a competitive price increase from Heinz cans.

### Low Levels of Consumer Awareness and Interest

Sampling activity was improved with the introduction of Cow & Gate products into the Bounty weaning pack alongside Heinz, Gallia and Milupa. This pack was available in Boots from July 1983 and is estimated to reach 40 per cent of mothers.

Advertising was developed to begin in August 1983.

# THE ADVERTISING

## Development of Advertising Strategy

Qualitative research was conducted with mothers (AMV, January 1983) to aid development of the advertising strategy; in this a number of conceptual areas were explored. These included statements of reassurance about the balance of the baby's diet, the use of wholesome ingredients with no added salt, artificial colouring, flavouring or preservatives, descriptions about the extent of the range and Cow & Gate's experience in babyfeeding.

This survey concluded that there is a requirement to reassure consumers that Cow & Gate babymeals meet all a baby's nutritional needs, are made from natural ingredients and contain no additives. But this would form only part of the task, as all manufacturers are trusted to provide nutritionally sound products, so a distinctive identity for Cow & Gate babymeals was required.

Despite the product improvements, the characteristics of the products were not considered sufficiently distinctive on their own to differentiate Cow & Gate from its competitors. The new Stage 2 formulation was generally seen to bring Cow & Gate into line with competitors, rather than make it superior to them.

However, a strong positioning did emerge in that Cow & Gate help babies grow up to adult food. This claim was believable and meaningful, as adult food is the objective towards which mothers are working. Cow & Gate was seen to help with the transition from milk, through early solids, to eating with the family, and therefore gained both practical and emotional benefits. This strategic route was felt to be campaignable, as there are several stories that can be told about the products: taste education, texture education etc.

Importantly, this approach was found to be particularly relevant to our prime target market: first-time mothers who require support and guidance in feeding education. However, subsequent mothers were also sympathetic to this proposition.

## The Role of Advertising

Mothers have to be given a reason to purchase Cow & Gate babymeals when other brands have high awareness levels, high trial and repeat purchase and also previous consistent advertising support. Awareness of Cow & Gate was poor, the brand was known to be expensive and there was satisfaction with other brands. The role of advertising was thus to capitalise on the warm and positive reactions to the new superior formulations and varieties.

*Target Audience*

The primary target audience was defined as mothers with babies aged two to four months who are thinking about starting their babies on solid food, especially those who are first-time mothers. (Overall the advertising was addressed to all mothers with babies aged two to nine months.)

*Advertising Objectives*

1. To build rapid awareness of Cow & Gate babymeals among a constantly changing pool of mothers (purchase cycle only 12–16 weeks).
2. To associate Cow & Gate with expertise in baby feeding: the most advanced in understanding the needs of babies and how to develop their taste for adult food.
3. To re-establish the brand values with which Cow & Gate has traditionally been associated: the manufacture of high-quality, natural food for babies.
4. To establish Cow & Gate babymeals as a regular part of the repertoire of mothers who are feeding babies.

*Creative Strategy*

Cow & Gate help your baby to grow up to adult food.

*Support*

1. The Cow & Gate babymeals range includes a complete range of varieties in breakfasts, dinners, savouries, desserts and yogurts.
2. Cow & Gate prepare their babymeals to take into account the need to learn to cope with food of a thicker consistency and varied texture.
3. Protein, vitamins and minerals are balanced to ensure that the nutritional needs of babies are met.
4. No salt, artificial colour or preservatives are added.

Four advertisements were produced. In research they were very favourably received by mothers, and worked well together as a campaign. 'Three big steps' encompassed the role of Cow & Gate overall, helping the baby grow up to adult food. 'Liver and bacon' was specifically appropriate and relevant to starting out on Cow & Gate both practically and emotionally, a position encroached upon by the dehydrated sector. 'Mother Nature' communicated texture education, and 'Varieties' communicated that Cow & Gate could aid in taste education and the extent of choice offered.

The unusually long copy was welcomed by the mothers who were hungry for relevant and supportive information (see pages 240; 242; 246).

(Creatively this campaign has been extremely well received with 'Liver and Bacon' winning the 1984 DADA gold award for the most outstanding colour consumer magazine advertisement, and the Campaign Silver Award for Best Food and Non-Alcoholic Drinks Advertisement 1984.)

*Media Choice*

The key criteria influencing the choice of media was the need to have, as far as possible, all-year support. This was very important because of the rapidly changing target audience. In addition qualitative research had clearly shown that as well as the period of purchase of the category being very short (only 12–16 weeks) mothers tended not to think of the category much in advance of the first purchase.

National support was also required, on a limited budget of only £200000 per annum.

The rapidly changing pool of mothers meant that it was possible to reach the core of our target audience via a relatively small list of specialist titles: *Parents, Mother & Baby, Mother* and *Maternity and Mothercraft*. Coverage was built up by adding a small group of mass market magazines including *Living, Family Circle, Good Housekeeping, She* and *Woman & Home* which all have sympathetic editorial including children's sections which were keyed into whenever appropriate.

A mix of full-colour spreads and single-colour pages was selected to increase impact and improve the brand's standing.

From August to December 1983 the campaign delivered 47 per cent coverage of housewives with children aged 0–23 months at 4.9 OTS. The 1984 (12 month) schedule is designed to deliver 61 per cent coverage of the same target audience at 7.1 OTS (NRS).

## EVALUATING THE RELAUNCH

Figure 2 shows the increase in Cow & Gate's volume sales ex-factory as moving annual totals. Following an overall decline to a low at the end of June 1983, after the relaunch, sales recovered and were still increasing at the end of the latest sales period ending mid-May 1984.

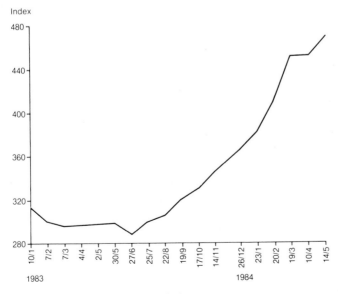

Figure 2. *Cow & Gate MAT volume sales indexed*
*Source:* Cow & Gate Ltd. Ex-factory sales

# Will your baby have taken three big steps before that first little one?

Your baby's first faltering step is something you'll never forget.

When it happens, you won't be able to wait to tell your friends.

Your baby's grandparents will be as proud as punch.

Snaps will be taken for the family album.

Why all the fuss?

Because it means your baby is no longer a baby, but a little grown-up.

But before all this takes place, most mothers would like their babies to have taken several other steps.

We mean, of course, the ones that lead to eating real grown-up food with the rest of the family.

**How Cow & Gate can help.**

For the first few months, breast or baby milk provides all the nourishment a baby needs. (And it goes on providing nourishment for up to 12 months, since solid food should always be supplemented with breast or baby milk.)

But when weaning does begin you'll be faced with a bewildering array of choices.

To help you decide what's best, we'd like to tell you about our Cow & Gate Babymeals.

They aren't just foods but more of a training course that teaches your baby to eat.

They gently take your baby through a series of stages until, at say 9 months, your baby moves naturally on to the same food as the rest of your family.

Here's how we do it.

## Step 1: Easy to swallow puréed babymeals for your baby.

**Eating in easy stages.**

Some babyfood manufacturers seem to think that all babies, however old, are the same. At Cow & Gate, we think differently.

So our baby foods come in two versions.

Stage 1 is for babies starting out on solids.

They're specially sieved or puréed so they can be taken from a spoon and swallowed easily.

Then, when your baby has enjoyed them for 2 or 3 months, it'll be time to move on to our thicker Stage 2 meals, which contain meaty or fruity pieces.

But more about that later.

**Faddy eaters start young.**

Most first-time mums are surprised to learn that we make 51 different varieties.

Why so many, they ask?

Obviously at first your baby won't think everything we make is marvellous, so the more you have to choose from, the better.

More importantly, we believe your baby should have as much variety as possible.

The earlier you can educate their palate to lots of different tastes, the less chance there is of growing up into a faddy eater.

And lastly, of course, babies are just like grown-ups.

They need a wide range of foods to give them a proper well-balanced diet.

## Step 2: Your baby learns to chew soft little pieces of food.

**Starting off and moving on.**

Like most mothers, you'll probably choose to start your baby on our Stage 1 meals at around 3 or 4 months.

If so, your baby's taste buds are in for a treat.

There'll be Cereals, Meats, Vegetables, Puddings, Fruit, even Yogurt Desserts. (And it's worth remembering that ours contain none of the artificial additives found in adult yogurts.)

Over the next few months your baby will explore all the different flavours we grown-ups take for granted.

But only the flavours.

Because until around 6 months a baby can only suck and swallow.

The next step is to develop your baby's ability to chew.

And that's where our Stage 2 meals come in.

Many taste the same as their Stage 1 counterparts. (So your baby won't have to cope with too many changes at once.)

All that's different is the texture.

It's a touch thicker and contains little soft pieces of food.

In no time at all your baby will realise that food has to be chewed, and so develop the correct chewing action.

And, in doing so, move another step closer to real grown-up food.

**Nothing but the best.**

Few things are more delicate than the stomach of a young baby.

It's something we at Cow & Gate never forget.

So we buy only the best foods.

All our suppliers must meet vigorous standards. And woe betide them if they don't.

Every item of food that comes in is checked by our inspectors. Next, our chemists carry out checks of their own.

After cooking, each meal is

## Step 3: Real grown-up food for a little grown-up.

then sterilised or pasteurised to make certain it's free from harmful bacteria.

Then, just to be on the safe side, still more checks are made.

In fact, over 20% of our staff do nothing else.

**Go on, taste it yourself.**

If you think all babymeals are bland and flavourless, try tasting ours.

We've recently altered our recipes. They now taste much more akin to grown-up food.

Quite simply, we've found that babies prefer them that way.

So do mothers. Because when the time comes to move on to adult food, your baby will already be used to its taste.

And as well as tasting good, our babymeals do a baby good.

We guarantee that they supply protein, vitamins and minerals that a growing baby needs.

(We even add a little extra Vitamin C to some of our desserts, to replace the amount that's lost in cooking.)

We also guarantee that our meals contain as little as possible of

the things you wouldn't want your baby to have.

We add no salt at all.

And the only sugar we use in our fruit desserts is to overcome the natural tartness of certain fruits.

Also, we guarantee that our babymeals contain no artificial flavourings, preservatives or colourings whatsoever.

**Gently does it.**

We hope we've shown you how our babymeals make the journey to adult food in short and gentle steps.

If you have any queries, have a word with your health visitor.

Or by all means, write to us at Cow & Gate Ltd, Trowbridge, Wilts BA14 8YX.

But it's worth remembering that no two babies are the same.

While you can encourage your baby to progress, never force the pace.

And be prepared for some dramas and setbacks on the way.

But when the time does come for your baby to sit up at the table and enjoy the same little steps across the carpet.

Maybe even as memorable as when he or she amazes everyone with those first little steps across the carpet.

## Two short steps to grown-up food.

This increase in sales ex-factory is not due only to retailers stocking up with product, but is due to an increase in consumer off-take. The Nielsen data in Table 10 shows that in the independent chemist trade following an initial stocking up in May–June 1983, stocks decreased over the period following the relaunch with sales increasing steadily.

TABLE 10:   COW & GATE STOCKS AND SALES TRENDS IN INDEPENDENT CHEMISTS

|  | Mar–Apr 1983 | May–Jun 1983 | Jul–Aug 1983 | Sep–Oct 1983 | Nov–Dec 1983 | Jan–Feb 1984 | Mar–Apr 1984 |
|---|---|---|---|---|---|---|---|
| **Stocks** | | | | | | | |
| months' supply stocks year on | 3.7 | 3.5 | 2.9 | 2.9 | 2.7 | 2.7 | 2.3 |
| year % change sales year on | −11 | +2 | −6 | −9 | −11 | +2 | +6 |
| year % change | −17 | −4 | +3 | +10 | +21 | +51 | +68 |

Source: Nielsen

Cow & Gate have increased their sales volume ahead of the market. Figure 3 shows Cow & Gate's sales performance against their major market (as monitored by Nielsen), the chemist trade (excluding Boots), and we can see that although the market has shown

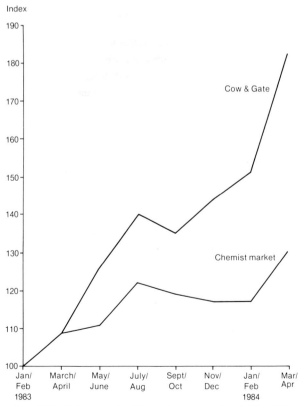

Figure 3. *Index of volume sales for Cow & Gate and babymeals chemist market Source:* Nielsen

# May we recommend the liver and bacon to follow?

During the first few months of life, breast milk is the perfect baby food.

Then, at around 3 or 4 months, something a little more substantial is called for, or even cried for.

But liver and bacon?

Are you mad?

On the contrary. We're one of the country's longest established makers of baby food.

Experience has taught us that most mothers prefer their babies to move from the breast or bottle to real grown-up food as naturally and smoothly as possible.

So our baby meals are designed to help you do just that.

**Learning to eat in easy stages.**

Cow & Gate baby meals aren't simply little glass jars of baby food.

They're a two-stage training programme that gently paves the way to adult food.

Stage 1 meals are for babies starting out on solids, and still getting most of their nourishment from breast or baby milk.

Since your baby will only be able to suck and swallow, they're finely sieved or puréed.

Then, about 3 months later, it'll be time to move onto our Stage 2 meals.

But more about that later on.

**The first step.**

If you're still troubled by the thought of a young baby tucking into liver and bacon, let us explain.

Sooner or later your baby will have to get used to adult food tastes.

And there's really no reason why it shouldn't be sooner rather than later.

That's why our Stage 1 range includes lots of grown-up tastes.

There are cereals, meats, vegetables, puddings, fruits and even artificial additive-free yogurt desserts.

So during those first few months of weaning, your baby's palate will be in for quite an education.

After 2 or 3 months, it'll be complete. And your baby will be ready to graduate to our Stage 2 meals.

**Grown-up tastes. Grown-up textures.**

The next stage is to develop your baby's ability to chew.

For this reason, our Stage 2 meals are thicker, and have either meaty or fruity pieces in them.

With a little practice your baby will soon realise that food needs to be chewed before it can be swallowed.

And knowing that babies don't like coping with too many changes at once, most of our Stage 2 meals are available in the same varieties as Stage 1.

**The 55 meal menu.**

You wouldn't take too kindly to eating the same food day in day out.

And neither do babies.

That's one reason why we make 23 different Stage 1 varieties, 23 Stage 2 varieties and 9 yogurt desserts.

But it isn't the only reason.

Perhaps more importantly, your baby grows so fast in the early months that a varied and well-balanced diet is essential.

What's more, it should help you avoid trouble in the years to come.

By educating your baby's palate to accept all sorts of different tastes and textures you should forestall food fads later on.

**The best for your baby.**

When it comes to feeding young babies, you can't be too careful.

That's something that we at Cow & Gate never ever forget.

So we buy only the best foods.

our staff go nowhere else.

It tastes like adult food...

If you think all baby meals are bland and flavourless, you've obviously not tasted ours.

We've recently altered our recipes so our meals now taste much more akin to grown-up food.

The fact is, we've found that babies prefer them that way.

And so do mothers.

Because when the time comes to move onto adult food, the switch will be that much gentler because your baby will already be used to its taste.

**...but it isn't adult food.**

Compared to adult food, our baby meals have some very important differences.

We add a little extra vitamin C to some of our desserts to replace the amount lost in cooking.

All our suppliers must meet the rigorous standards we set.

Every item of food that comes in is checked by our inspectors.

Then our chemists carry out checks of their own.

And the same thing happens all through the cooking process.

In fact, over 20% of

And none of them contain any artificial colourings, flavourings or preservatives.

But we do, however, make sure they supply protein, vitamins and minerals a growing baby needs.

**Gently does it.**

We hope we've shown you how our baby meals make the journey to adult food indeed a gentle steps.

If you have any queries, have a word with your Health Visitor.

Or by all means write to us at Cow & Gate, Trowbridge, Wiltshire.

But it's worth remembering that no two babies are the same.

While you can measure progress, never force the pace.

And be prepared for some little dramas and setbacks on the way.

But don't lose heart. It is a Cow & Gate medium, it shouldn't be too hard to coax ing with the rest of the lamb.

**Two short steps to grown-up food.**

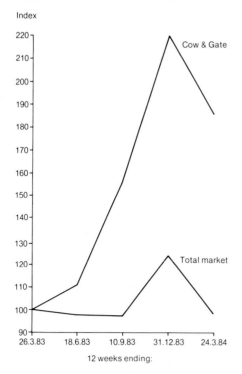

Figure 4. *Index of volume sales for Cow & Gate and babymeals market*
*Source:* RSGB Baby Panel

growth since June 1983, Cow & Gate sales have increased at a much more rapid rate. Similarly, Figure 4 plots Cow & Gate's sales against the total market, and again we can see Cow & Gate's successful growth pattern.

TABLE 11:    BABYMEALS BRAND SHARE

|  | Volume | | Value | |
|---|---|---|---|---|
|  | June 1983 | March 1984 | June 1983 | March 1984 |
|  | % | % | % | % |
| Cow & Gate | 9 | 14 | 7 | 11 |
| Heinz cans | 54 | 49 | 37 | 33 |
| Heinz jars | 9 | 11 | 8 | 9 |
| Gallia jars | 1 | * | 1 | 1 |
| Total wet meals | 73 | 74 | 53 | 54 |
| Milupa | 8 | 7 | 18 | 16 |
| Robinsons | 11 | 11 | 17 | 18 |
| Heinz weaning food | 2 | 1 | 2 | 1 |
| Boots own-label | 6 | 7 | 10 | 12 |
| Total dehydrated meals | 27 | 26 | 47 | 46 |

* Less than 0.5 per cent.
Source: RSGB Baby Panel 12 weeks ending 18th June 1983 and 24th March 1984

*Brand Share*

Again looking at Nielsen data for the chemist trade, Cow & Gate had increased their sterling brand share to a record 24.5 per cent by March–April 1984 (see Figure 5).

Cow & Gate also improved their performance within the market overall, achieving a 14 per cent share of volume and 11 per cent of market value (see Table 11).

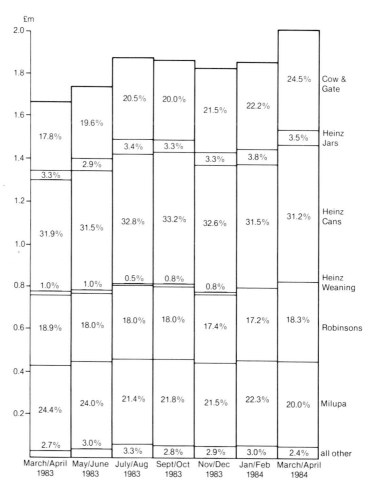

Figure 5. *GB consumer sales value share — independent chemists*
*Source:* Nielsen

*Awareness and Attitudes*

Spontaneous awareness of Cow & Gate babymeals increased by six percentage points over the year to May 1984 following nine months of advertising support. Cow & Gate showed the most improvement of all the brands monitored (see Table 12). Image measurements

TABLE 12:    SPONTANEOUS RECALL OF BABYMEALS MANUFACTURERS

|  | May 1983 | Nov 1983 | May 1984 | May 83–84 Change |
|---|---|---|---|---|
| base: | (241) | (244) | (253) | |
|  | % | % | % | % |
| Heinz | 87 | 87 | 86 | −1 |
| Robinsons | 73 | 66 | 66 | −7 |
| Milupa | 69 | 74 | 71 | +2 |
| Cow & Gate | 60 | 64 | 66 | +6 |
| Boots | 44 | 42 | 44 | = |
| Gerber | 9 | 11 | 9 | = |
| Gallia | 8 | 13 | 6 | −2 |

Source: Audience Selection Ltd

were included in the monitor. Respondents were read out a series of statements and asked to indicate how strongly they personally felt each applied to Cow & Gate and competitive brands by awarding a mark out of ten. Cow & Gate improved their standing on the key dimensions that the advertising had aimed to address (see Table 13).

TABLE 13:    IMAGE OF COW & GATE

|  | mean rating out of 10 | | |
|---|---|---|---|
|  | May 1983 | Nov 1983 | May 1984 |
| They make products to cater for all baby's feeding needs up to the age of one year. | 7.3 | 7.4 | 7.6 |
| They are a brand you see around a great deal. | 7.2 | 7.6 | 7.7 |
| A brand I can really trust. | 7.4 | 7.3 | 7.8 |
| They are clearly the babyfeeding specialists. | 6.9 | 7.2 | 7.4 |
| They really do help your baby grow up to adult food. | 6.4 | 6.8 | 7.2 |

Source: Audience Selection Ltd

Whilst it is early days for shifting the image of Cow & Gate, the brand does appear to be moving in the right direction. This movement becomes more apparent when we look at the performance of other brands on these dimensions as a control (see Table 14). Cow & Gate consistently shows a more positive trend.

# Mother Nature teaches a baby to suck. So how does a mother teach a baby to chew?

A new-born baby needs no lesson in the art of feeding.

The sucking instinct is there from the beginning. (In fact it's there *before* the beginning. Many babies are known to suck their thumb inside their mother, weeks before birth.)

This ability to suck, along with a plentiful supply of breast or baby milk, is all that's needed during those first 3 or 4 months of life.

But when the time arrives to make a start on solids, then life gets a little more complicated.

Because it's then that a mother must begin to teach the art of eating.

The eventual goal is, of course for your baby to enjoy real grown-up food with the rest of the family.

And being specialists in baby-feeding, our foods are designed with this goal in mind.

### Cradle days to family meals.

As you may know, our jars come in two sizes.

The smaller ones are Stage 1 meals. These are finely sieved or puréed, making them suitable for babies from around 3 or 4 months.

In the bigger jars you'll find our yogurt desserts

and Stage 2 meals.

The yogurt desserts, which are free from all artificial additives, are also suitable from 3 or 4 months.

And our Stage 2 meals are for older babies, as they're thicker and contain soft little meaty or fruity pieces.

### Introducing grown-up tastes.

Babies like routine. And they don't always take too kindly to change.

That's why we believe that learning to eat should be a gentle 2-step process.

It starts at around 3 or 4 months. While most of your baby's nourishment is still coming from breast or

baby milk, try introducing just a spoonful or two of a Stage 1 meal or yogurt dessert.

(Don't worry about wasting the rest of the jar. Just replace the lid, keep it in the fridge and it'll be good for 48 hours.)

As your baby becomes accustomed to taking food from a spoon, gradually increase the amount.

And once your baby gets used to one particular flavour, then you can begin to introduce a new one.

### What's on the menu today?

A baby who's fed on Cow & Gate should never be fed-up.

Our Stage 1 meals come in 23 different varieties. There are 23 in our Stage 2 range.

And 9 yogurt desserts.

The reasons for making so many are simple.

Obviously your baby won't at first think that every meal we make is marvellous, so the more you have to choose from the better.

And just like grown-ups, babies need a wide range of foods to give them a well-balanced diet.

Also, it should help you avoid trouble later.

By educating your baby's palate to different flavours early on, "faddy" eating shouldn't become a problem

## Until about 6 months, a baby just sucks and swallows. So all our Stage 1 meals are puréed.

**Learning to chew.**

After 2 or 3 months of Stage 1 meals your baby will have learnt to enjoy all manner of grown-up tastes.

And those first little teeth may well be making an appearance.

So the next step, at around 6 months, is to develop the ability to chew by moving onto Stage 2 meals.

To start with, choose Stage 2 flavours that are the same as Stage 1.

(Then the only new thing your baby will have to cope with is the texture.)

Also, to make it easier, little meaty or fruity pieces in them.

With a little practice

your baby will learn that food needs to be chewed.

And then in a few months he or she will be ready for the biggest step of all.

Real grown-up food. **Natural is best.**

We know how sensitive a young baby's stomach is.

So we're highly sensitive about the food that goes into our baby meals.

We buy only the best foods.

All of our suppliers must meet the rigorous standards we set. And woe betide them if they don't.

**Testing… Testing.**

When each ingredient arrives, our inspectors

## Learning to chew comes next. So our Stage 2 meals have little pieces in them.

preservative or flavouring.

And we make certain that no salt is ever added to any of our meals.

So, all in all, you should certainly have no qualms about choosing Cow & Gate.

### Gently does it.

We hope we've shown you how our baby meals make the journey to adult food in short and gentle steps.

If you have any queries, then have a word with your Health Visitor.

Or by all means write to us at Cow & Gate Limited, Trowbridge, Wiltshire BA14 8YX.

But do remember that no two babies are the same.

And the same thing happens all through the cooking process.

We make certain that our meals contain protein, vitamins and minerals your growing baby needs.

We make certain that they contain no artificial colouring,

check it over.

Then our chemists carry out checks of their own.

While you can try to encourage progress, never force the pace. And be prepared for some little setbacks on the way.

But don't lose heart.

Mother nature may have got your baby off to a fine start.

But it's up to you to carry on with the good work.

## Two short steps to grown-up food.

TABLE 14:   COMPETITIVE IMAGERY OF BABYMEALS MANUFACTURERS CHANGES IN MEAN RATING
            OUT OF 10 MAY 1983 TO MAY 1984

|  | Cow & Gate | Heinz | Milupa | Robinsons |
|---|---|---|---|---|
| They make products to cater for all baby's feeding needs up the age of one year. | +0.3 | +0.1 | +0.2 | +0.1 |
| They are a brand you see around a great deal. | +0.5 | +0.3 | +0.3 | +0.1 |
| A brand I can really trust. | +0.4 | +0.2 | +0.1 | +0.2 |
| They are clearly the baby-feeding specialists. | +0.5 | −0.7 | +0.2 | +0.3 |
| They really do help your baby grow up to adult food. | +0.8 | +0.2 | −0.2 | 0 |

Source: Audience Selection Ltd

## Penetration

Cow & Gate improved their penetration of mothers with babies aged 0–2 years from June 1983, particularly among those with older babies, the weak group prior to the relaunch.

TABLE 15:   PENETRATION OF BABYMEALS BY AGE OF BABY

|  | all wet meals | | Cow & Gate | |
|---|---|---|---|---|
|  | Jun 1983 % | Mar 1984 % | Jun 1983 % | Mar 1984 % |
| Total | 44 | 42 | 16 | 19 |
| 0–3 months | 34 | 33 | 16 | 16 |
| 3–6 months | 75 | 75 | 38 | 38 |
| 6–9 months | 74 | 81 | 31 | 41 |
| 9–12 months | 61 | 57 | 24 | 29 |
| 12–18 months | 35 | 30 | 6 | 10 |
| 18–24 months | 13 | 10 | 2 | 3 |

Source: RSGB Baby Panel 12 weeks ending 18th June 1983 and 24th March 1984

## EVALUATING THE ROLE OF ADVERTISING

The relaunch of Cow & Gate babymeals only commenced ten months ago. However, all data sources monitoring the effect of the relaunch have shown consistent improvements since that date.

We have already listed the four areas addressed in the relaunch: product formulation and range, distribution, price, and low levels of consumer awareness and interest which were addressed through advertising and sampling. We now assess the role of each of these areas in contributing to the success of the relaunch.

### Product Formulation and Range

Cow & Gate's product range was rationalised and new varieties were added. The increase in Cow & Gate sales was not due to a significant add-on effect of sale of new varieties;

the top-selling varieties after the relaunch were mostly those that had been favourites before; only Spaghetti Bolognaise was a top-selling newcomer (see Table 16).

TABLE 16: INDEX OF SALES INCREASE FOR TOP SIX VARIETIES MARCH–JUNE 1984 ON MARCH–JUNE 1983

|  | Index |
|---|---|
| Stage 1: | |
| 1. Chicken Dinner | 213 |
| 2. Lamb Dinner | 180 |
| 3. Chocolate Pudding | 142 |
| 4. Beef Dinner | 119 |
| 5. Peach Melba* | 206 |
| 6. Fruit Delight | 157 |
| Stage 2: | |
| 1. Spaghetti Bolognaise | new |
| 2. Beef Dinner | 162 |
| 3. Chicken Dinner | 236 |
| 4. Cherry Treat | 167 |
| 5. Lamb Dinner | 196 |
| 6. Peach Melba* | 149 |
| Yogurts: | |
| 1. Strawberry | 172 |
| 2. Banana | 193 |
| 3. Raspberry | new |
| 4. Pear | 173 |
| 5. Apple and Blackcurrant | new |
| 6. Apricot | 174 |

*Renamed from Peach Teatime Treat with Vitamin C (stage 1) and Peach Delight with Vitamin C (stage 2).
Source: Cow & Gate Ltd. ex-factory sales.

## Distribution

We mentioned earlier that Cow & Gate restructured their sales force, and aimed for an increase in grocery distribution. Although Cow & Gate have been building the drugstore

TABLE 17: STERLING PROFILE BY SOURCE OF PURCHASE

|  | total market | | Cow & Gate | |
|---|---|---|---|---|
|  | Jun 1983 % | Mar 1984 % | Jun 1983 % | Mar 1984 % |
| grocers | 35 | 32 | 9 | 8 |
| Boots | 42 | 45 | 63 | 55 |
| other chemists | 21 | 22 | 26 | 36 |
| other outlets | 2 | 1 | 2 | 1 |

Source: RSGB Baby Panel 12 weeks ending 18th June 1983 and 24th March 1984

sector, this still accounts for only a tiny proportion of the total market. Attempts to build distribution in grocers are still at an early stage and have yet to prove effective.

The increase in Cow & Gate sales has not been due to significant improvements in distribution since the increased share of purchases in other chemists (see Table 17) has been secured from a static distribution base.

## Price

Cow & Gate's price has been reduced, but a price premium over brand leader Heinz cans has been maintained (see Table 18). If Cow & Gate's price had gone below Heinz we would have expected price to be a major influence on the recent sales success. But as

TABLE 18:   INDEX OF AVERAGE RSP PER UNIT

|  | Mar–Apr 1983 | Mar–Apr 1984 |
|---|---|---|
| Heinz can (128 g) | 100 | 100 |
| Cow & Gate 1 (78 g) | 118 | 108 |
| Cow & Gate 2 (113 g) | 129 | 119 |
| Cow & Gate Yogurt (113 g) | 121 | 115 |
| Heinz jars (128 + 170 g)* | 135 | 128 |

\* Nielsen reports two sizes together as average
Source: Chemist Nielsen March–April 1983 and 1984

already stated. it was policy to maintain some price premium to add value to the product. So although the pricing was adjusted to a more realistic differential, apart from a brief initial undercutting at the early stage of the relaunch to aid rapid sales of old product, Cow & Gate did not undercut Heinz cans (regarded by the consumer as the definitive price in the market) and so is not considered to have had the major effect on sales.

## Low levels of consumers awareness and interest

### SAMPLING

Increased sampling activity brought the brand to the attention of more mothers, but the Bounty pack (estimated 40 per cent coverage) also includes competitive products which are known to be popular among mothers. Whilst an important component in the relaunch, sampling can not build brand values and is not considered to have had the major effect on sales.

### THE ADVERTISING

Competitors continued to support their brands during Cow & Gate's activity and Cow & Gate only achieved a minor share of voice overall, being heavily outspent by both Heinz and Robinsons. (see Table 19.)

Figure 6 shows the relationship between the commencement of advertising activity and Cow & Gate's increase in sales. Our hypothesis for the success is that the advertising has drawn attention to the brand in it's new preferred recipe format and has added emotional

TABLE 19:   SUMMARY OF COMPETITIVE ACTIVITY

|  | Jul–Sep 1983 | | Oct–Dec 1983 | | Jan–Mar 1984 | | total year ending March 1984 | |
|---|---|---|---|---|---|---|---|---|
|  | £000 | % | £000 | % | £000 | % | £000 | £ |
| total | 395 | 100 | 197 | 100 | 392 | 100 | 1644 | 100 |
| Cow & Gate | 55 | 14 | 102 | 52 | 55 | 14 | 212 | 13 |
| Heinz | 217 | 55 | 87 | 44 | 66 | 17 | 1021 | 62 |
| Robinsons | 119 | 30 | – | – | 257 | 66 | 376 | 23 |
| others | 4 | 1 | 8 | 4 | 14 | 4 | 35 | 2 |

Source: MEAL (TV and Press Expenditure)

values. As stated before, the packaging had not changed and so there was no reason why the consumer should realise it had improved, nor would they notice the difference as the target market is constantly changing. The advertising constantly encourages a new target group of mothers to try the brand; they are satisfied with the new formulation, repeat purchase occurs and sales continue to increase.

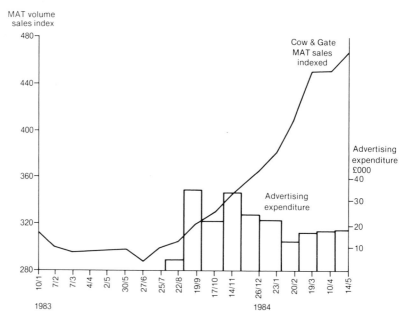

Figure 6. *Cow & Gate MAT volume sales indexed and advertising expenditure*
*Source:* Cow & Gate Ltd. Ex-factory sales actual advertising expenditure

## EFFECT OF RELAUNCH ON PROFIT

The relaunch has significantly increased profitability on Cow & Gate babymeals. In real terms, it is estimated that profit will have increased by 65 per cent on 1982 levels, representing notable return on advertising investment. (See Table 20.)

TABLE 20:    INDEX OF PROFIT CHANGE ON BABYMEALS

|        | index | adjusted index** |
|--------|-------|------------------|
| 1982   | 100   | 100              |
| 1983   | 114   | 109              |
| 1984*  | 182   | 165              |

Source: Cow & Gate Ltd
* 1984 profit estimated on first six months.
** Index adjusted to RPI at January each year.


## CONCLUSIONS AND IMPLICATIONS FOR THE FUTURE

Cow & Gate were in a weak position prior to the relaunch in August 1983. Deployment of the £200 000 advertising budget for the relaunch demanded careful attention as the advertising needed to create awareness and build brand imagery and reason to purchase among a target audience that changed every 12–16 weeks.

The low budget needed to work particularly hard for Cow & Gate in the face of being heavily outspent by competitors. By utilising specialist and selected women's colour press, the campaign efficiently reached our target audience all year round.

So overall, the success of the advertising has been due to the identification of a motivating strategy, a persuasive creative message and the placement of advertisements in relevant and efficient media.

The advertising has been identified to be the major contributor to the relaunch of Cow & Gate babymeals. It is judged to have stimulated trial of the improved product which has resulted in repeat purchase.

The relaunch activity has boosted sales to a level whereby profits generated by Cow & Gate babymeals have increased. Confidence in the contribution of the advertising to the relaunch is demonstrated by the increased budget allocated by Cow & Gate to advertising their babymeals in the remainder of 1984.

# 16

## Rebirth of the English Riviera

### INTRODUCTION

The 'English Riviera' and its prime resort, Torquay, have had a long history as one of the leading holiday areas in Britain.

Tourism is vital to the people of Torquay, Paignton and Brixham. Tourists spend £130 million (November 1982 figure) in this area (Torbay) and at the height of the season at least a third of Torbay's workforce are deriving their employment from tourism.

The Torbay Tourist Board is in effect a committee of Torbay Borough Council, including 12 councillors and four co-opted commercial members. Staff resources include a tourism officer, his deputy, a marketing officer and clerical assistants.

### MARKETING BACKGROUND

#### Adverse Trends

In 1982 tourism in Britain was faring poorly. The number of tourist visitors to the Torbay area had dropped from 1.3 million in 1976 to 1 million in 1982. The travel industry generally had been hard hit by the recession with fewer of the British planning to take any holiday.

Trends towards later booking of holidays were evident as people waited to see whether they could afford a holiday at all (for most, the largest single purchase in an average year) and whether by leaving booking till later they could achieve one of the 'last-minute bargains' often heavily promoted by overseas tour operators.

TABLE 1:   HOLIDAY INTENTIONS 1979–82

|  | 1979 | 1980 | 1981 | 1982 |
|---|---|---|---|---|
| base: all adults | 1971 | 2010 | 2150 | 1989 |
|  | % | % | % | % |
| intending a holiday of 4+ nights |  |  |  |  |
| yes | 64 | 66 | 62 | 58 |
| no | 28 | 29 | 29 | 35 |
| don't know | 8 | 6 | 9 | 7 |

Source: ETB Holiday Intentions Survey

The English Tourist Board's annual Holiday Intentions Survey, carried out in March each year, revealed the trends shown in Table 1: a considerable decline 1980–82 in the numbers intending to take a significant holiday. Thus, for those in the holiday business, May 1982, when the survey results were published, was a traumatic time. Not only had the number of people intending to take a holiday dropped by four percentage points for the second year in succession but there was also a hardening of attitudes *against* taking a holiday that year. People were not just unsure; 35 per cent expressed the definite view that they would *not* be taking a 'long' (4 + nights) holiday.

Over the same period, intentions to take a holiday in Britain declined sharply whereas holidays abroad were still being planned and intentions even rose between 1980 and 1981 (see Table 2).

TABLE 2:    INTENDED HOLIDAY DESTINATIONS 1979–82

|  | 1979 | 1980 | 1981 | 1982 |
|---|---|---|---|---|
| base: all adults | % | % | % | % |
| in Britain | 40 | 42 | 35 | 32 |
| in England (specifically) | 28 | 29 | 25 | 22 |
| abroad | 19 | 20 | 23 | 22 |
| don't know where | 4 | 4 | 4 | 4 |

Source: ETB Holiday Intentions Survey

Holidays abroad are most popular among the AB social groups who in 1982 were suffering less than others from economic constraints.

Holidays in Britain are particularly popular among the C2 social classes and to a lesser extent C1s and DEs, and hence were more vulnerable to the effects of adverse economic conditions on the skilled and semi-skilled worker. And as the English Tourist Board (ETB) said in 1982:

'Regional intentions to holiday show exceptionally severe decreases since last year by residents of Northern England and the Midlands while intentions have kept up much better in the relatively better-off Western and Southern parts of Britain, especially in London. Such results reflect regional variations in economic conditions.'[1]

## Effect on Torbay

As mentioned earlier the number of holiday visitors to the Torbay area had declined and in 1982 there was a considerable amount of press and TV coverage given to the problem of 'empty beds' in English resorts, with the public being urged to travel to the West Country and other tourist areas where vacant accommodation was said to be plentiful.

It was at this time (August 1982) that Pictorial Publicity[2] was appointed to handle the advertising for the Torbay Tourist Board.

However, although trends were adverse, the market for English holidays was (and is) substantial. It was estimated by the ETB that in 1983 over 25 million people would each take a week's holiday in England. The task was thus to increase the numbers coming to Torbay.

## DEFINITION OF MARKETING AND ADVERTISING STRATEGY

*Research Findings*

Research conducted by the Torbay Tourist Board and by Pictorial Publicity during the course of its 'pitch' revealed several interesting points.

1. There were two major types of Torbay holiday-makers. The first saw Torbay as the best resort area in Britain and was not interested in foreign travel; the second, while preferring to go abroad – to be sure of good weather – could not afford it at the time and saw Torbay as the closest approximation to a continental holiday available in Britain.
2. Visitors to Torbay were generally satisfied with their holidays: the beaches, the scenery, the friendly pubs, nightlife and general cleanliness all scored highly.
3. Repeat visitors constitute a high proportion of holidaymakers in Torbay. In 1981 nearly two-thirds of visitors had stayed in Torbay before.
4. There were fewer visitors than might be expected from the AB social groups, especially when compared with other West Country resorts. (These are also, of course, the type of people most likely to take second holidays.)
5. There were fewer visitors than might be expected from London and the South East. Particularly adverse economic conditions in other parts of Britain made it vital to attract holidaymakers living in London and the South East.
6. Although the Torbay area has one of the best climates in England, awareness of this was limited and it appeared that the good weather had not been effectively presented and exploited.
7. Perhaps most important of all, the name 'Torbay' was not helping the area. Even people who had visited Torquay, Paignton or Brixham had not heard of 'Torbay' and, when asked what it meant to them, thought it was a separate resort.
8. The term 'The English Riviera' on the other hand, though it had fallen out of 'official' use, was associated by many respondents with the resorts of Torquay, Paignton or Brixham and also engendered associations of a warm climate, attractive beaches, beautiful scenery and the famous palm trees.

Thus 'The English Riviera' and what it symbolises is what people would be looking for in the better type of English holiday.

*Implications and Opportunities for the Torbay Tourist Board*

Economic trends and the research data available thus indicated that:

1. Regular visitors would keep coming back to Torbay. The urgent need was to attract the first-time visitor.
2. Specific opportunities for 1983 lay with:

    (a)  The holidaymaker who prefers to go overseas but in 1983 could not afford to do so. To these, Torbay offered something of the style and quite a lot of the weather associated with a continental holiday.

(b)  The second holiday market: especially in the upper social groups, there was a burgeoning market for the shorter/second holiday, for which people are often prepared to consider destinations completely different from those preferred for their main annual holiday.

(c)  The more affluent, especially in London and the South East.

## ADVERTISING ROLE AND OBJECTIVES

How could advertising help to achieve these marketing objectives? The advertising budget available was small – around £100 000, to include production. Its deployment had to be carefully considered to contribute towards the following objectives:

—  to create (or recreate) the image of the Torbay area as the most stylish English resort area, comparable with the better continental seaside resorts;
—  to widen awareness of it as a top-class seaside resort with the facilities and weather for a highly enjoyable holiday, so as to attract, in particular, more first-time visitors.
—  to help Torbay reach its potential among the higher social classes and the more prosperous areas of London and the South East.

## THE ADVERTISING ROUTE

When the advertising tasks are defined as creating a wider awareness and better image of a product, the media planner's mind turns primarily to TV, the most powerful medium for achieving such tasks. However, on a small budget such as Torbay's there was obviously no question of producing a full-scale TV commercial or of buying adequate airtime to achieve the necessary coverage. The chosen route was therefore as follows:

—  to produce a stylish brochure, with details of Torbay's facilities and accommodation, which would also make a significant contribution to the image-building task.
—  to advertise by inviting the public to send for this brochure, deploying the advertising budget to buy a large number of relatively small spaces in appropriate publications and partial TV coverage of the country using a very simple and low-cost ten-second commercial.

To make advertising work in such modest spaces and in a very short commercial it was absolutely essential to develop a distinctive 'branding' device for Torbay which would economically and effectively convey the identity of the area and something of its characteristics.

## AGENCY'S ADVERTISING RECOMMENDATIONS

### Creative

The agency's creative recommendation was based on the opportunity to use two special 'properties' that were unique to Torbay in order to create an easily recognisable identity device which also communicated the desired image of the area.

THE ENGLISH
RIVIERA
TORQUAY · PAIGNTON · BRIXHAM

Send for our free 208 page colour brochure.
The English Riviera, Dept. No. DE1, Torquay TQ2 5JG.
Telephone 0803-211211 (24 hours).

The first of these 'properties' was the name 'The English Riviera' which was already understood by the public to denote the Torbay area. The word 'Riviera' clearly also invites the comparison with the resorts of other, continental, 'rivieras' – a comparison that we were not afraid to encourage.

The second 'property' was the palm tree image. This had been used before in a humorous way and was closely associated with the Torbay resorts. The agency planned to represent it so that it projected the panache and climate of a stylish continental resort.

Thus it was recommended that for the purpose of communicating with the holiday-taking public the name 'Torbay' should be dropped, as it appeared to be meaningless, and that 'The English Riviera' should be revived as the name for the area. This name in conjunction with the palm device would neatly and economically express the values we wished to associate with the area: those of being a warm, sunny resort which, though in England, offered much that was comparable with the continent.

These recommendations were accepted, and after the agency's appointment John Gorham was commissioned to produce the definitive expression of this identifying combination. Subsequently, this device was used for the cover of the 1983 brochure, and throughout the 1983–84 advertising.

For the 1984 Brochure and poster, the palm tree device was used in a different way to provide continuity of imagery while avoiding mere repetition.

# If it's hot enough for palm trees, is it hot enough for you?

Send for our free colour brochure. There's something for everyone from grand hotels to campsites, apartments to caravans.

Name _____

_____

Address _____

_____

_____ SP/1

Send to:
The English Riviera, Torquay TQ1 3EY.
Telephone: 0803-211211 (24 hours).

THE ENGLISH
RIVIERA
TORQUAY  PAIGNTON  BRIXHAM

*Media*

The agency's media recommendations for 1983 were to use a combination of appropriate national press, and TV, in regions of particular importance. In brief, the rationale for this combination was that while national TV could not be afforded, national press obviously provided a certain level of national coverage. However, there were good marketing reasons for using TV regionally, particularly since a key objective was to attract more interest in Torbay from London and the South East. TV achieves high audience coverage and generates awareness quickly, and for the holiday advertiser it has the added advantage of a telephone answering service for brochure requests.

The media schedule for December 1982–March 1983 can be summarised as follows:

PRESS

10 cm × 2 cols:

*Daily Mail*
*Daily Express*
*Sunday Mirror*
*Sunday People*
*News of the World*
*Sunday Express*
*Sunday Times*
*Mail on Sunday*

various sizes
up to $\frac{1}{4}$ page:

*Radio Times*
*TV Times*

# Which Riviera has 22 miles of unspoilt coastline?

Send for our free 248 page colour brochure. There's something for everyone from grand hotels to campsites, apartments to caravans.

Name_____

_____

Address_____

_____

_____

_____ NW/2

Send to:
The English Riviera, Torquay TQ1 3EY.
Telephone: 0803-211211 (24 hours).

THE ENGLISH
RIVIERA
TORQUAY · PAIGNTON · BRIXHAM

| | | |
|---|---|---|
| single buyline: | *Readers Digest* | |
| approximate total press cost: | | £60 800 |

| | TV | |
|---|---|---|
| 10 seconds | London | |
| | Midlands | |
| | South | |
| achieving 250 adult TVRs over 3 weeks | | |
| approximate TV cost | | £37 400 |
| | | |
| Total advertising cost for December 1982–April 1983 (excluding production) | | £98 200 |

The success of this advertising activity will be expanded upon later but first we will discuss how the campaign was continued and modified for 1984.

Based in detailed coupon response analysis of publications used in 1983, a 1984 media plan was drawn up. Budget constraints ruled out TV in London and the South and so in 1984 TV was concentrated on Central (Midlands) and on Yorkshire.

To provide some extra coverage of holidaymakers in prime target areas, national press was supplemented by posters in the London Underground in March 1984 to coincide with the English Riviera display at the Ideal Home Exhibition, and posters were used again in London in July 1984 to pick up this major late-booking market, made even more important with the impact of the miners' strike in the North and Midlands.

The media used for the 1983–84 peak booking season were:

PRESS

*Radio Times* – Christmas edition
*Radio Times/TV Times* English Tourist Board feature
*Sunday Express Magazine* (colour)
*Readers Digest*
*TV Times*
*Daily Mail*
*Daily Express*
*Sunday Express*
*News of the World*
*Sunday Mirror*
*Daily Mirror*
*Sunday People*
*Mail on Sunday*
*Sun*

*Woman, Woman's Own, Woman's Weekly,*
*Woman's Realm,*
*Mother*

*Summertime Special*
*England Holidays 1984*

Local Press: a number of local and regional newspapers, mainly in the North and West Midlands, to tie in with local exhibitions featuring the English Riviera.

approximate total cost                                         £ 87 000

TV

10 seconds:                        Central (Midlands)
                                            Yorkshire
achieving 300 adult TVRs over 2 weeks
approximate TV cost                                           £ 22 000

LONDON UNDERGROUND

4-sheet posters
approximate cost                                               £  6 000

total advertising cost for December 1983–March 1984 (excluding production)                                            £115 000

## RESULTS OF THE ADVERTISING

### *Introductory Note*

There are a variety of possible ways of measuring the success of an advertising campaign. Ideally, in the case of the Torbay Tourist Board, we would have liked to have had:

— *tracking* studies of awareness of Torbay, attitudes towards taking holidays there, and

awareness of the advertising spanning the seasons before and after the adoption of the new approach recommended by Pictorial;
— estimates of the *'fullness' of the resorts* (such as bed occupancy rates);
— an analysis of *bookings by source of enquiry* to assess the effectiveness of the advertising in placing the brochure in the hands of the most appropriate target groups.

However, one of the problems often encountered when working with relatively small advertising budgets is that the cost of market research surveys can be wholly disproportionate to the size of the marketing budget and is hard to justify, given that it represents money deducted from the funds available for advertising space or brochure production.

In this case, estimates of resort 'fullness' would not prove the effectiveness of the advertising, since 1983 saw relatively good summer weather and this will have boosted the holiday trade. However, Torbay does appear to have outperformed other English resorts in 1983 according to comments made by UK Tourism Resort Officers.

More feasible in theory would be an analysis of accommodation bookings by source of initial enquiry. Possibly a panel of hotels, guest houses, proprietors of holiday flats, and so on, could be set up, but this has not been done so far. It would require a considerable amount of effort on the part of the small team of marketing professionals employed by the Torbay Tourist Board, plus commitment from the hoteliers, landlords and landladies on such a panel.

These observations are made because by the standards of large national advertisers with multi-million pound budgets, the data available to prove the effectiveness of the advertising for the Torbay Tourist Board may well appear rather 'thin'. It consists of brochure enquiries resulting mainly from *direct response* to the advertising. We cannot *prove* that any particular proportion of these brochure enquiries resulted in bookings, and therefore directly benefited Torbay. But it is worth noting that brochure enquiries are a pure, if limited, measure of the *advertising's* effectiveness. There is no 'interference' such as can be caused by distribution difficulties or competitive activity as in the case of sales of a retail product.

Further, since we are dealing with enquiries during the winter–spring booking season, the results are unaffected by the weather which obviously has a crucial effect on the business in a total holiday season and could, whether good or bad, mask the effects of the advertising campaign.

### Analysis of Response to Advertising

#### PERIOD COVERED

This analysis deals with the peak winter–spring holiday booking season, that is, from December to April each year. In all years, efforts have been made to attract 'late bookers' by further bursts of activity in early and mid-summer. Activity during these late booking periods has been diverse and we do not feel that valid year-on-year comparisons can be made. Hence, we have confined the results analysis to the peak December–April booking season in each year:

(a)  1981–82   Prior to appointment of Pictorial Publicity
(b)  1982–83 ⎫
(c)  1983–84 ⎭ Pictorial's tenure of account

RESULTS ACHIEVED

Response analysis is based on two sources of enquiry: first, coupon response to advertisements, and second, enquiries to the 24-hour Ansaphone number included in the advertisements, and to the TV answering services. It *excludes* enquiries made directly to the Tourist Board's information centres. (Some of these might have been attributable to the advertising but it would not be valid to assume that *all* would be so attributable.)

TABLE 3:   TORBAY TOURIST BOARD—ADVERTISING RESPONSE 1981-82
           TO 1983-84

|  | 1981–82 | 1982–83 | 1983–84 |
|---|---|---|---|
| December–January | 28 805 | 32 078 | 51 025 |
| February | 10 840 | 14 913 | 23 805 |
| March–April | 8 399 | 14 038 | 8 830 |
| total December–April | 48 044 | 61 029 | 83 660 |
| Percentage change year-on-year |  | +27.0% | +37.1% |
| index (1981–82 = 100) | 100 | 127 | 174 |

Source: Torbay Tourist Board Statistics

Table 3 shows that the levels of response in 1982–83 were 27 per cent up on the previous year's figures; and in 1983–84 a further 37 per cent increase was achieved.

## Results in Relation to Advertising Budgets

It would hardly be fair to claim that advertising had been more effective than in previous years if the budget had substantially increased. To prove that it is the advertisements themselves that have succeeded, it is necessary to analyse cost per response and/or response per pound spent. This is the subject of the following analysis.

Different agencies can obtain different levels of media discount, so to avoid distortions from this source the analysis is based on advertising spend as reported by MEAL (hence discrepancies occur with the budgets given on pages 258-9).

Two analyses have been conducted; the first uses quoted MEAL figures, the second quotes expenditure at 1982 media costs with subsequent years adjusted for media cost inflation (using the Advertising Association's inflation estimates).

UNADJUSTED EXPENDITURE

Table 4 shows that Pictorial's campaign not only achieved increases in response but did so in spite of lower expenditure in 1982–83 and a relatively modest increase in 1983–84 over 1981–82. Further, the cost per response was reduced by more than a third with corresponding increases in the returns per pound spent.

TABLE 4: ADVERTISING EXPENDITURE AND RESPONSE 1981–82 TO 1983–84

|  | 1981–82 | 1982–83 | 1983–84 |
|---|---|---|---|
| advertising expenditure | £108 800 | £86 400 | £125 300* |
| percentage change on 1981–82 |  | −21% | +15% |
| responses | 48 044 | 61 029 | 83 660 |
| percentage change on 1981–82 |  | +27% | +74% |
| responses per £ spent | 0.44 | 0.71 | 0.67 |
| percentage change on 1981–82 |  | +61% | +52% |
| cost per response | £2.26 | £1.42 | £1.50 |
| percentage change on 1981–82 |  | −37% | −34% |

* MEAL plus posters not recorded by MEAL

ADJUSTED FOR INFLATION

The increased response rate per pound and reduced cost per response become more dramatic when expenditure is adjusted for media cost inflation (see Table 5.)

TABLE 5:    ADVERTISING EXPENDITURE AND RESPONSE 1981–82 TO 1983–84—
              ADJUSTED FOR INFLATION

|  | 1981–82 | 1982–83 | 1983–84 |
|---|---|---|---|
| advertising expenditure (MEAL) at 1982 prices | £108 800 | £77 481* | £102 800* |
| percentage change on 1981–82 |  | −29% | − 6% |
| responses | 48 044 | 61 029 | 83 660 |
| percentage change on 1981–82 |  | +27% | +74% |
| responses per £ spent | 0.44 | 0.79 | 0.81 |
| percentage change on 1981–82 |  | +80% | +84% |
| cost per response | £2.26 | £1.27 | £1.23 |
| percentage change on 1981–82 |  | −44% | −46% |

* adjusted by Advertising Association press inflation factors. 1983–84 also includes posters not recorded by MEAL to which inflation factor has not been applied.

## Holiday Intentions 1984

As a final note, it is worth quoting from the 1984 English Tourist Board Holiday Intentions Survey. Overall, the numbers intending to take a holiday of four or more nights rose to 61 per cent in 1984 from the 58 per cent and 57 per cent recorded in 1982 and 1983. But intentions to holiday in *Britain* have remained *level* in 1982–84 and England's popularity remains in long-term decline (see Table 6).

'Britain in general and England in particular are no more popular as holiday destinations in 1984 than they were in 1983 and the year before.'[3]

The success of Pictorial Publicity's advertising in arousing interest in holidays in Torbay – 'The English Riviera' – has thus been achieved against a background of continued British apathy towards holidaying in Britain.

TABLE 6:   HOLIDAY INTENTIONS 1981–84

|                              | 1981 | 1982 | 1983 | 1984 |
|------------------------------|------|------|------|------|
| base: all adults             | 2150 | 1989 | 1978 | 2189 |
|                              | %    | %    | %    | %    |
| intending a holiday of 4 + nights | 62   | 58   | 57   | 61   |
| in Britain                   | 35   | 32   | 33   | 32   |
| in England (specifically)    | 25   | 22   | 24   | 23   |
| abroad                       | 23   | 22   | 22   | 26   |
| don't know where             | 4    | 4    | 2    | 3    |

Source: ETB Holiday Intentions Survey 1984

## CONCLUSION

Although the marketing objective was complex, the role of advertising for the Torbay Touring Board could be reduced to two tasks.

1.  To create a distinctive identity and image for the area – an image which evoked the right associations of weather and style.
2.  To put the Torbay Tourist Board's brochure into the hands of the right target audience.

Because of prohibitive cost, no consumer survey data was available to show whether or not the British holidaymaker's view on 'The English Riviera' had changed. However, the response figures, particularly when analysed in terms of cost per response and response per pound spent, indicated that the advertising created by Pictorial had proved highly successful and cost effective in meeting the needs of the Torbay Tourist Board and reviving interest in 'The English Riviera'.

## REFERENCES

1.  *Holiday Intention Survey*, English Tourist Board, 1982, page 5.
2.  Now Travis Dale & Partners.
3.  *Holiday Intention Survey*, English Tourist Board, 1984, page 6.

# Section Four

## *Special Category*

# 17

# Advertising's Part in the Regeneration of London Docklands

## INTRODUCTION

The brief given to Gold Greenlees Trott when appointed by the London Docklands Development Corporation (LDDC) at the end of 1981 was very simple: 'Show us how advertising can be used to help regenerate London Docklands.' What we hope to do in this paper is to demonstrate how bold, impactful advertising can contribute to the solution of daunting social and industrial problems.

We will leave you, we hope, with our conviction that advertising is an integral part of the successful regeneration of London Docklands. This belief is shared by Nigel Broackes, who was, until recently, the Chairman of the LDDC. He wrote in the second paragraph of his 1982-83 Chairman's Statement:

> In this first full year, the London Docklands Development Corporation (LDDC) has seen the crossing of the first, the psychological, threshold. The next few months will transform the development scene as well. After so many years in which attention is focused on other regions and the new and expanding towns, the emphasis really is shifting back to the potential of the capital's inner city. Advertising for investment, long banned for London, is now allowed and three major campaigns - with black London crows as stars - have undoubtedly helped create the necessary general climate of interest in the area. Those who follow this up rarely fail to be impressed by the range of construction activity in hand throughout the eight square miles.

## BACKGROUND

The final closure of London's docks in the period 1968-81, when most commercial sea traffic moved to Tilbury, was the last chapter in the steady decay of the riverside from Tower Bridge to the Woolwich Ferry.

In an attempt to stem the decline the local councils (Tower Hamlets, Newham and Southwark) and the Greater London Council established the Dockland Joint Committee in 1974. Its brief was to attract new business to the area. Unfortunately, it had neither the resources nor a wide enough remit and was largely unsuccessful. The Dockland Joint Committee was disbanded upon the formation of the London Docklands Development Corporation in 1981.

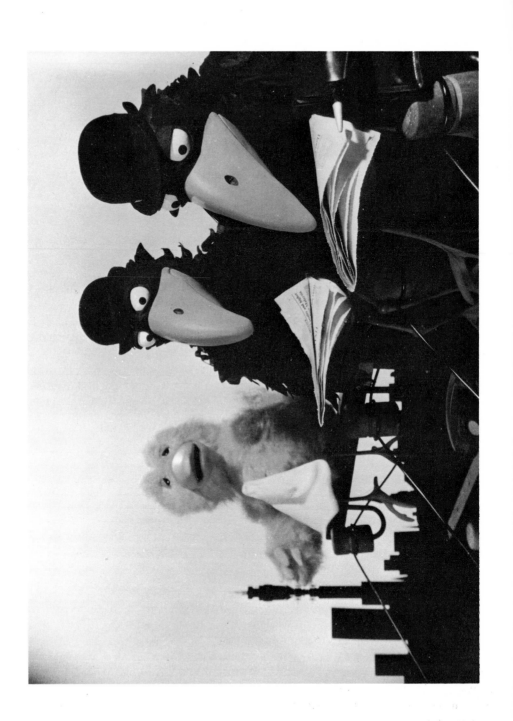

The LDDC's brief is to regenerate eight square miles of Newham, Southwark and Tower Hamlets through the encouragement of industry, commerce, housing and social provisions, including better public transport and general urban infrastructure.

Although it has a wide range of social and environmental responsibilities its principal focus is on economic development, for without industry and employment the community would continue to stagnate.

The major marketing tool which the LDDC has to encourage economic development is the Isle of Dogs Enterprise Zone. The March 1980 Budget set up a number of these zones (which we have listed in Table 1), and gave them a wide range of benefits, particularly 100 per cent capital allowances, and a ten-year rates holiday, to encourage industrial and commercial activity in otherwise depressed areas of the country.

TABLE 1:    FIRST GENERATION OF ENTERPRISE ZONES

| Enterprise Zones | Area (ha) | Date of coming into operation |
|---|---|---|
| 1.  Salford | 174 | 12/8/81 |
| 2.  Trafford | 178 | 12/8/81 |
| 3.  Swansea | 298 | 11/6/81 |
| 4.  Wakefield | 57 | 31/7/81 |
| 5.  Clydebank | 231 | 3/8/81 |
| 6.  Dudley | 219 | 10/7/81 |
| 7.  Hartlepool | 109 | 23/10/81 |
| 8.  Corby | 113 | 22/6/81 |
| 9.  Newcastle | 89 | 25/8/81 |
| 10. Team Valley ⎫ 11. Gateshead ⎭ | 365 | 25/8/81 |
| 12. Speke | 136 | 25/8/81 |
| 13. Isle of Dogs (LDDC) | 195 | 26/4/82 |
| 14. Belfast Inner City ⎫ 15. Belfast North Foreshore ⎭ | 208 | 21/10/81 |

Source: Zone Authority

The important thing to note about the Isle of Dogs Enterprise Zone is that it was set up in April 1982, six to nine months after the others. Although the Isle of Dogs is only a relatively small part of the Docklands area, the LDDC have concentrated resources on it as a 'vanguard' for the rest of the area. The major effect we will seek to demonstrate in this paper is how advertising has encouraged new businesses to move to the Isle of Dogs.

## THE PRODUCT

At the time of designation the Isle of Dogs had 105 firms, employing between them 641 people, mainly in transport and distribution, light engineering and construction. The area has several important buildings, notably in the West India Docks, but much of the enterprise zone consisted of vacant land, vacant water and vacant, almost derelict buildings.

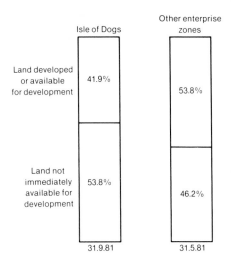

Figure 1. *Usable land*

*Source:* Yearly Economic and Land Development Survey (YEALDS)

Figure 1 compares the proportion of usable land in the Isle of Dogs with other enterprise zones. In 1981 roughly 58 per cent of the Isle of Dogs was unusable, compared with an average of 46 per cent for other areas. This land required major clearance and site preparation before development could take place.

The Isle of Dogs was not connected to mains electricity, and the provision of modern services was essential. Above all, access to the Isle of Dogs was extremely difficult. There were no major roads to or from the area, and no public transport.

## STRATEGY DEVELOPMENT

We have outlined the objectives of the LDDC. The key target groups to motivate to encourage investment, development and new businesses are businessmen in general, and investors, developers and potential business relocaters (in-movers) in particular. We have called these groups the 'main actors':

—  investors
—  developers
—  in-movers

We used research to try and understand the concerns of these groups, their knowledge and opinion of London Docklands and the LDDC, and what influences their investment decisions.

We also interviewed other potentially influential people, such as local and central government, and the local community.

- 30 in-depth interviews with key decision-makers in the City, in finance and property;
- 70 telephone interviews with business people;
- informal discussion with the LDDC and with government;
- 4 group discussions with the local community.

### Influences in Decision-making

Figure 2 illustrates the interrelation of the main actors. We found that the decision whether or not to invest in the Docklands rested on a number of factors, both rational and emotional.

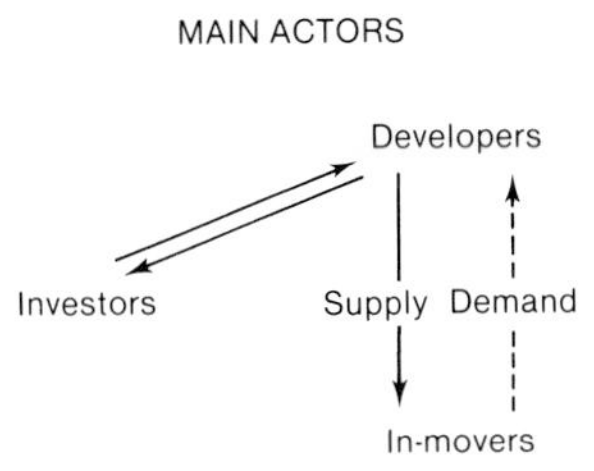

Figure 2. *Decision-making amongst main actors*

   In-movers, unless they were large enough to be their own developers, could not move into the Docklands unless there were premises (developments) for them to move into.
   Developers could not develop unless there was an infrastructure and developable land. They would not develop, nor would investors invest, unless they *perceived* that there would be demand (and hence reasonable occupancy at profitable rent levels) for their developments.
   Thus confidence that the Docklands would be a success was all-important, and the confidence of the main actors was affected by their perceptions of the opinions of the other groups. Figure 3 attempts to model these influences.
   Just as the main actors' perceptions of the attitudes of central and local government to the future of Docklands, conveyed partly by the media, could affect their investment decisions, so the attitudes of government and the media were shaped by their perceptions of the progress that Docklands was making – a vicious circle!
   Not only did Docklands have to be successful, it had to be seen to be successful, and in the absence of any perceived progress on the ground in the early days of the LDDC, we concluded that confident, aggressive advertising was one of the few ways that this vicious circle could be broken.

### Attitudes to Docklands

Against this background it was reassuring to find that most groups we spoke to expressed a strong emotional desire to see the successful regeneration of Docklands. Many saw it as a tragedy that such a large and important part of London, so close to the City, had been allowed to decay for so long, and, as you might expect, the local community were particularly keen to see new industry, new jobs and new amenities in the area.

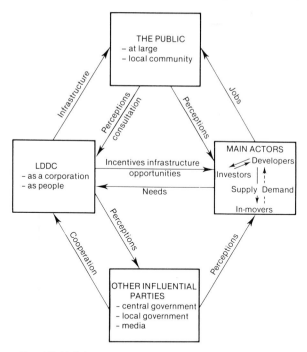

Figure 3. *Model of influences on decision making*

However, although developers and investors saw the potential of the location, they were very cynical and disillusioned about its prospects after the series of false starts. (One merchant banker told us that he was devoting his time to something with more short-term potential – the Channel Tunnel!)

Central and local government felt that this time they had created the right climate for the regeneration of the area, but emphasised the magnitude of the task, and the importance of the LDDC as a catalyst for development.

### Attitudes to the LDDC

Awareness of the LDDC among government and most City investors was quite high. Among developers and potential in-movers it was low. (A survey which the LDDC conducted amongst AB London businessman showed it to be 30 per cent in March 1982.)

The local authorities of Newham, Tower Hamlets and Southwark, which are all Labour-controlled, took a certain amount of exception to this free enterprise cuckoo in their midst. (Southwark still refuses to have any working contact with the LDDC.)

Not surprisingly, surrounded by indifference ('the phone never rings'), cynicism ('Oh here we go again'), and downright hostility, and with such a large responsibility to bear, morale among LDDC employees was not very high.

### Barriers to Purchase

Our principal objectives were to persuade private capital to invest in Docklands and relocators to move into the area.

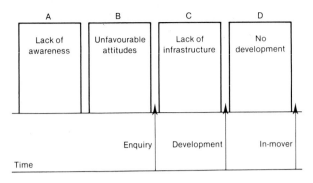

Figure 4. *Barriers to purchase*

We characterised the problems in fulfilling these objectives in terms of barriers to purchase:

— *lack of awareness*; obviously if one has never heard of Docklands or the LDDC, then one cannot relocate there, we have already seen that awareness of the LDDC was low among London businessmen.
— *unfavourable attitudes*; if one knows about Docklands, but holds the sort of attitudes that we uncovered in our exploratory research then one is unlikely to consider relocating there.
— *lack of infrastructure*; the lack of infrastructure would severely inhibit development in the early days of the LDDC.
— *no development*; without development there would be no firms moving to the area.

The first two of these, the ones which Nigel Broackes referred to earlier as the psychological barriers to the development of Docklands, we felt able to tackle with advertising. As Figure 5 demonstrates, we reasoned that raising awareness and changing attitudes would lead to enquiries; if the LDDC concentrated on improving the infrastructure this

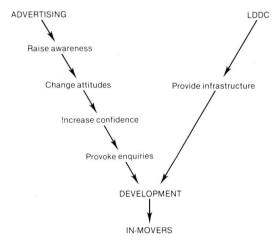

Figure 5. *The development process*

in turn would lead to development, and if there was development then there would be in-movers.

### Roles for Advertising

Figure 6 attempts to summarise the roles for advertising. The explicit role of our advertising for Docklands was to raise awareness of the LDDC, communicate the benefits of the enterprise zone, to generate enquiries, and hence to funnel investment into the Isle

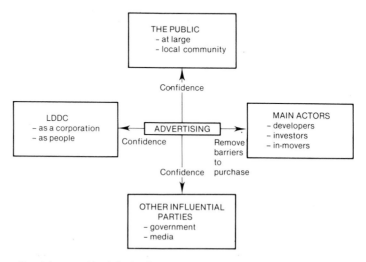

Figure 6. A summary of the roles for advertising

of Dogs. The implicit role was to demonstrate to all interested and influential parties, through the style and scale of the advertising, that the LDDC meant business, and that this time Docklands would be regenerated.

## THE ADVERTISING STRATEGY

We are evaluating in this paper the launch phase of the LDDC campaign, which covers a period from June 1982 to July 1983. By the end of this launch phase we planned to have removed the psychological barriers to the development of Docklands.

We conceived the advertising in three stages which correspond to our barriers to purchase model. Stage one (June–July 1982) was designed to create impact, to raise awareness of the LDDC, and to instil the feeling that this time something really was going to happen in Docklands. In stage two (February–March 1983) we began to communicate the specific benefits of the area, particularly the Isle of Dogs Enterprise Zone, with a view to generating enquiries. Stage three (June 1983) concentrated on the development opportunities in Docklands. In particular, we were keen to communicate that things *were* happening, and that this was not, therefore, another false start in the regeneration of the area.

## Media Strategy

As Figure 7 shows, the majority of businessmen move less than 30 miles when relocating. Most property developers, the national media, the City and local community are based in London; therefore we concentrated our media in London.

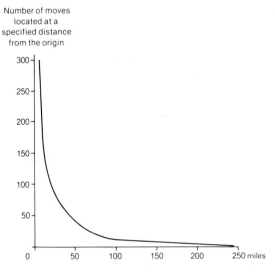

Figure 7. *Distance of move associated with all openings with an origin, 1966-75*

*Source:* Department of Industry

The first burst of advertising was deliberately designed to be a multi-media extravaganza. We wanted everyone to know that something special was happening in Docklands. TV was used as the lead medium (we took the centre break in News At Ten every weekday for four weeks). The quality press was also used to increase coverage against businessmen, and give some national exposure, local radio and 48 sheet posters increased frequency of exposure and conveyed certain tactical messages.

In the second and third bursts we used TV alone in order to maximise cover of our

TABLE 2:    MEDIA PLANS, LDDC LAUNCH CAMPAIGN

|  | 1982 | | | | | | | 1983 | | | | | |
|---|---|---|---|---|---|---|---|---|---|---|---|---|---|
|  | Jun | Jul | Aug | Sep | Oct | Nov | Dec | Jan | Feb | Mar | Apr | May Jun | Jul |
| TV (London) | £250 000 | | | | | | | | £300 000 | | | £100 000 | |
|  | ← → | | | | | | | | ← → | | | ← → | |
|  | 500 men TVRs | | | | | | | | 500 men TVRs | | | 200 men TVRs | |
| national press | £245 000 | | | | | | | | | | | | |
|  | ← → | | | | | | | | | | | | |
| outdoor | £65 000 | | | | | | | | | | | | |
|  | ← → | | | | | | | | | | | | |
| radio | £65 000 | | | | | | | | | | | | |
|  | ← → | | | | | | | | | | | | |
| total | £625 000 | | | | | | | | £300 000 | | | £100 000 | |

diverse target market. We have since started to use 48 sheet and supersite posters for frequent copy rotation and tight geographical targetting, and colour press to illustrate more detailed success stories for Docklands.

The total budget for the first three bursts was £1 025 000 (see Table 2 for breakdown by media).

## Creative Strategy

To achieve the objectives we had set for the campaign, the creative work had to embody a number of features.

1.  It had to position the LDDC as a development area, so that potential in-movers and developers would consider it alongside the longer established 'greenfield' sites such as Milton Keynes.
2.  It had to contain powerful, logical arguments, not glib advertising slogans, to appeal to our businessmen target groups.
3.  It had to be bold, confident, aggressive and single-minded.

Docklands major benefit as a location was its proximity to London. This had emerged clearly from our exploratory research. Its importance is underlined by the fact that even our rival development areas (as one of our early press advertisements demonstrated – see page 277) stress how close *they* were to London.

The line we developed, which is common to all the creative work, is:

'Why move to the middle of nowhere, when you can move to the middle of London.'

This communicates both the rational benefits of Docklands, ie its location and the fact that it is a development area, and the emotional reinforcements of the LDDC's confidence and determination.

The fact that we were talking about our capital city, and indeed that London had been losing businesses and employment to some of these greenfield areas, gave us the right, we felt, to adopt this tone of voice.

The first commercial featured a group of crows having a meeting on Nelson's Column, and discussing how long it had taken them to get there. Crows were used as a one-off joke ('as the crow flies') but proved to be so memorable and popular in post-testing that they were retained as a creative vehicle for subsequent TV advertising.

## STRUCTURE AND METHODS OF EVALUATION

The analysis we have made of the roles of advertising, and in particular the barriers to purchase, will form the basis of our evaluation of the success of the advertising. We will concentrate on evaluating the advertising against the rather narrow objective of economic regeneration on the Isle of Dogs, as this was the LDDC's principal focus over the advertising period.

The nature of this analysis, and the fact that we had three stages of advertising (and the nature of language) lead one naturally to think of the activities as sequential. Of course this is not the case; all the dimensions that we will be discussing would have been

# What's the point of moving out if you've got to keep coming back?

**CENTRAL LANCASHIRE**

*2½ hours to London on electric inter-city.

**PETERBOROUGH**

Peterborough is 50 minutes from King's Cross by train.

**WALES**

just 3 hours from London by rail or motorway.

**MILTON KEYNES**

A stretch of the M1 motorway forms part of the city's eastern boundary with access from junction 14, 50 miles (80 kilometres) from London.

London is a good place to be 'near' but it's a better place to be in, and we should know.

We're in the heart of London Docklands ourselves, just a few hundred yards from the City as the crow flies.

Not a few hundred miles as the car drives.

London has more of everything than all the other towns laid border to border.

Which means if you're out of London, you're out of touch.

You'll have to keep coming back.

For further details of how to set up in London Docklands, write to the London Docklands Development Corporation, West India House, Millwall Dock, London E14 9TJ.

And we'll show you how to get your business moving forward.

Not backwards and forwards.

**L.D.D.C.**
LONDON DOCKLANDS DEVELOPMENT CORPORATION

WHY MOVE TO THE MIDDLE OF NOWHERE, WHEN YOU CAN MOVE TO THE MIDDLE OF LONDON?

changing throughout the campaign period as we have shown in Figure 8. For the sake of clarity, however, we will continue with the analysis as if the activities were neatly sequential.

The methods of evaluation are as follows:

— pre-advertising awareness check, AB businessmen, London area – NOP;
— tracking study – London businessmen, local residents – SRA;
— YEALDS – monitor of all enterprise zones;
— qualitative study by University College London, reasons for moving to Docklands.

*Awareness and Attitudes*

The first two barriers in our model of development and advertising effect are lack of awareness and unfavourable attitudes.

Table 3 shows spontaneous awareness of the LDDC and prompted awareness of the advertising among London businessmen before and after the first burst of Crows

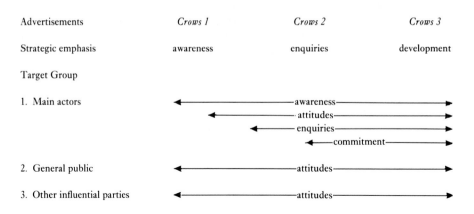

Figure 8    *Effects of advertising over time*

TABLE 3:    AWARENESS OF THE LDDC AMONG LONDON BUSINESSMEN

|  | March 1982 | July 1982 |
|---|---|---|
| Spontaneous awareness of the LDDC | 30% | 50% |
| Prompted advertising awareness of the LDDC | 38% | 70% |

Sources:  NOP
         SRA

advertising. This increased by 20 percentage points to 50 per cent, and prompted aware-ness after the first burst was 99 per cent.

The pre-advertising recall figure at 38 per cent is surprisingly high considering that the LDDC had done no advertising themselves prior to Crows 1. However the 'Dockland Joint Committee' had run a TV campaign (featuring Cliff Michelmore) and this may have confused respondents. In any case, as Table 3 shows, prompted awareness of LDDC advertising almost doubled following our first burst of Crows advertising.

TABLE 4:    SPONTANEOUS AWARENESS OF DEVELOP-MENT AGENCIES/CORPORATIONS AMONG LONDON BUSINESSMEN

|  | July 1982 |
|---|---|
|  | % |
| LDDC | 50 |
| Welsh DA | 41 |
| Milton Keynes DC | 20 |
| Scottish DA | 13 |
| Merseyside | 13 |

Source: SRA

Table 4 shows spontaneous awareness of the LDDC compared with other development areas; after just one burst of advertising it was already the best known development area among London businessmen. This is despite the longer advertising history of, and concentration on London as a prime market by, other development corporations.

Figures 9 and 10 show how awareness of the LDDC and its advertising continued to

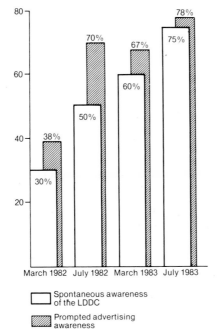

Figure 9. *Awareness of the LDDC amongst London businessmen*
*Sources:* NOP, SRA

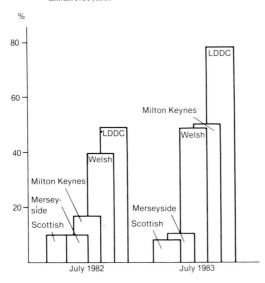

Figure 10. *Spontaneous awareness of development areas amongst London businessmen*
*Source:* SRA

grow over the campaign period, in line with our objectives, and at the expense of rival development areas.

TABLE 5:    BUSINESSMEN'S ATTITUDES TO THE LDDC

|  | July 1982 % |
| --- | --- |
| is committed to success | 81 |
| will succeed | 54 |
| has attracted business | 44 |
| has created more housing | 35 |
| has created more recreation | 29 |
| won't succeed | 4 |

Source: SRA

Table 5 shows the attitudes of London businessmen to the LDDC after the first burst. Their estimate of the LDDC's commitment to success and the fact that over half of them now thought it would be a success is impressive. Particularly when you think that many of them had never heard of the LDDC before we started advertising, and that our exploratory research (admittedly qualitative) showed such a high level of cynicism about the whole enterprise.

It seemed that we had swept away many people's psychological barriers to investing in Docklands in just one burst!

### Enquiries

Following the success of the first burst in building awareness and changing attitudes about Docklands we concentrated the second burst on communicating the specific benefits

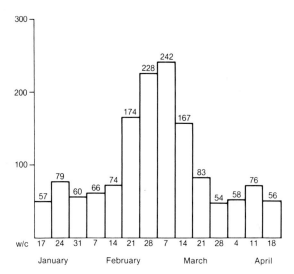

Figure 11. *Number of enquiries received by the LDDC by week, Jan–Apr 1983*
Source: LDDC

of Docklands, particularly the tax and rates benefits of the Isle of Dogs. The principal objective was to turn interest into enquiries. Figure 11 shows the enquiries generated during the second Crows burst in February–March 1983.

The average number of enquiries per week before the advertising began was 67. This trebled to an average of 203 a week during the campaign, and then fell back to 65 a week afterwards.

In all, the second burst of the campaign generated 811 enquiries from firms for information about the Isle of Dogs or Docklands generally during the burst itself.

During the total campaign period of a year the LDDC received over 4000 enquiries (when we started advertising there were only 105 firms in the Isle of Dogs in total!). This gave the LDDC a list of potential in-movers and developers which they followed up through personal contact and direct mail. The size and type of the enquiries also helped them plan the development of Docklands more systematically.

*Commitment*

Once the psychological barriers have been crossed and the prospect has made an enquiry, the final hurdle is the product itself.

The developer needs land to develop; the businessman needs developments to move into. As we have already described, much of the land in the Isle of Dogs was actually unusable.

In the period 31st September to 31st May, the LDDC invested £12.3 million in land reclamation, site clearance and site preparation, and in the provision of services. This amount was far in excess of any other enterprise zone (eg Salford £3.3 million, Swansea £4.9 million, Clydebank £5.9 million, and Corby £4.7 million), but was an essential step in the regeneration of the area. The results are shown in Figure 12.

In 1981 roughly 58 per cent of the Isle of Dogs was 'not available for development' compared with 46 per cent in other areas. Two years later the LDDC had reduced the amount of unusable land by 31 per cent to 69.21 hectares, ie to 40 per cent of the total, which compares with a drop of 25 per cent in the other areas.

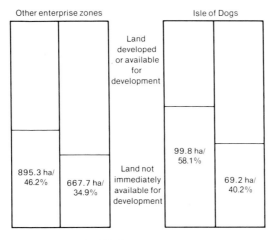

Figure 12. *Proportion of usable land*
*Source:* YEALDS

Having prepared the land for development, the LDDC needed to attract private investment from the City, not least because they had spent all their own money on fundamental site preparation!

One of their early development successes was in housing, and we decided to feature this in our third Crows film to illustrate the development opportunities in the area.

TABLE 6:    ATTITUDES TO LDDC IN THE CITY

|  | March 1983 | July 1983 |
|---|---|---|
|  | % | % |
| has attracted new business to the area | 41 | 55 |
| has created more housing | 44 | 45 |
| has created more recreational facilities | 29 | 31 |

Source: SRA

As Table 6 shows, the proportion of the City respondents in our tracking study who agreed with a number of statements about how the LDDC was progressing increased markedly over the period of the third burst, particularly on the issue of attracting businesses to the area. Reassuringly, the local residents, who are on the ground, and therefore ought to know, agreed with them (see Table 7).

TABLE 7:    ATTITUDES TO THE LDDC AMONG LOCAL RESIDENTS

|  | March 1983 % | July 1983 % |
|---|---|---|
| has attracted new business to the area | 37 | 54 |
| has created more housing | 35 | 45 |
| has created more recreational facilities | 26 | 32 |

Source: SRA

The creation and maintenance of this bandwagon effect is the key strategy behind subsequent advertising campaigns for the LDDC and, as Figure 13 shows, private investment has poured into the Isle of Dogs.

Figure 13 shows the total investment in site development by type of investor over the period 1 June 1981 to May 1983 in the top nine enterprise zones (all those in which more than £5 million has been invested).

YEALDS defines three types of investors: private developers, private producers who are developing the land for their own use, and others, mainly public authorities.

The outstanding enterprise zone in terms of site development over this period was Corby. An exceptionally large proportion of this investment was from large firms building premises for their own use eg, RS Components, Euramax Aluminium, Associated British Foods and A.C. Nielsen.

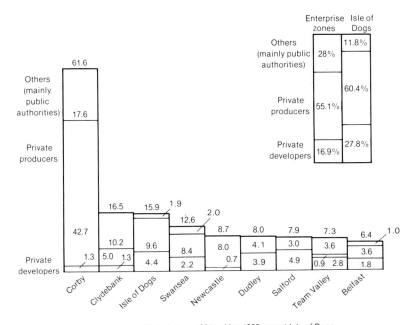

Period: June 1981 to May 1983 except Isle of Dogs
(start September 1981) and Belfast (start October 1981)

Figure 13. *Total investment in site development by type of investor (£m)*
*Source:* YEALDS

In terms of private producers the Isle of Dogs was second only to Corby in the magnitude of their incoming investment, and second only to Salford in terms of private developers – and this despite the fact that the Isle of Dogs was set up more than six months after these areas. In fact, in line with their objectives, 88.2 per cent of investment in the Isle of Dogs was from private investors, compared with an average of 72 per cent for other areas.

If we are correct in our analysis of how development in the Docklands area will occur, then given that we have now removed the psychological barriers to purchase, generated enquiries, provided an infrastructure, and begun to develop land, we should now see growth in the number of in-movers to the area.

TABLE 8:    IN-MOVING FIRMS BY ENTERPRISE ZONE (TOP EIGHT)

|  | 1st Jun 1981 –31st May 1982 | 1st Jun 1982 –31st May 1982 | 1st Jun 1982 –31st Dec 1983 | total |
|---|---|---|---|---|
| Clydebank | 62 | 82 | 37 | 181 |
| Isle of Dogs | 10 | 67 | 52 | 129 |
| Swansea | 39 | 42 | 20 | 101 |
| Corby | 21 | 42 | 27 | 90 |
| Dudley | 20 | 44 | 21 | 85 |
| Salford | 11 | 35 | 38 | 84 |
| Belfast Inner City | 15 | 36 | 14 | 65 |
| Trafford | 21 | 33 | 7 | 61 |
| total for all 13 enterprise zones | 251 | 474 | 299 | 1 024 |

Source: YEALDS

Table 8 shows the number of new firms that started in the top eight enterprise zones over the period 1st June 1981 to 31st December 1983. Over that period the Isle of Dogs has attracted more firms than any other enterprise zone except Clydebank. In fact as time has gone on, and in line with our analysis, the LDDC has been increasingly successful in attracting firms to the area.

Figure 14 shows the number of firms attracted to the area in successive periods for the top three enterprise zones. The Isle of Dogs began slowly – not surprisingly, given its

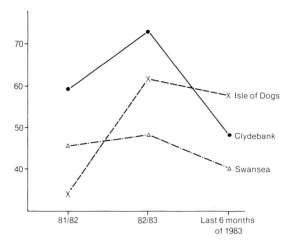

Figure 14. *Number of incoming firms (top 3)*

late start. In the 1981–82 period, before we started advertising, it only captured 10 of the 251 firms which moved into enterprise zones (a 4.0 per cent share of the market). In 1982–83, during our first burst of Crows advertising it improved very rapidly, taking 14.1 per cent of the market. In the last six months of 1983, following our third burst of advertising and the development activity we have described, the Isle of Dogs gained more incoming firms than *any other* enterprise zone, capturing 17.4 per cent of the market.

The 129 new firms that have moved into the Isle of Dogs over these two years have more than doubled the number of enterprises and jobs in the area.

## CONCLUSIONS

### *Has the Advertising Worked?*

Our analysis was that if we used advertising to raise awareness of the LDDC, to change attitudes towards the LDDC and to generate enquiries for the LDDC, and if the LDDC could improve the infrastructure of the Docklands area, particularly in the Isle of Dogs, then we would attract investment and new firms to the area.

We have raised awareness, we have improved confidence in the LDDC and we have generated enquiries. The LDDC have invested huge sums in improving the land, and we have attracted private capital, new firms and new jobs. The LDDC is now indisputably one of the top development areas in the country.

However, even though our analysis appears to have been correct, this in itself does not necessarily demonstrate a causal link between our advertising and a bulldozer starting work in the Isle of Dogs. To demonstrate such a link we need to find out from people locating to the Isle of Dogs why they moved there.

The University College of London carried out a study into the reasons why companies locate to the London Docklands Enterprise Zone in June 1984. They interviewed 62 firms who had moved into three major developments in the Isle of Dogs since 1982, using a semi-structured questionnaire.

They found that awareness of Docklands advertising was very high (88 per cent), and that over 70 per cent of the sample recognised the crows campaign correctly and identified it with Docklands.

When asked why they had considered moving to the Isle of Dogs the majority (58 per cent) said that they already knew the area, but of the rest, over 80 per cent said that they had made their first enquiry as a direct result of the advertising (ie 35 per cent of the total interviewed – see Table 9).

TABLE 9:    STIMULI FOR EXPLORING SITES IN THE ENTER-
PRISE ZONE

|  | number | % |
|---|---|---|
| total | 62 | 100 |
| aquaintance with area | 20 | 32 |
| local search | 6 | 10 |
| contacts in area | 10 | 16 |
| total with local knowledge | 36 | 58 |
| advertising/publicity | 22 | 35 |
| other | 5 | 8 |

Source: University College of London June 1984

The UCL report goes on to conclude that as well as generating enquiries the LDDC has two further, related functions.

First it counteracts negative images of the Isle of Dogs/East End which are held by company personnel, their customers and competitors. Second it fulfils a psychological function in reducing perceptions of risk. A high visibility campaign reinforces executives' decisions to locate in the area, and supports the gamble that the area has potential.

This survey demonstrates conclusively the direct (or explicit) role that our advertising has played in the regeneration of Docklands. Their analysis of how the advertising has worked is totally in line with the model that we have devised and confirms the indirect (or implicit) roles for advertising which we have described. Finally, it highlights an important by-product of the advertising which is that it reinforces the decisions of in-movers once they have moved.

# 18

# Chip Pan Fire Prevention
# 1976–84

## INTRODUCTION

In 1981 there were 21 deaths and 1 372 injuries caused by 15 000 chip pan fires. The key question was whether advertising could do anything to reduce this catalogue of personal tragedy, or whether accidents were unavoidable.

This paper sets out to demonstrate that advertising can, and did, affect the number of accidents and thus make a valuable social contribution.

### Background

The number of deaths and injuries caused by chip pan fires has been mentioned already; however, the scale of the problem is wider than human cost alone.

Chip pan fires are the biggest cause (31 per cent) of domestic fires and result in over £8 million of property damage, and this is only the tip of the iceberg, since the vast majority (95 per cent) of chip pan fires are unreported. Furthermore, chip pan fires represent a cost to the taxpayer in terms of emergency services such as the Fire Brigade, the National Health Service, and the Police.

Against this background of waste and human anguish, the Home Office (HO) and the Central Office of Information (COI) asked the agency to put forward advertising recommendations 'to reduce the death, injury and damage caused by chip pan fires'.

## THINKING BEHIND THE ADVERTISING STRATEGY

A reduction in casualties and damage could be achieved *either* by trying to prevent accidents happening in the first place *or* by educating the public about how to contain a fire efficiently and safely so that it does not get out of control because the wrong actions are taken (eg putting water onto it or moving the pan outdoors). Both these routes would achieve the advertising objective: the 'prevention' strategy, by reducing the number of chip pan fires, and the 'containment' strategy, by minimising the injuries and damage caused, albeit without reducing the number of accidents.

Initially we examined the prevention option. The main causes of chip pan fires are *overfilling*, so that oil overflows onto the hotplate or ring when the chips are put in, and *inattendance*, when the oil can reach a flashpoint and self-ignite.

However, there seemed to be two obstacles to encouraging preventive action. The first concerned the nature of accidents. Although deep-frying is extremely common (more than 80 per cent of housewives deep-fry at least monthly), most people have not experienced a chip pan fire.

In fact it is estimated that only about 15 per cent of households have had such a fire, and we assumed that, in general, people do *not* overfill their pans or leave them unattended. Thus an accident can be defined as being an aberration from normal behaviour probably caused by misjudgement or distraction. We were doubtful, initially, whether advertising could stop someone from making such a misjudgement or being distracted in the domestic environment that may have contributed to it, eg being in a hurry to prepare a meal, forgetting to check the level of oil, being called away from the kitchen to answer the door or settle a crying baby.

The second problem concerned people's unwillingness to believe that accidents might happen to them personally. Our own exploratory qualitative research indicated that people recognised that a chip pan was such an obvious hazard from the point of view of burns and scalding, as well as fire, that they claimed to take extreme care anyway. This, allied to the fact that most people have not experienced a chip pan fire, encouraged the belief that accidents happen to 'other' people who are more 'careless' or 'stupid'.

In considering these twin problems - the momentary, aberrational nature of accidents and the unwillingness to take the risk of a fire personally - we concluded that the prevention route did not appear to be particularly promising. On the other hand, we felt that the containment route was more fruitful. Initial qualitative research indicated that there was ignorance about what to do in the event of a fire and uncertainty about whether, at the moment of danger, the individual would do the 'right' thing, or simply panic. Thus we concluded that the role of advertising should be to inform people about the correct containment procedure and instil confidence in its effectiveness.

However, in reflecting on this proposed strategy, it occurred to us that demonstrating how to cope with a chip pan fire was a possible way to address the prevention issue. Above all, we felt that it could *personalise* the problem in such a way that advice about how to prevent accidents was more likely to be heeded. We believed this for two reasons. First, we felt that showing someone tackling a chip pan fire would raise doubts in the viewers' minds about whether *they* could do this in such an eventuality. By raising this doubt about *their* ability to cope, we felt that advice about how to prevent a fire occurring in the first place would be welcomed. We felt that showing the containment procedure would encourage viewers to want to take more notice of preventive advice in order to avoid the greater of two evils.

The second potential benefit of this strategy lay in the tone voice in which the advertising could address the target audience. Rather than saying, 'Don't do this because it might cause an accident' - advice which might be rejected or ignored for the reasons outlined earlier - we wanted the advertising to say, 'Well, it's happened - unluckily - but here's what to do'. The possibility ot the advertising being accusatory, and therefore being rejected, could be replaced by advice which was unmistakably reasonable, helpful and positive.

In effect, we hypothesised that, by turning the problem on its head, we could maximise the potential benefit of the advertising.

Instead of saying:

'Don't overfill your chip pan or leave it unattended, because you may cause a fire and possibly injure youself.'

we wanted to say:

'Here's what to do if you're unlucky enough to have a chip pan fire; putting it out isn't easy, so why not remember why it happens in the first place.'

The advertising model which we postulated can be represented diagrammatically (see Figure 1).

Figure 1. *Advertising Model*

## CAMPAIGN DETAILS

TV was the natural choice for both media and creative reasons: it reaches the wide audience of 'all housewives' and it was the logical choice to show the containment procedure with the most dramatic impact. The campaign line encapsulated the strategy:

### FIRE: IF YOU DON'T LET IT START, YOU WON'T HAVE TO STOP IT

Two 60-second commercials – 'Inattendance' and 'Overfilling' – were produced, and these have been used since 1976, although in 1982 they were edited to 40 seconds, (see pages 289 and 290 for storyboard examples). Both showed the initial cause of the fire and then the actions required to put it out:

—   turn off the heat;
—   cover the pan with a damp cloth;
—   leave the pan to cool down.

The dramatic effect of the commercials was heightened by combining real-time with slow-motion sequences.

# INATTENDANCE

If you go out of
the kitchen

and leave your
pan of cooking
fat or oil with
the heat on

it's going to
get very hot.

When it gets
hot enough

it'll catch fire.

When you notice it

the first thing

you'll have
to do

is turn off the
heat. The second
thing you'll

have to do is get a
tea towel, run it under
the tap and wring it out
until it's just damp.

The third thing you'll
have to do is place it
over the area of the fire.
And the fourth thing is
to leave it alone until
it is completely cooled
down.

Of course, if you don't
leave your pan unattended
in the first place you
won't have to do any of this.

# OVERFILLING

If you fill your
chip pan more than
half full of cooking
fat or oil

it will bubble over
when you add the chips.

When it touches the
heat it will naturally
catch light.

Having started a fire
you should set about
putting it out.

The first thing you
should do if you can
reach the knob safely
is turn off the heat.

The second thing you'll
have to do

is get a towel, run it
under the tap,

and wring it out
until it's just damp.

The third thing you'll
have to do is place it
over the area of the
fire

and if you haven't already
done it, turn off the heat.
The fourth thing is

leave the pan alone for half
an hour or so . . . until it's
completely cooled down.

Of course, if you don't
overfill your chip pan in
the first place, you won't
have to do any of this.

TABLE 1:　CHIP PAN FIRE ADVERTISING 1976–84

| 1976 | Yorkshire |
| | Granada |
| 1977 | Granada (reminder) |
| 1979 | Central |
| 1982 | Harlech |
| | Tyne-Tees |
| 1983 | TVS |
| | Harlech (reminder) |
| | Tyne-Tees (reminder) |
| 1984 | London |

The campaign has appeared on a regional basis in ten areas since 1976, and Table 1 shows the chronology of the advertising. The advertising has always appeared in the period January–March/April and at a national equivalent expenditure level of about £1 million. (Reminder campaigns were about half this level.)

## CAMPAIGN RESULTS

### Sources

The primary source for evaluating the campaign has been the Fire Statistics (derived from the reports made by fire brigades on every fire to which they are called), which are available for the six campaigns between 1976 and 1982, (data for 1983–84 not yet being available). The Fire Statistics have been analysed by the HO and the COI, and these behavioural data have been supplemented by two quantitative consumer surveys in 1976 and 1983. The rationale for the methodology and the results of combining statistical behavioural data with consumer attitudes and claimed behaviour have been written about by N Phillips.[1]

### The Results

There are a number of benefits in regional advertising: the ready availability of control areas, the opportunity to experiment with different media and media weights and, with particular reference to this case history, the opportunity to see whether the advertising is working in different areas over time.

The overall results of the campaigns evaluated between 1976 and 1982 are shown in Table 2 and show 'net' declines of between 7 per cent and 25 per cent over a twelve-month period.

There is clear evidence that the advertising has been successful in reducing the number of chip pan fires. The most disappointing result is in the Central area (the Midlands). This is an area with one of the lowest incidences of reported chip pan fires per thousand households in the UK. We cannot explain why this is the case, but it implies that it is likely to be more difficult to produce an effect from a lower base.

Further analysis of the data adds credence to the causal effect of the advertising. As we would anticipate, the advertising is having its maximum effect during and immediately after the campaign.

TABLE 2:    YEAR-ON-YEAR PERCENTAGE CHANGE IN REPORTED CHIP PAN FIRES

|  |  | advertised area | control area | 'net' change |
|---|---|---|---|---|
| 1976 | Yorkshire | −20 | +1 | −21 |
|  | Granada | −24 | +1 | −25 |
| 1977 | Granada* | −32 | 0 | −32 |
| 1979 | Central | −2 | +5 | −7 |
| 1982 | Harlech | −19 | −2 | −17 |
|  | Tyne-Tees |  |  |  |

\* Six months only
Source: HO and COI

Figure 2 shows the pattern of actual fires against forecast in the 1976 campaigns and indicates that from about August the effect of the advertising was diminishing before the reminder burst in the Granada area re-depressed the number of fires.

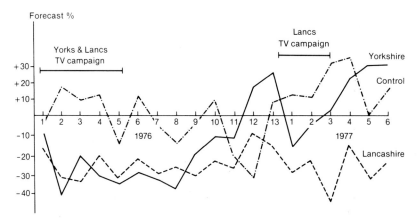

Figure 2 . *Change in the number of calls to fat pan fires relative to the forecast number*
*Source:* Home Office

TABLE 3:    YEAR-ON-YEAR CHANGE IN CHIP PAN FIRES 1982

|  | during campaign | next 25 weeks | next 15 weeks |
|---|---|---|---|
| Harlech | −27 | −20 | −8 |
| Tyne-Tees | −33 | −17 | −15 |
| control | −6 | −2 | +1 |

Source: COI

A similar pattern over time was observed in the 1982 areas (see Table 3). Further credence is added to the advertising effect if 'pure' and overlap areas are analysed separately. We would anticipate that the effect would be less in overlap areas because of reduced advertising impact (due to dual or triple ITV tuning). This proved to be the case, as shown in Table 4.

TABLE 4:   COMPARISONS OF YEAR–ON–YEAR CHANGES IN CHIP PAN FIRES IN 1982

|  | during campaign | next 25 weeks | next 15 weeks | total 52 weeks |
|---|---|---|---|---|
| 'pure' areas | − 30 | − 18 | − 12 | − 19 |
| overlap areas | − 14 | − 14 | + 2 | − 9 |

Source: COI

Not only has the advertising produced an effect, but it has generally been cost-effective, because a 12 per cent drop in fires represents an estimated saving of £1 million in property damage alone, excluding the benefits of reducing injuries and deaths and savings to the emergency services.

Moreover, these results have been achieved with increasing cost-efficiency. The Yorkshire campaign had 2 800 housewife TVRs (circa £2 million +) and used the original 60-second commercials; by 1982 the advertising weight had been reduced by over half and 40-second commercials were being used. This represents a saving of over 70 per cent.

In summary, therefore, we believe there is a prima-facie case for the effectiveness of the advertising: different regions over a six-year period have all responded positively. The number of chip pan fires has been reduced, and this decrease translates directly into reductions in casualties and property damage.

The hypothesis that the advertising is effective is supported by further analysis of the data. The pattern of reduction over time and the differences between 'pure' and overlap areas confirm a common-sense view of how the advertising is likely to work: with greatest effect during the campaign and in pure, non-overlap areas.

In addition, it has been possible to improve the efficiency of the campaign by reducing the weight of advertising and the lengths of the commercials with no apparent loss of impact.

## ADVERTISING AWARENESS AND RECALL

Our confidence that these decreases were a function of the advertising is heightened by the high levels of awareness recorded. Spontaneous awareness of chip pan fire advertising increased sharply after just one burst and was sustained at very high levels thereafter (Table 5).

TABLE 5:   SPONTANEOUS AWARENESS OF CHIP PAN FIRE ADVERTISING 1976

|  | pre-campaign % | after first burst % | post-campaign % |
|---|---|---|---|
| Yorkshire | 62 | 90 | 96 |
| Lancashire | 47 | 85 | 90 |
| control | 53 | N/A | 57 |

Source: RSL

The pre-campaign levels were caused by and correlate with levels of exposure to COI fire fillers (screened at the discretion of the ITV contractors) in 1974–75. They were not shown during the campaign, and recall and prompted awareness measures show that the paid-for advertising was what was remembered. Similarly, high levels of advertising awareness were achieved in 1983, with no evidence of a decline even four weeks after the TV advertising had stopped.

The impact of the advertising is further confirmed by the way the advertising appears to increase the awareness of chip pan fires as a potential kitchen hazard (Table 6).

TABLE 6:   SPONTANEOUS FIRST MENTION OF CHIP PAN
           FIRES AS A DANGER IN THE KITCHEN

| | Pre-advertising % | Post-campaign % |
|---|---|---|
| Yorkshire | 12 | 28 |
| Granada | 18 | 33 |
| control | 10 | 17 |

Source: RSL 1976

Indeed, we are sufficiently confident of the impact and memorability of the advertising to be considering further media experimentation in the future to increase media flexibility and cost-efficiency and also, it is hoped, to reduce or minimise the 'decay' effect noted earlier.

## HOW THE ADVERTISING WORKS

In theory, understanding how this campaign works does not matter: the objective of reducing chip pan fires appears to have been achieved. However, understanding can help to improve our confidence that the advertising was effective.

It is tempting to conclude from the fact that reported chip pan fires decreased that advertising prevented fires occurring in the first place. However, it is possible to explain the decrease by the containment theory: more people knew how to cope with and put out a chip pan fire as a result of the advertising, and therefore did not *need* to contact the fire brigade.

We cannot determine with certainty whether prevention or containment was the more significant, since we would need to know whether unreported fires increased or stayed the same; these have never been monitored because of the large samples sizes required. However, we believe, on the available evidence, that a combination of prevention and containment was responsible for the decrease in the number of reported fires.

There seems to be no doubt that the advertising increased knowledge of the correct containment procedure, as Table 7 shows. Furthermore, housewives' confidence that this technique would work increased to 75 per cent and, equally importantly, incorrect (and dangerous) practices declined.

However, we do not think that increased knowledge of the containment procedure *is* the sole reason for the decrease in the number of reported chip pan fires. Had it been, then we

TABLE 7: OBSERVED REACTIONS OF RESPONDENTS TACKLING A CHIP PAN FIRE

| | Yorkshire | | Granada | | control | |
|---|---|---|---|---|---|---|
| | pre % | post % | pre % | post % | pre % | post % |
| turn off heat | 68 | 84 | 57 | 80 | 75 | 70 |
| cover with damp cloth | 53 | 74 | 39 | 75 | 40 | 52 |
| leave to cool down | 42 | 62 | 22 | 47 | 41 | 33 |
| open doors/windows | 5 | 24 | 5 | 20 | 7 | 3 |

Source: RSL

would expect that those fires to which the fire brigade *was* called would be more serious than before. But this did not happen: the brigades did not have to fight a higher proportion of fires, injuries were no more common or severe, and the nature and level of damage caused by fires that were reported did not increase.

Also, we believe that the decay effect observed earlier is more likely to be caused by people forgetting prevention advice than by their forgetting the 'new' information about the correct containment procedure.

Furthermore, we think that the twin 'effect' of advertising may explain the relatively disappointing results in the Central area. We do not know precisely why there should be such a low incidence of reported chip pan fires. Survey data suggest that their knowledge of the 'damp cloth' technique appears to be no better than in other areas (before advertising), so we assume that 'Midlanders' are more careful and have fewer fires. If this is the case, then the prevention advice is less relevant and the observed effect may be only a reflection of the containment component.

In summary, neither containment nor prevention alone seems to explain the reduction in chip pan fires; as a result, we believe that both were important.

## CONCLUSION

The purpose of this paper was to demonstrate the effectiveness of advertising in reducing the deaths, injuries and damage caused by chip pan fires. We believe there is clear evidence that advertising achieved this objective in six monitored campaigns between 1976 and 1982.

We believe that a causal relationship has been established between advertising and the reduced number of chip pan fires and that proof of this effect is enhanced by the way in which advertising works over time, or, more accurately, by the way the advertising effect decays over time.

The creative strategy of using the containment procedure not only to inform but also to encourage preventive behaviour produced highly visible advertising and appears to have helped achieve greater public awareness of both containment and preventive practices.

Furthermore, we believe the advertising has been not only effective but progressively more efficient. The campaign now costs two-thirds less in real terms than in 1976.

This advertising campaign has had a measurable and worthwhile effect on society: savings in damage to property have generally covered the cost of the advertising and there have been additional savings in loss of life, injuries and fire brigade expenditure.

## REFERENCES

1. Phillips, N., 'Measuring attitudes and behaviour – practical implications for advertising', *Admap*, March 1979.

# 19

# The Lloyds Bank Personal Loan— Accessible Borrowing

## BACKGROUND

Since mid-1982, consumer spending had been on the increase. This boom had been financed by the growing credit market, rather than by people dipping into their savings. (Overall consumer spending was up 11 per cent on 1982 in 1983, and consumer credit was up 31 per cent. The source for these and the following figures in this section is the AGB Index.)

Though there are numerous ways of borrowing money, banks have always been a major source (see Table 1). However, throughout the boom year of 1983, unlike the other banks, Lloyds Bank did not appear to be benefiting from the buoyancy. Its share of total credit-taking had fallen from 5.3 per cent for the quarter ending March 1983 to 3.3 per cent by the end of the year. This was reflected in a reduction of the percentage of Lloyds' customers taking up loans from Lloyds (16 per cent in June 1982 had slipped to 12 per cent by June 1983). Also, in contrast, 19 per cent (value) of Lloyds' current-account customers were now borrowing from other sources (in the main from the *more expensive* finance houses, both directly and indirectly, which were also in general benefiting from the growth in consumer spending). This, combined with the fact that a high proportion of Lloyds Bank's lending was on overdraft (then approximately 14 per cent interest rate) rather than personal loan facilities (then approximately 18 per cent interest rate), resulted in Lloyds not achieving the real growth desired in their lending portfolio, even in a favourable market-place.

TABLE 1:   MAJOR SOURCES OF CREDIT

|  | share 1983 % | increase 1983 on 1982 % |
|---|---|---|
| total credit market | 100 | +31 |
| banks | 38 | +59 |
| finance house, indirect | 16 | +38 |
| finance house, direct | 13 | +38 |
| credit cards (includes no interest) | 21 | +24 |

Source: AGB Index

## MARKETING OBJECTIVES FOR THE BORROWING SECTOR, FIRST HALF OF 1984

The marketing objectives for the first half of 1984 were to turn around this trend by:

(a) increasing Lloyds' customers' borrowing from Lloyds;
(b) generating higher margins from loans where possible.

## ROOT OF THE PROBLEM

Lloyds Bank 'suffered' in two areas: in comparison with *other clearing banks* and in the *general comparison of banks with finance houses*.

### Lloyds vs. Other Clearing Banks

Overall, Lloyds had a weaker image in terms of willingness to lend and the speed with which the decision to lend was made. This was evident from two sources:

1. Lloyds purchase a syndicated bi-monthly advertising monitor from Millward Brown (sample size 1800 adults). This includes a battery of image statements. In September 1983 the rating 'readily provide loans' registered only 31 per cent agreement for Lloyds compared with 36 per cent for Barclays.
2. At the same time, another syndicated image study undertaken for the bank by MORI (sample size 4000 adults) compared the major clearing banks against the rating 'quick loan approval'. Lloyds scored only 10 per cent compared with Barclays 16 per cent, Midland 18 per cent and Nat West 15 per cent.

### Banks vs. Alternative Credit such as Finance Houses

Again, two pieces of research exposed the problem area: NOP carried out a personal customer attitude survey in 1980 (which, despite its age, is still believed to be relevant); this was supported by some qualitative advertising development work undertaken specifically for this project in November 1983 by Campbell Daniels Research (six group discussions, adults 25 +, borrowing in last 12 months).

Both pieces of work established that, although Lloyds and banks in general are competitive on price, their customers still used alternative and more expensive sources of finance because of the perceived complication and emotional barrier of applying for a loan at a bank.

For example, among those who had obtained credit of up to £750 in the past two years, the 'easy to obtain' requirement was rated as a more important reason for choice than 'interest rate' (44 per cent compared with 15 per cent) (NOP study, sample 1200 adults).

## ROLE FOR ADVERTISING

On the basis of the evidence thus far it became clear that there was a need to establish Lloyds Bank as a ready and quick source of finance in the eyes of the public. The following strategy resulted.

### *Advertising Strategy*

#### TARGET AUDIENCE

The target audience was all adults with bank accounts, and in particular Lloyds customers, age 25–54, BC1C2 (probably borrowing elsewhere at the moment).

#### PRIMARY MESSAGE

The advertising had to counteract the perception of 'hassle' and confirm that borrowing was seen by Lloyds as a normal part of their relationship with their customers.

#### SPECIFIC SECONDARY MESSAGES TO NEW CUSTOMERS

—   Borrowing need not mean seeing the bank manager.
—   A loan could be obtained for 'self-indulgent' purchases as easily as for those representing more basic requirements.

#### SPECIFIC SECONDARY MESSAGE TO LLOYDS CUSTOMERS IN PARTICULAR

—   Interest rates are cheaper than for non-bank loans.
—   Loans for things such as household durables, which the customer might have considered as a 'finance-house loan', can be – and are – better undertaken via the bank.

### *Specific Bank Product with which to Execute the Strategy*

Of the options available, the flat-rate personal loan was seen as the most suitable product with which to promote this image change. It is aimed primarily at Lloyds Bank customers, but is also available to non-customers providing they open a current account from which repayments are made automatically. It is designed for loans over £300 up to a usual limit of £5000. Repayments are fixed and can be spread over periods of 6, 12, 18, 24 or 36 months.

## THE 'SALES' TARGET

The sales target set for this campaign was for 22000 additional loans to be written in the period February–May 1984. The target was set based on an assessment of overall bank objectives and experience.

## CONSTRAINTS FOR THE CREATIVE WORK

### Tone of Voice

The execution had not in any way to *trivialise* the borrowing transaction or the role of the manager. The commercial had to encourage the appropriate use of credit, not a 'live now, pay later' attitudes.

### Loan Details

Despite the fact that personal contact would be unlikely, the bank had to retain the right to interview an applicant if necessary, and the commercial had not to communicate otherwise.

If the execution involved a particular purchase, then it had to be something that cost around £1000–£5000 *and* something which the purchaser would normally expect to be delivered, eg furniture.

The reasons for this were twofold. Most importantly, this neutralised the speed advantage that retail credit has for items that can be bought off the shelf, like videos. Secondly, sums of this order are what customers expect banks to be prepared to lend.

### The Consumer Credit Act 1974

Financial matters are very strictly guarded. There are two key rules. First, even if credit is referred to only briefly, it must be made clear that interest rates are available on request. Second, if a comparison of interest rates is made, then *all* rates must be quoted *with full details* in the same advertisement – the reason so many financial ads are so offputting.

## CREATIVE WORK

Three pieces of work were developed, and these are discussed in detail below.

### The Major Theme, to Overcome the Image of 'Hassle', Encapsulated in a TV Commercial

TV was selected as it was vital to ensure that the bank appeared approachable and the procedure uncomplicated. The proposition behind the script was: 'It was easier than I realised to get my loan from Lloyds. Applying was simple and I got the money with little fuss because Lloyds want to lend me the money.'

The commercial is referred to from here on as 'On-form'. (See the illustrations on pages 302–304 of the script and key frames for the detail.)

To support the TV campaign by offering specific details and by developing the secondary messages, two press advertisements were also developed: 'Car' and 'Carpet'.

### 'Car'

This promoted the proposition: 'When I applied for a loan at Lloyds it was dealt with speedily and efficiently, *and I didn't have to see the bank manager.*'

The Morgan was chosen purposely to represent an indulgent but not irresponsible purchase (as, by comparison, an old, battered Mini might have been considered) (see the illustration on page 305).

### 'Carpet'

This was developed to promote the proposition: 'I didn't know that borrowing money from Lloyds was cheaper than my credit card/money shop/finance house/shop plan/HP.'

The purchased item featured was in this case a carpet, chosen to represent a household durable - goods that a bank customer would normally choose to pay for by HP rather than by credit card (see the illustration on p. 306).

## MEDIA PLAN AND EXPENDITURE

Press and TV were used over the period January–March 1984.

### TV: 'On-Form' (40 seconds)

Spend  £1 062 000 (MEAL)
TVRs  528 (adult) (national average)
Dates  24th February–25th March (except Central – 1st April – and Granada/Yorkshire/ Tyne Tees – 28th March)

### Press: 'Car' and 'Carpet'

Spend  £335 000 (MEAL)
Dates  27th December–6th February
Media  *Daily Mail, Daily Mirror, Daily Express, Sunday People, Daily Telegraph*

Total spend: £1 397 000 (MEAL)

### Competitive Expenditure

The competitive advertising expenditure outlined in Table 2 does show Lloyds as one of the heavier advertisers of this type of product during this time period, but its expenditure was similar to that of the TSB, and the expenditure outlined here is product specific – many of the competitors were spending considerably larger sums overall.

TABLE 2:    MEAL EXPENDITURE £000

|  | 1983 | 1984 | | | | |
|---|---|---|---|---|---|---|
|  | Dec | Jan | Feb | Mar | Apr | May |
| Lloyds | 60 | 180 | 378 | 776 | 3 | – |
| TSB | – | 48 | 990 | 56 | 5 | – |
| Barclays 'Cashplan' | – | – | – | 199 | 123 | 108 |
| Midland 'Save & Borrow' | – | 110 | 664 | – | – | – |
| Nat West 'Personal Loans' | 43 | 22 | 82 | 335 | – | – |

'Applying for a loan is more
straightforward than you ever
dreamt'

'All you do is fill in a simple form'

'You can use the loan for all sorts
of things'

'And very soon you could have
your dream living room'

'At Lloyds you'll find personal
loans a matter of form'

*'ON-FORM' TV SCRIPT* - *40 seconds (full version)*

| VIDEO | AUDIO |
|---|---|
| *Early Dawn* | (The music is a sung version of the Lloyds loan form) |
| On a bedside table is a brochure showing 'SUITE DREAMZ' with a picture of a living-room suite. | |
| Next to it is a sleeping man. He gets out of bed, sleepwalking. | Applying for a loan from Lloyds Bank is more straightforward than you ever dreamt. |
| We see the man sleepwalking down the stairs, and sitting down at the kitchen table. | |
| We move back to see the whole house, front on, with the rooms revealed, as in a doll's house. | |
| Cut to close-up front cover Lloyds form. The man opens the form. | All you do is fill in a simple form. |
| | (song starts) |
| Four sleepwalking deliverymen in pyjamas enter carrying furniture. They move in time to the music, like a dream sequence. | You can use the loan for all sorts of things. |
| Cut back to form to see 'LLOYDS' being written in. | |
| Cut back to the deliverymen still walking across the screen. | |
| Cut back to form to see 'FURNITURE' being filled in. | |
| Cut to man still writing at kitchen table. | Often you won't even need to see a Bank Manager, unless you'd like to. |
| Wife sleepwalks down the stairs and she goes to the front room as the last deliveryman leaves. The furniture is now in position. She smiles. | And very soon you could have your dream living room. |
| Close-up to the form being signed. | (song ends) |
| Man and wife sleepwalk and meet in the hall. She kisses him. | SFX: Kiss |
| Cut to the completed form and pen in limbo. They animate into the Black Horse. | |
| | At Lloyds, you'll find personal loans a matter of form. |
| *Super*: Lloyds Bank | |
| Written details from Lloyds Bank plc, 71 Lombard Street, London EC3 3BS | |

*Contd on page 304.*

*BACKGROUND SONG*

*Verse 1*

Name and address and telephone,
Date of your birth and married or single,
And number of children under 18 years of
age,
Now your occupation,
Now who do you bank with?
Now it's not Lloyds,
We're not annoyed.

*Verse 2*

Purpose of loan,
Amount you want,
The date required,
Now choose you repayments,
And details of home,
Are you the owner or tenant or any other?
Now here's where to sign,
On the old dotted line,
And last the date.

## RESULTS

### New Business Gained

The target of 22 000 additional loans to be written over the period of February to May was achieved. In the following tables, sales are represented in terms of the average weekly figures of loans taken up over any one month. Due to bank confidentiality exact figures cannot be quoted, and it has been necessary to index the figures.

TABLE 3:   SALES GROWTH 1983–84

| month | | 'Sales' index for average weekly loans figure for that month |
|---|---|---|
| 1983 | mid–Oct | 100 |
| | mid–Nov | 98 |
| | mid–Dec | 91 |
| 1984 | mid–Jan | 69 |
| – – – – – – – – – – – – – – – – – – | | press campaign started |
| | mid–Feb | 96 |
| | mid–Mar | 113 |
| | mid–Apr | 135 |
| | mid–May | 117 |
| | mid–Jun | N/A |

The growth of 'loan opening' can be shown by indexing the average offtake starting from the month of October 1983 (see Table 3). These figures first illustrate the 'decline' that occurred in 1983 and then show the rapid growth, peaking in April 1984, just after the advertising campaign.

To show that this growth was not merely a seasonal one, and that offtake was incremental, it is necessary to compare the offtake of loans over the same time period in the previous year, 1982–83, when personal loans were *not* actively promoted as they were this year.

# "I didn't need to see the bank manager to get a loan."

# "He didn't need to see the car."

The heartwarming tale of some unusually benevolent bank manager?

Not at all. With a Lloyds Personal Loan, it is par for the course.

Just fill in a simple form. Usually without further formality we can advance you between £300 and £5000.

Money to spend on anything from a fitted kitchen to fitted carpets. But a trip to the bank manager isn't all we will save you.

Scout around and you will find our rates surprisingly competitive.

And while we might be quick to come up with the money, you'll find us flexible about the period over which you pay it back.

We will take the repayments from your Lloyds Current Account. (If you don't have an account with us, we'll happily start one for you.)

We will even offer to cover your loan against unemployment, accident or sickness.

So if you're after finance without fuss, call into your local Lloyds branch and fill in a Personal Loan form.

The chances are, it will be the only visit you'll need to make.

**Lloyds Bank**

Written quotation available on request. Offer limited to people over 18. Lloyds Bank Plc, 71 Lombard Street, London EC3P 3BS.

# "It's surprising the bargains you can pick up at the bank."

No, your local Lloyds branch has not suddenly branched out into the carpet business.

We are not offering savings on Axminsters and Wiltons.

We are offering savings on the money you need to buy them.

Apply for a Lloyds Personal loan and we can advance you between £300 and £5000.

So the more wily amongst you will be in a good position to get a discount for cash.

You'll certainly get a good deal so far as interest is concerned.

Scout around, you will find our rates surprisingly competitive.

And although we might be very quick to come up with the money, we're real slowcoaches asking for it back.

You can take up to three years if you wish.

We spare more than a thought about making life easy for you.

The money could be yours without so much as a cursory glimpse of the bank manager.

And with a Lloyds Personal loan, the repayments are taken from your current account.

(If you don't have an account with us, we will be happy to start one for you.)

We even offer to cover your loan against redundancy, accident or sickness.

So, no matter whether it's a new fitted carpet or a new fitted kitchen, don't fill in forms all along the High Street.

Just fill in one at Lloyds.

**Lloyds Bank**

Written quotation available on request. Offer limited to people over 18.
Lloyds Bank Plc, 71 Lombard Street. London EC3P 3BS.

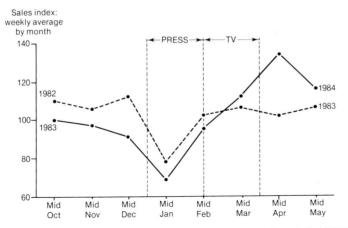

Figure 1. *Personal loans — graphical representation of indexed comparison of offtake 1982-83 with 1983-84*

This comparison can be shown in two ways, graphically (see Figure 1), and as a comparison of indexed figures (where October 1983 = 100) (see Table 4). In both years sales figures decline in January (the 1984 sales being lower than those of 1983). Both years recover in the spring, but then the 1984 average weekly figure clearly exceeds that of 1983 as the TV advertising breaks. The difference in sales over the period equals the 22 000 additional loans.

TABLE 4:    INDEX FIGURE COMPARISON OF AVERAGE WEEKLY
            LOAN OFFTAKE 1982-83 ON 1983-84

|  | 1982-83 | 1983-84 |
|---|---|---|
| Mid-Oct | 110 | 100 |
| Nov | 106 | 98 |
| Dec | 113 | 91 |
| Jan | 78 | 69 |
| Feb | 102 | 96 |
| Mar | 107 | 113 |
| Apr | 102 | 135 |
| May | 107 | 117 |

## Bonus Halo Effect

Prior to the April 1984 Budget (when VAT was levied on all home improvement loans), the campaign also had the effect of increasing the number of this type of loan (an alternative loan also being offered by the bank but not directly promoted on TV or in the press) (see Figure 2). There was probably some further effect after the middle of March, although this was obscured by the increased demand resulting from the imminent tax changes.

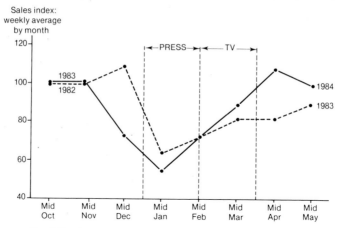

Figure 2. *Home improvements loans — indexed comparison of offtake 1982-83 with 1983-84*

## Effect on Lloyds' Share of the Loan Market

As monitored by the AGB finance index, the first quarter of 1984 figures show an increase on the 1983 figures, reversing the downward trend (see Table 5).

TABLE 5:    LOAN SHARE GROWTH FOR LLOYDS

| figures for quarter ending | Lloyds' share of total credit % |
|---|---|
| Mar 1983 | 5.3 |
| Jun 1983 | 3.6 |
| Sep 1983 | 3.4 |
| Dec 1983 | 3.3 |
| Mar 1984 | 4.1 |

Source: AGB Finance Index

## CONTRIBUTION OF THE ADVERTISING

It is possible to show a timing association between a number of positive changes and the advertising.

### Sales and Advertising Pattern

As already shown, immediate inspection of the sales graph is encouragingly positive. The results show that offtake was in line with the advertising, taking its strongest hold as the TV advertising broke (see Figure 1).

*Advertising Recall*

But to cover the albeit unlikely possibility that this was a mere coincidence, the link with claimed advertising recall was examined. Claimed recall of *any* Lloyds advertising had dropped to a relatively low level (32 per cent) at the end of 1983. After the TV campaign had started, awareness began to increase, peaking at 47 per cent mid–campaign and only dropping to 38 per cent by the beginning of May (see Table 6 (percentages) and Figure 3).

TABLE 6:   LLOYDS' CLAIMED ADVERTISING AWARENESS, PERCENTAGES BY MONTH

|  |  | any % | TV % | press % |
|---|---|---|---|---|
| 1983 | Dec | 33 | 24 | 14 |
|  | (28 Nov–8 Jan) |  |  |  |
| 1984 | Jan | 32 | 24 | 12 |
|  | (2–29 Jan) |  |  |  |
|  | Feb | 34 | 25 | 13 |
|  | (30 Jan–26 Feb) |  |  |  |
|  | Mar | 47 | 37 | 17 |
|  | (5 Mar–1 Apr) |  |  |  |
|  | Apr | 41 | 29 | 18 |
|  | (2 Apr–29 Apr) |  |  |  |
|  | May | 38 | N/A | N/A |
|  | (to date) |  |  |  |

Source: Millward Brown Tracking Study

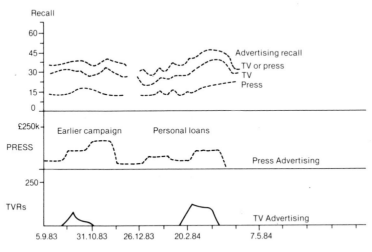

Figure 3. *Claimed advertising awareness for Lloyds — graphically represented*
Source: Millward Brown tracking study

Recall of press advertising was claimed to be comparatively poor, approximately 18 per cent – it was the TV advertising that appeared to contribute to the high recall – but this difference will be discussed in a later section. What is interesting is that it is possible to

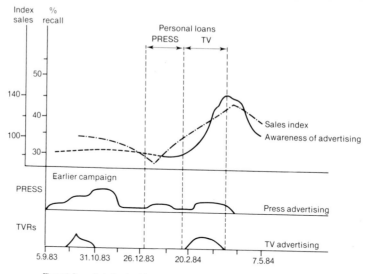

Figure 4. *Loan offtake & advertising awareness superimposed*
*Sources:* Millward Brown
Lloyds Marketing Department (sales figures)

plot a graph featuring sales, media timing and recall and show that all three coincide (predominantly with the TV advertising) (see Figure 4).

## *Image*

This latest campaign also coincided with the effective halting of the decline in Lloyds' image which the tracking study had recorded during the latter half of 1983. Increases occurred on important overall image factors in addition to the one related specifically to loans.

Examining the data by period before and after the TV campaign shows consistent improvements.

*For general dimensions*
— 'sort of bank I would be happy to join' (*up 5 per cent* to 28 per cent) (by February/ March)
— 'provide helpful advice to customers' (*up 4 per cent* to 36 per cent) (by February/ March)
— 'sympathetic to customers' problems' (*up 4 per cent* to 25 per cent) (by March/ April)

*For loans-type dimensions*
— 'readily provide loans'
(*up 5 per cent* to 34 per cent) (by March/April)
— 'offer a wide range of services' (*up 4 per cent* to 44 per cent) (February/March)
— 'attracting new customers at the moment' (*up 4 per cent* to 20 per cent) (February/ March)

*For key rating*
— 'Lloyds specifically promoted loans
recently'
Total sample:                              *up 16 per cent* to 21 per cent (by March/
                                           April)

*Target market*, ABC1 25–44:              *up 21 per cent* to 27 per cent
Lloyds customers:                          *up 26 per cent* to 42 per cent

Again if the changes in attitude are superimposed over the figures for recall of advertising, in each case the increases coincide. (See Figure 5 for a graphical representation of this.)

## CONTENT ANALYSIS OF THE ADVERTISING

The link between advertising and sales was further examined by checking the content analysis of the advertisements: was the message communicating or was the sales increase unrelated?

### Quantitative Analysis of Recall Content

Only a comparatively small percentage of the advertising monitor in April (3 per cent) were able to describe the TV ad in any detail, but bank advertising in general (regardless of which bank it is) falls into an area of low interest and consistently performs poorly compared with other markets. This figure was similar, for example, to an earlier and well rated commercial for Lloyds, presenting the Extra Interest Account.

What was relevant was that, among those recalling the ad, the intended central message, 'it's easy to get a loan', was well communicated (41 per cent). Forty per cent felt that the ad made Lloyds friendly and approachable, and 15 per cent felt it communicated 'something about the bank I didn't know'.

### Communication of the Main Objectives of the TV Advertisement

In another section of the questionnaire, a series of statements designed to reflect the communication points in the TV script were read out to respondents and they were asked to state which bank or banks they associated with each. As Table 7 illustrates, association

TABLE 7:   PROMPTED COMMUNICATION STATEMENTS*

|  | total % | ABC1 25–44 % | Lloyds customers % |
|---|---|---|---|
| you don't always have to see the manager when you apply for a loan | 21 (+5) | 29 (+10) | 54 (+13) |
| easy to apply for a loan as they have a simple application form | 23 (+6) | 30 (+10) | 50 (+10) |
| you get a decision on a loan quickly | 20 (+3) | 27 (+8) | 46 (−1)  Apr<br>56 (+10) May |
| you don't have to be a customer of the bank to apply for a loan | 17 (+4) | 17 (−1) | 24 (−1) |

* Change from pre TV advertising period

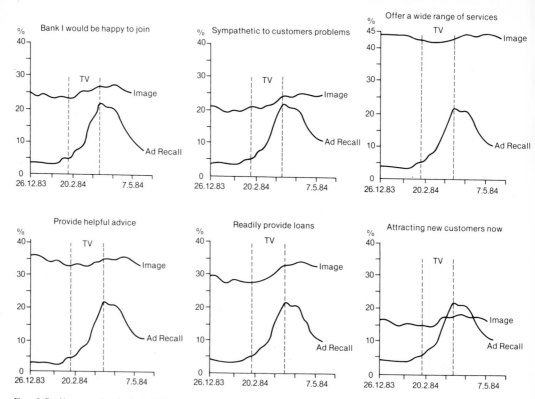

Figure 5. *Graphic representations showing the link between media advertising recall and image scales*
*Source:* Millward Brown

with Lloyds increased during the TV campaign on all four points. Yet no movement was recorded for any of the other Big Four.

## A Qualitative View on Content

A small qualitative analysis of the TV commercial (two groups among the target market) was undertaken by Campbell Daniels Research, prior to the launch but with effectively finished film. The purpose of this research had been to assess the need for any 'fine tuning', but it is relevant to quote it here, as it demonstrated how effectively the commercial was in communicating its original objectives.

1. The fantasy execution was understood. Respondents were able to scale down the advertising hyperbole/fantasy into a *credible message of ease and speed of borrowing.*
2. The 'dream suite' which had a luxury orientation was an understood device to show that the *range of acceptable goods qualifying for a loan was widening.*
3. The lighthearted tone of the commercial suggested casual borrowing, so that the bank's *lending stance* was seen as more accessible and less intimidating than expected. But, fortunately, this more *laissez-faire* position stopped short of irresponsible money-pushing. In other words, this was casual borrowing but not casual lending.

*Advertising Recall Index*

Finally, another research 'device' can be used to show that the TV advertisement's success was not based upon media weight alone but that content and execution contributed as well.

Using the advertising monitor, Millward Brown undertook mathematical modelling that calculates the 'average' increase in advertising recall that a notional 100 TVRs would generate overnight. On this basis they calculated that an 'average' financial commercial would receive an estimated figure of 3 per cent. Yet in this case the TV commercial achieved a figure of 4 per cent (acknowledged to be a 'good' score by Millward Brown).

## TV *vs.* PRESS EXECUTION

It should be apparent now that the TV commercial both researched well and could be directly linked to sales, whereas the press was mentioned only briefly, and not positively: it achieved relatively low recall, and only slight links with sales and image changes can be made.

The inevitable conclusion is that this study represents an apparently effective case history for the TV execution, but not for the press. But, before dismissing the press advertising so summarily, it is appropriate to make some comments. The issue of press relevance does become an inevitable one at this stage: a frequent response made in defence of press advertising is that 'press never researches well', whereas in advertising monitors consumers always claim TV recall, even if a product has not appeared on TV.

Perhaps a 'truer' explanation encompasses this, but includes a number of other reasons as well.

### Execution could have been Improved

Prior to the launch, the press advertisements were tested qualitatively (Campbell Daniels) and, based on this and the advertising monitor check on advertising content recall, the detailed communication of the two press advertisements could be described as satisfactory, if not excellent.

*But* communication results also indicated that the executions could have been improved; for example in 'Carpet' the link with the bank was not clear, and the choice of woman was inappropriate.

### Timing could have been more Appropriate

It must be remembered that these ads were designed only as a support to the TV (20 per cent of the budget). In this guise, if they had been exposed *during* the TV campaign or *after* the TV had set up the platform, 'conventional wisdom' would say they would have performed better. Post-Christmas press, however, was selected intentionally to attract the 'January sales' shoppers.

## CONCLUSIONS

In a buoyant market, Lloyds personal loan volumes were not maintaining their market share despite competitive 'pricing'. Customers were going elsewhere, often at disadvantageous rates.

A TV and press campaign was developed to counteract what was believed to be a consumer misunderstanding both that Lloyds were unwilling to lend and that the process was long and complicated (factors more important to consumers than 'price'). The advertising proposition developed was that 'a loan from Lloyds is hassle-free, quick and simple'.

Immediately after the launch, offtake of new personal loan accounts was noted, particularly once the TV campaign broke. *The accounts opened equalled the bank's targets. Lloyds' share of the loan market was seen to improve.*

Directly in line with the sales offtake:

1. There was an increase in recall of advertising.
2. Image data for the bank showed positive changes in the area of bank lending.

Communication checks showed the advertising (specifically TV) to be on strategy.

In conclusion, *the advertising can be demonstrated both to have affected the short-term promotion of loans, and to have contributed to more long-term image changes for the bank -* often an area where short-term tactics and long-term strategy clash, but which in this case clearly the reverse has been proved.

# Index